THE GUINEA PIGS AFTER
TWENTY YEARS

THE GUINEA PIGS
AFTER TWENTY YEARS

A Follow-up Study of the Class of 1938
of the University School Ohio State

MARGARET WILLIS

WITH A CHAPTER BY

LOU L. LABRANT

OHIO STATE UNIVERSITY PRESS
COLUMBUS

Library of Congress catalogue card number: 61–63285

To all those who shared the exhilaration and exhaustion of those memorable years with the guinea pigs

PREFACE

The idea for this book goes back to 1938 and is not original with me. When the seniors of the University School were writing *Were We Guinea Pigs?*, they hoped and expected that it would be followed up at some later date. The faculty shared the hope, but no definite or specific plans were made or responsibilities assigned.

An enterprise which interests and involves many people but is the clear responsibility of none easily remains indefinitely in a vague planning stage. In this case most of the class members and their former teachers had become widely scattered before enough time had elapsed to make a follow-up meaningful. As the years passed it seemed increasingly clear to me that the study would never be made unless I did it.

However, there were many reasons why I hesitated to undertake it. The shape such a study should take was so uncertain that I had doubts whether I could make it mean anything. It would surely require an enormous amount of time which would have to come mainly from school vacations; the prospect of surrendering vacations for an indefinite period was not enticing. While there were certain to be many expenses, there was little prospect for any financial assistance. On the other hand, I had taught these students during their junior–high school years, had worked with some in the upper grades, liked them, and was very much interested in and curious about what had happened to them in the intervening years. The occasional visits of individuals returning to the school whetted that curiosity. At various times I made some tentative beginnings toward the study, always looking around for discouragement and half hoping that obstacles would prove insurmountable.

Instead I found enthusiasm wherever I turned, and not merely enthusiasm for me to do the job, but an eagerness on the part of many people to help get it done. The most important assistance and encouragement in launching the project were given by Lou L. LaBrant and the late Norma Albright Beach, former teachers who at the time were in Georgia and California. The guinea pigs I talked with were very enthusiastic and ready to give both time and thought to it. Paul Klohr, then director of the University School, arranged for me to have one quarter of research assignment in order to permit traveling over the country with a tape recorder for interviews. With his help a budget was obtained through the Graduate School from the Ohio State University Development Fund to finance the task of transcribing the tapes and preparing the manuscript.

Thus by a long series of short, noncommital steps I found by 1955 that I had shuffled into a commitment to make a full-fledged follow-up. Because I undertook the study while working full time—except for the one quarter in which I was given research assignment—the collection of data took approximately a year and a half. Analyzing and writing was another long, slow job. This is a twenty-year follow-up which began in 1955 before the period had elapsed and is reaching publication in 1961, well past that magic number. Such a time lapse has caused occasional problems in the handling of certain data, but I do not believe any is critical.

At every stage of planning and carrying through the work, Miss LaBrant's contributions have been invaluable. She helped in the preparation of the biographical questionnaire, took full charge of the study of communication media reported in Chapter VIII, read critically all of the manuscript of Part I and gave important suggestions, and gave generously of her time and experience to discuss in person or by mail an indefinite number of the problems which arise in such a study as this. I am deeply grateful for her unstinting help.

Mr. Klohr and Herbert Coon, then assistant director of the school, were both very helpful in reading and criticizing the manuscript.

Herbert Toops gave valuable aid in helping me see how to put together meaningfully the very diverse test scores which I found in the records of the guinea pigs. Mrs. Alice Seeman helped work out the pattern for analyzing the interview data. Mrs. Thelma Boyd who typed the manuscript gave, in the process, assistance far beyond the routines of typing. I am deeply grateful to Ralph Tyler for reading the manuscript and giving advice and encouragement about publication.

The guinea pigs themselves made the collection of data a pleasure instead of a chore. They spent hours filling out questionnaires. In the interviewing stage they rearranged personal schedules to suit my convenience, frequently offered meals and lodging on the out-of-town trips, and graciously gave two or more hours of time to exploring questions many of which must have appeared to bear little relationship to the follow-up which they had thought of years before.

The section of Chapter IX which was written by the guinea pigs is the work of a committee. From her home in Connecticut the chairman, Jane Banks Whipple, organized the contributions of Cecil North in Michigan, George Wendell Ashman in Illinois, Elizabeth Stocking Seale in Idaho, Dorothy Lindquist Hargreaves in southern California, and Inez Norman Spiers in New York State. To produce an organized piece of writing under those conditions is a remarkable achievement which seems to me in itself a testimonial to their education.

In spite of my initial doubts and reluctance, I found the work on this study a most rewarding experience. To see what kinds of men and women yesterday's boys and girls have become is a dream of every teacher, but usually one sees only a few and wonders about the rest. To have seen them all and to have learned so much about them was most satisfying, especially since there were so few disappointments. I hope my enthusiasm has not warped my judgment; where I felt the danger, I have tried to be especially careful.

In any case, I assume full responsibility for the conclusions and interpretations you will find in these pages.

MARGARET WILLIS

Columbus, Ohio, May, 1961

CONTENTS

xi

TABLES

PART I

THE BACKGROUND OF THE STUDY

I

WHY STUDY THIS CLASS?

Is there any reason why a detailed study of the members of one particular high-school class seventeen years after their graduation should be of interest and importance to anyone beyond their immediate circle? This report is submitted in the belief that there are many reasons why it should be.

The class which is the subject of this study graduated from the University School of Ohio State University in 1938, the first group to complete the six years of junior and senior high school in the highly experimental program of the new school. The elementary grades of the University School, often referred to as the "Little School," had been begun on a small scale in 1930 in rented quarters under the direction and inspiration of Laura Zirbes. The high-school grades were added, and the entire program opened in a new building with a new staff and a new student body in the fall of 1932 under the direction of Rudolph Lindquist.

This was just at the time when arrangements had been completed for the Eight Year Study, sometimes called the Thirty Schools Experiment. The Commission on the Relation of Secondary Schools and Colleges of the Progressive Education Association had arranged with some two hundred colleges, including most of the endowed private colleges as well as the state universities, for a study of the relation of specific entrance requirements to success in college. For a period of eight years the graduates of some thirty experimental schools were to be admitted to the colleges which joined the experiment on the recommendations of their high schools rather than on the basis of examinations or prescribed units. Meanwhile, the Commission was studying and arranging for assistance to the programs of the experimental schools, and a committee from the colleges was studying the success of the graduates in the colleges which they entered, matching each progressive-school graduate with one from a conventional program, and following the progress of each matched pair.

With the Eight Year Study beginning, the University School at Ohio State knew before it opened that it would have a very large measure of freedom in planning whatever program the faculty believed would offer the best education for children. The philosophies of John Dewey and Boyd Bode gave over-all guidance, but the problems of implementing a philosophy in terms of day-to-day operation were challenging. This investigation is an attempt to evaluate the adult living of students exposed to that program to determine whether evidence of any effects can be discovered today.

What does research show about the long-term results of specific educational programs?

Even today, when the results of extensive educational research are available, many of the reports are in the form of detailed studies of specific aspects of content and method. There is also an enormous and rapidly growing literature advocating or attacking particular programs, though there is little published research which evaluates the larger outcomes of such programs. Long-range follow-ups of whole groups of students who have shared a particular type of high-school experience have not been published. There are only occasional short-term studies on college attendance, honors, scholarships, and so on.

The short-term study which pioneered in a new field, *Did They Succeed in College?* by C. D. Chamberlin, was published as Volume IV of the Eight Year Study series. A committee of college admissions officers studied the success of the progressive-school graduates (including a number from the University School Class of 1938) in comparison with the matching students from traditional schools, considering not only academic success but also a list of other assumed educational values. They found that the progressive-school graduates, possessing a variety of subject-matter patterns, consistently did a little better academically than their traditional counterparts, and that therefore the contention that a particular pattern of units was a necessary preparation for college was no longer valid. They also found that

> on a number of more intangible criteria, . . . on which ratings of both groups were made as objectively as possible, the progressive school graduates made a slightly better showing. For example: they were "more often judged to possess a high degree of intellectual curiosity and drive"; "were more often judged to be precise, systematic, and objective in their thinking"; "more often demonstrated a high degree of resourcefulness in meeting new situations"; "participated somewhat more frequently and more often enjoyed appreciative experiences in the arts"; "had a somewhat better orientation towards the choice of a vocation"; and "demonstrated a more active concern for what was going on in the world." [1]

In addition to discovering that, in general, the graduates of the experimental schools did a little better than the graduates of conventional schools, the study also compared the students from the six most progressive schools (of which University School was one) with the six most conventional among the thirty. Again the most experimental did better than the more traditional.

Unfortunately, it was impossible for this report to be given the careful attention it deserved since its publication came early in the Second World War. The focus of attention in both American high schools and colleges was on more immediate problems during the next few years. The report made its contribution to a notable relaxation of the rigidity of college entrance requirements in that period, but the return of the veterans under the G. I. Bill and the demands for college recognition of U. S. Armed Forces Institute courses and armed-forces training programs also contributed.

The classic in the field of the long-range follow-up is, of course, Lewis Terman's, *The Gifted Child Grows Up*. This study involved 1,528 individuals, homogeneous only in having I.Q.'s of 140 or above (about sixty of the group, children of the original subjects and others,

[1] C. D. Chamberlin, *Did They Succeed in College?* ("Adventure in American Education," Vol. IV [New York: Harper and Brothers, 1942]), p. xxi.

had I.Q.'s of between 135 and 139); they were scattered through California, and were attending all sorts of schools. The findings give a highly significant pattern against which to check the results found with any small coherent group.

In 1952, David Riesman's *Faces in the Crowd* appeared. It contains characterological studies of groups of young people from three different kinds of school and social environments. These sketches are pictures of character as it exists at a given moment, rather than of how it developed, and are useful for background and some understanding of the interplay of forces.

There have been a great many studies of college classes, chiefly assembled as a part of reunion celebrations, usually consisting of family data and income figures, and generally published privately. Occasionally, someone interested in broader issues takes the time and trouble to assemble and analyze the information. Cornelius Du Bois and Charles Murphy did this for Harvard 1926 in *The Life and Opinions of a College Class,* which appeared in 1951. Princeton Class of 1929 went only a little beyond the basic statistics, but Princeton Class of 1944 wrote *The First Decade,* which became the basis for an article in *This Week Magazine* (June 6, 1954), "The Class of '44 Today." Another reunion article is John Hersey's "Yale '36—Look at Them Now," in *Harper's Magazine,* September, 1952.

An extremely significant college study appeared while this manuscript was in preparation. It is Philip Jacob's exhaustive survey (*Changing Values in College*) of the attempts by colleges to affect the values of students through general-education courses and other means, and his analysis and comparison of the evaluations made by the colleges of such attempts. In almost every study which he examined, the maximum time range is from freshman to senior year. The book is notable for its penetrating analyses of failures and successes, and apparent reasons for them, and its challenging suggestions as to the directions which future research might take.

The most far-reaching studies of the college graduate are the two which were prepared from nation-wide survey materials collected by

Time. The first, *The U. S. College Graduate,* by Franklin L. Babcock, was published by Macmillan in 1942. It has largely been superseded by Ernest Havemann and Patricia West's book, *They Went to College,* published in 1952 by Harcourt, Brace and Company, which stands at present as the most thorough and comprehensive analysis in print of many kinds of data about college graduates of all ages.

Research describing what has happened to all the members of a high-school class many years after graduation has not been published, so far as the writer has been able to determine. An unpublished doctoral dissertation by Walter B. Barbe at Northwestern, dated 1953, is a follow-up of the graduates of special classes for gifted children in Cleveland. His first group of sixty-one men and fifty-four women graduated from high school in 1938, 1939, 1940, and 1941. These students all had I.Q.'s of 120 or higher and were in the special major work program at the time they graduated, which indicates they had been in it for at least two years and usually more. His results furnish a basis for a few valid comparisons.

An earlier study by W. J. McIntosh of one thousand graduates of a trade school, "Follow-up Study of One Thousand Non-academic Boys," in the *Journal of Exceptional Children,* March, 1949, dealt with a very different kind of student in a different sort of school setting, but reached interesting conclusions as to the factors which accounted for the success of the program.

There are a number of reasons for the lack of published data on high schools. One of the major ones is, of course, the doubt whether such studies will be of enough general interest to warrant publication. Then there are serious difficulties in the research itself. The study of every member of a specific class uncovers a mass of confidential data, and raises some critical problems in maintaining anonymity, which is essential if the results are to be published. Also, by the time students have been out of school long enough so that the quality of their adult living begins to be apparent, they are so scattered that they are hard to study, and they have had so many later experiences that it is extremely difficult to demonstrate a relationship between the school experience and their patterns of adult living. Perhaps even more important is the fact that there has been no particular motive and very little financing for such studies.

A number of people at the University School have felt that a follow-up of the University School Class of 1938 had the possibility of shedding light on important educational questions, and that it could begin with certain initial advantages which were of great importance.

The background of the Class of 1938 which made them particularly satisfactory for the follow-up can be summarized briefly. They were the first seventh-grade class of the University School when it began operation in the fall of 1932 in a new building and as a new department of the College of Education of Ohio State University. Nine graduates of the sixth grade in Miss Zirbes' Little School were among the seventh graders. The newly assembled faculty of the school was charged with the responsibility for developing a consistent program in the school, based on a specific educational philosophy; the school was to be an experimental and demonstration center, rather than a place for training practice teachers.

The beginning of the Eight Year Study in 1932–33 gave to the new high-school program an unusual degree of autonomy because of freedom from the pressures of college entrance requirements. In a letter from the dean of the College of Education to the trustees of the University, dated March 9, 1933, it was explained that the new high school was intended to be

an exceptional high school, exceptional in reference to the quality of its teaching, the attention given to the morals, the physical and mental health and progress of the pupils, to the manner and order of presenting subject-matter and the ways in which the different subject-matter is interrelated and integrated into a progressive educational program.[2]

The faculty tried to design a program to meet these challenges and strove to teach in terms of their philosophy and purposes, meanwhile clarifying the purposes in terms of accumulating experience. The

[2] "The Eight Year Study: A Report" (Columbus, Ohio: University School, Ohio State University, October, 1940), p. 1.

faculty assumed that if children learned to live democratically in school, they would carry over this experience into their later living. They made various other assumptions concerning the curriculum and developed practices which the circumstances of the experiment encouraged them to put in written form. Among the research publications which came out of those busy years was one monograph which included a study of the reading of this class in the seventh, eighth, and ninth grades, *An Evaluation of Free Reading in Grades Seven to Twelve Inclusive*, by Lou L. LaBrant and Frieda M. Heller.

Another contemporary document of importance is the faculty report to the Eight Year Study, issued in a mimeographed edition at the school and later included in *Thirty Schools Tell Their Story*, published by the Progressive Education Association Commission on the Relation of Schools and Colleges. This report contained the basic material for later work on defining philosophy and purposes, out of which emerged in 1948 *The Philosophy and Purposes of the University School*, printed at the University as a pamphlet.

When the Class of 1938 was in its senior year, the members undertook a major writing project in their English class with Lou La-Brant.[3] They looked back over their six high-school years, organized their thinking about their experiences and their evaluation of the whole process, and wrote a book, to which everyone contributed, called *Were We Guinea Pigs?* It was published by Henry Holt and Company, Inc., in the fall of 1938. Although the book was prepared as a writing project in English, its nature made teacher supervision undesirable. The publishers demanded that there be no attempt on the part of any teacher to suggest organization, edit copy, or make suggestions concerning material. Such an undertaking, of course, called for great restraint on the part of the faculty. Progress was checked by the publisher to guarantee complete honesty about procedures, and the usual editorial corrections were not made on the manuscript. This report has a unique place in educational literature,

[3] All seniors were required to take English for two periods per week. They met in two sections, both of which were taught by Miss LaBrant. Minor schedule adjustments with their required social-studies class made it possible for the whole class to meet together when necessary.

since it is the only account of a six-year progressive program, written by the students themselves.

A research study from outside the school which offers some background is the Chamberlin report, *Did They Succeed in College?*, mentioned earlier. The number and identity of students from each school chosen for study was a closely guarded secret, though it could not be concealed from the students themselves. Certain members of the class have spoken to the writer of all the special questionnaires they filled out during their college days to furnish data for that study.

Finally, thirty-three of the fifty-four students who graduated in 1938 had been in the school for the six years of junior and senior high school, forty-seven had been in the class four years or more, and an additional one for three years, long enough for any program to show for what purposes it was effective. The class included a wide range of ability.

In summary, then, this class is highly suitable for study for the following reasons: (1) some basic research has already been published; (2) the faculty report to the Eight Year Study and the students' own book offer contemporary documentary evidence; (3) the group was heterogeneous and the large majority of students who graduated had been in the school four years or more; and (4) the program to which they were exposed had been planned thoughtfully by the faculty in an atmosphere of unusual freedom from arbitrary restrictions.

Some of the persistent questions that teachers face have effects on present practices; but so far, answers to them must be accepted largely on faith since success or failure of a practice will only show up long after the student has left the school far behind. It was hoped that a follow-up might shed light on such questions as these:

(1) Can teachers do justice to different ability levels in the same classroom? Is there evidence that there are any techniques which will permit a genius and a slow student to work side by side with mutual respect, increased understanding of people, and optimal intellectual development for each?

(2) Can the school teach moral and ethical values, not just preach them?

(3) Can democratic give and take and concern for others be developed? If it can be, will it carry over into adult living?

(4) Is a child's sense of status, of being an individual person but also one who belongs, something of primary importance?

(5) Can tolerance be taught so that it functions?

(6) Can individual and social responsibility be taught?

(7) How can academic learning in school be so organized that the individual will carry the responsibility for his own education into the out-of-school hours and into his life after he has left school?

The thesis of this study is simple. If basic high-school curriculum reorganization is worth the effort, it should have results which are apparent in the adult living of the students who experience it. This follow-up attempts to look at all the "guinea pigs" to find out how successful they are in their living nearly twenty years after high-school graduation, and to see what connection, if any, can be established between the nature of the high-school experience and the kind of adult living discovered.

The problem of defining "success in adult living" will be considered in later chapters (Chapters II, VII, and X). It is an extremely complex one in any culture, but perhaps especially so in a pluralistic society such as ours. Standards for evaluating unsupervised adult behavior vary within wide limits, which in each case need to be explored.

The research findings in Part II are organized in classifications to permit as many comparisons as possible with other research data. Those in Part III are concerned with the values which the faculty were trying to develop. The final chapter contains general comments and conclusions on the success of the program.

II

COLLECTION AND ANALYSIS OF
FOLLOW-UP DATA

Collection of Data

The background data on the University School Class of 1938 has already been described in the previous chapter. The first problem in the follow-up was to locate all living members of the class. *Were We Guinea Pigs?* lists fifty-five names of writers, though there were only fifty-four graduates. One student withdrew before graduation, but for some purposes has been included in the study.

The parents' names and 1938 addresses were available at the school. The current telephone book led to information about some. Class members who lived in Columbus helped with the addresses of others, or with names of relatives who could give information. Return postcards to all who were located served to verify addresses and give clues which led to finding the rest. All members of the class were located and all fifty-five were still alive. They proved to be widely scattered over the United States as can be seen in Table 1.

The problem of what kind of information to collect was discussed with many members of the class, with present and former faculty members, and with outside experts during 1954. Obviously, comparative data from research studies which had been made with other groups would be valuable, but the published literature, which has been discussed in Chapter I, revealed only a few studies that offered helpful leads. Each individual consulted, however, agreed that the

TABLE 1

LOCATION OF THE MEMBERS OF THE CLASS OF 1938 IN 1956

Ohio	26	Louisiana	1
(Columbus, 17)		Maryland	1
California	8	Michigan	2
Connecticut	2	New York	6
Florida	2	Pennsylvania	1
Idaho	1	Washington	1
Illinois	1	Washington, D. C.	2
Kentucky	1		

research should not limit itself to questions for which comparisons were available, but should aim at as rich an accumulation of pertinent information as possible. The use of open-ended questions was a device to give every individual his chance to contribute his own ideas as to what he considered pertinent.

TABLE 2

COVERAGE OF RESEARCH INSTRUMENTS

Research Instruments	Number of Responses	Per Cent
Biographical questionnaire	52 of 55	94.5
"Uses of Communication Media" questionnaire	42 of 55	76.0
Interview (extensive)	45 of 48	94.0
Interview (reactions to school program)	47 of 55	85.0

The data were collected in four different stages as follows:

(1) A biographical questionnaire, "Follow-up of Class of 1938," was mailed out in January, 1955. It included a group of open-ended questions which were used as a basis for the fourth stage.

(2) A questionnaire, "Uses of Communication Media," was mailed out in March, 1955.

(3) Data on values were obtained from an extensive interview, which was originally intended for the forty-eight students who had been in school three years or more. Forty-five were actually interviewed.

(4) Interviews to discover reactions to the school program, based

on responses to open-ended questions in the biographical question-naire, were held between July, 1955, and April, 1956.

THE BIOGRAPHICAL QUESTIONNAIRE

A great deal of thought on the part of interested teachers and members of the class went into the preparation of the biographical questionnaire. If all the detailed questions which were suggested had been included, the sheer bulk of the document would have discouraged the recipient. It seemed best to make the basic questions simple and factual, inviting the detail in various open-ended questions. The final form of the questionnaire was nine pages long, and contained items on education, military service, publications, health, marriage, divorce, children, vocation, avocational interests, politics, religion, community service, and earned income, the last to be detached from the rest of the questionnaire and handled without identification. (See Appendix A for the biographical questionnaire, "Follow-up of Class of 1938.")

Two open-ended questions which invited fuller responses were included in connection with particular sections of the questionnaire: (1) "Unusual experiences, assignments, associations, or responsibilities" (under Military Service); and (2) "Be as specific as you can in a few sentences about what sorts of things you do in your principal avocational interests (collecting particular kinds of records, participating in chorus or orchestra, climbing mountains, or whatever)" (under Avocational Interests). These responses are analyzed in connection with related data in subsequent chapters.

The most important group of questions came at the end of the questionnaire. The subjects were invited to write on any or all of the following:

15. *a*) Do you feel *now* that the things we emphasized at University School actually were the important things, the things which *should* have been stressed?

 b) Do you feel that your University School experience has had any significant bearing, positive or negative, on your over-all capacity to *enjoy* life (as contrasted with your ability to do particular things)?

c) Are there particular experiences since you left high school which have been so challenging to you or so rewarding that you want to tell about them?

d) Are there particular values in living that you have come to prize very highly or particular causes that you watch for opportunities to further? If so, do you want to tell about them?

The numbers of class members responding to these questions are shown in Table 3. Since four out of five people wrote out their re-

TABLE 3

RESPONSES TO OPEN-ENDED QUESTIONS ON
PROGRAM AND VALUES

Question	Number of Responses	Per Cent
One or more questions...................	41	79
15 *a*...................................	36	69
b...................................	17	33
c...................................	16	31
d...................................	9	17

actions to one or more of these questions, some significant material was collected for the fourth step in the follow-up.

The way the responses were handled will be discussed under the heading "Interview on Reactions to the School Program" (page 18).

THE "USES OF COMMUNICATION MEDIA" QUESTIONNAIRE

When the biographical questionnaires were mailed in January, 1955, the subjects were warned that a second questionnaire, "Uses of Communication Media," was being prepared by Lou LaBrant, and would be sent to them soon.[1] (See Appendix B for the second questionnaire.) The second questionnaire surveyed their present reading of books, magazines, and newspapers, their radio listening and television viewing, and their movie, concert, lecture, and theater attend-

---

[1] Miss LaBrant was one of the teachers who was very close to this class during their high-school days. She worked with them in the junior–high school core and during two of their three years of senior–high school English work. It was in her class periods that they wrote *Were We Guinea Pigs?* She has been most helpful and encouraging in this study, and has done all the work on the language sections.

ance, and asked for significant recent experiences in these fields. Information concerning books they wanted to read and the size of home libraries was also requested.

The first steps in the data collection—the location of the class members and the preliminary discussion of the kinds of data to be collected —took place largely during 1954. The biographical questionnaires, mailed in January, 1955, came back during the winter and spring of 1955; eventually, fifty-two of fifty-five were returned. The "Uses of Communication Media" questionnaire was mailed in March, 1955, and forty-two responses reached the school during the spring; a number of others appear to have been lost in campus mail because of a rather complicated type of return envelope.

EXTENSIVE INTERVIEW

Although questionnaire information was important and likely to yield significant comparisons with other studies, it was evident that it would prove inadequate in dealing with the question, Is there any evidence that the school program might have had any over-all influence on value systems and the quality of adult living?

Interviews seemed the most promising technique for getting at this kind of information, but they presented very serious problems. Since the group was so scattered, an attempt was made to work out a sampling technique so that a few nearby subjects might represent the whole group, but the disadvantages were so obvious that the scheme did not get far.

Then there was the problem of interviewing skills. There was no budget to hire the kind of highly skilled interviewers used by T. W. Adorno for his study, *The Authoritarian Personality,* or by Lewis Terman in his studies of gifted children. The interview schedule and methods of interpretation developed by David Riesman in the collection of data for *The Lonely Crowd* and *Faces in the Crowd* furnished a model which was closer to our purposes and to our capabilities, since the interviewers would have had no special training. The main reliance in this kind of interview was on the verbatim recording of responses to a long list of wide-ranging questions which could later be studied to discover value systems, social attitudes, and personality patterns.

The interview schedule which was developed was essentially that of Riesman with numerous additions and modifications.[2] (See Appendix C for Interview Schedule.) For example, the schedule used by Riesman included a number of political questions which, of course, were out of date; it was not difficult to find contemporary equivalents. The schedule was further modified to adapt it to the age of the group being studied. All were in their middle thirties, and all but six were married. A number of questions about marriage and family life, relations with in-laws and other relatives, bringing up children, and vocational adjustment were added. The actual questions asked in each interview varied as the situation of that individual varied, of course, and the schedule kept on evolving as particular new questions proved valuable. Inevitably, at the end one wished it were possible to begin it all over again with the benefit of the added insights gained along the way.

The first nine interviews were conducted without mechanical aids, with the interviewer writing as rapidly as possible in order to get down on cards the exact words of the respondent. This proved to be very time-consuming, inaccurate, and generally exhausting. The use of a tape recorder for the remaining forty interviews introduced a different element of tension for some, though probably not a serious one. One interview, however, was completed before the investigator discovered that the machine had not been set to record it. A patient and generous guinea pig gave time later for a second exposure, but the replies were not as spontaneous the second time.[3]

Transcribing the tapes was a difficult and time-consuming secretarial job; but in spite of the loss of some small parts through mechanical difficulties or unintelligibility, the tapes gave far more com-

---

[2] Riesman says of his schedule, "Our interview guide went through nearly as many editions as a Hearst paper." *Faces in the Crowd* (New Haven: Yale University Press, 1952), p. 14 n. For each portrait in this volume, the interview questions are reproduced.

[3] Interview responses will be extensively quoted in Part III of this report and in other sections where they are relevant.

plete, accurate, and spontaneous records than the hand-written cards.

The interviews were begun in the late summer of 1955 and carried on intensively during the fall and winter of 1955–56. Several people from distant states took time for it during brief visits home. The writer made one long interviewing trip to the west coast and another to the east coast, planning the two routes to take in twenty-one of the most distant members. In spite of a tight schedule and limited time at each place, eighteen were actually interviewed, thanks to the people who were very co-operative in arranging their time to fit a visitor's schedule. With several other shorter trips and many local appointments, the writer was able to interview forty-nine members of the class in ten states and the District of Columbia.

Of the six who were missed, one lives in Florida, a state which it was not feasible to visit; the other Florida resident was interviewed during a visit to Columbus. One who lives in Columbus refused the interview, and one in California proved too difficult to locate, though we have a mailing address which appears to reach him. These were the three who did not return either questionnaire, and thus had no part in the follow-up. Of the other three who did return questionnaires, two were in hospitals at the time of the interviewing trips to California and New York for which they had been scheduled. The third, late on the list from Columbus, was just going on vacation when his name was reached, and was very busy after his return, so that it proved difficult to find a mutually convenient time. Since the interviewing time was past and his questionnaire had given a goodly amount of basic data, it seemed legitimate to omit his interview.

Interview on Reactions to the School Program

The way in which the answers to the open-ended questions at the end of the biographical questionnaire were converted into interview questions is described in detail in Chapter IX, "Attitudes toward the School Program." The process can be outlined here briefly. (See Appendix C, Questions 1 through 14.) The responses which were offered spontaneously by the individuals who answered the questions were studied and tabulated to discover each person's areas of awareness and concern. These were the matters which then became the questions to be asked of everyone. In this way every member of the class had an opportunity to bring into the study his own ideas of what questions, opinions, and information were pertinent. Question 14 was intended as a further invitation to free association of ideas: "Of course you know the school as a human institution must have changed, but since you do not know just what the changes are, assume it is still just as you knew it. Tell the faculty what things about it were particularly valuable and should be conserved and what parts were weak and should be improved."

The attempt was made to ask these questions of all students who had participated in writing *Were We Guinea Pigs?* The first two experimental interviews were held before the questions had been worked out, and five other individuals could not be reached for the interview. Actually, forty-seven out of fifty-five individuals, or 85 per cent, answered the questions.

A good deal is known about the three individuals who did not return questionnaires, and where such information is reliable it has been included.

The coverage, as shown in Table 2, varied from 76 per cent answering "The Uses of Communication Media" questionnaires, to 85 per cent being interviewed about the school program, 94 per cent being given extensive interviews, and 94.5 per cent returning the biographical questionnaires. Information about such matters as marriage, children, education and war service was acquired for all members of the class.

The high level of interest and co-operation from a very large majority of the class members is one of the interesting features of this study. Only three gave no co-operation, and although this is a very small number, it still means that there were three individuals who did not care enough about what had happened to the others to enter into the study, or who did not feel that the others were interested in them. Of these, one had been a member of the class for only two years, and another for only a year and a half. There were four other two-year people in the class, however, two of whom, judging by the interview data, seemed to feel completely at home in the class, while the other two, who were happy enough, did not feel themselves fully a part of it. The third who refused the interview and did not fill out either questionnaire had been in the school for five years. In a long telephone conversation he furnished a great deal of information about himself, but expressed much resentment toward the school. Since his subsequent record has demonstrated capacities which were never discovered during his University School attendance, his resentment is understandable.

The fact that the person communicating with the class members by mail and interviewing them was one of their old high-school teachers undoubtedly made a difference, though not the same difference in every case. Early in the study the writer decided that the only honest approach was to admit to herself and everyone else that she was interested in what had happened to her old students. She hoped that the admission would be of more help toward greater objectivity than a superficial "scientific approach" concealing unrecognized concerns. The unusually high returns are probably related in both a direct and an indirect way to this personal interest, directly because each guinea pig reacted in some measure to it, and indirectly because a follow-up by one of their old teachers seemed closely related to *Were We Guinea Pigs?*, the writing of which had been a significant experience to almost everyone. In only one case did the writer feel that the former-teacher role skewed the interview data. Forty-eight people handled the conference as adults, talking frankly and honestly to an interested old friend; only one clearly slipped back into the role of child talking to teacher. The sharpness of the contrast was encouraging validation of the rest of the protocols.

Problems of Analysis

The data collected in this study have been organized and analyzed in two broad categories, one treated in Part II and the other in Part III of this report. Part II includes the kinds of information which can be counted or tabulated, whether the facts have been derived from the questionnaires or from the interviews. The significant point is that objective data are assembled so that comparisons with other pertinent studies may be made and meaningful relationships discovered, pointed out, and interpreted.

Part III deals basically with thoughts, feelings, attitudes, relationships with others, and values. Here the data are not clear-cut: they must be discovered through an analysis of the protocols, the verbatim texts of the interviews. The inescapable difficulties of this enterprise cannot be used as a reason for avoiding it, since many of the major purposes of the school lie in these areas. Unless the follow-up can grapple with these issues, it has very limited meaning.

"Success in adult living," the basic matter being investigated throughout the study, is a deceptively simple phrase. To the person using it, it can mean anything from keeping out of jail to making a million dollars. If the school's program did for the child what the faculty hoped, taking into consideration the other influences impinging on him, what should these fifty-five individuals be like now?

Obviously, in many important respects they should be very different from each other: the diversities already conspicuous in their high-school days should have widened as each developed his potentialities in his own direction. Yet there should be areas of common values, the things which knit a society together enough that democracy may function. And there should be the kind of adjustment of the individual to himself and his world which is covered by the concepts of mental health.

From discussion, thought, and study, some criteria for examining successful living began to emerge. Each of the following must be thought of, not as an attainable absolute, but as a growing and changing function of living. In applying each of these criteria to the individual, two closely related questions must be asked: In what direction is the individual moving? and, To what extent is he like this?

1) Finding worth-while work, commensurate with his ability and satisfying to him personally.

2) Developing a stable pattern of human relationships through which he gives and receives affection and status.

3) Feeling and acting upon a sense of social responsibility in areas where he can be effective.

4) So managing his use of communication media and other avenues of learning that passing years promise increasing depth and breadth of understanding.

5) Living with sanity, good humor, tolerance for human foibles, but vigorous championship of some good causes.

6) Developing inner resources to enrich his living in good times and to tide him over the difficult days.

7) Ordinarily enjoying living, and having aspirations and values which contribute to life's purpose.

8) Learning to accept himself and the circumstances which he cannot change.

9) Tolerating unsolved problems, without either feeling so hopeless that he cannot work on them, or frustrated because they do not yield immediately to his efforts.

10) Living comfortably with ambiguity.

For comparison, here is a psychiatrist's description of mental health. In *The Sane Society,* Erich Fromm presents a pessimistic view of our society, and then gives a definition of mental health for the kind of sane, humanistic society we ought to have.

. . . The aim of life is to live it intensely, to be fully born, to be fully awake. To emerge from the ideas of infantile grandiosity into the conviction of one's real though limited strength; to be able to accept the paradox that every one of us is the most important thing there is in the universe—and at the same time not more important than a fly or a blade of grass. To be able to love life, and yet to accept death without terror; to tolerate uncertainty about the most important questions with which life confronts us—and yet to have faith in our thought and feeling, inasmuch as they are truly ours. To be able to be alone, and at the same time one with a loved person, with every brother on this earth, with all that is alive; to follow the voice of our conscience, the voice that calls us to ourselves, yet not to indulge in self hate when the voice of conscience was not loud enough to be heard and followed. The mentally healthy person is the person who lives by love, reason and faith, who respects life, his own and that of his fellow man.[4]

As judgments are made in the course of this study, they will be made in terms of such criteria as these, while recognizing that anyone who excelled in each of them would be a paragon. Applying criteria of success to individuals is the point at which the subjective knowledge of the interviewer becomes most pertinent and most dangerous—the special circumstances which account for failures may help in understanding, but the failure exists nonetheless. The bias of the investigator intrudes itself most subtly, too, in this area of judgment.

In general both Parts II and III are designed to throw light on the kind of development which has taken place. Lines of inquiry developed in other researches and the aims of the school have been used as pointing out organization of the data. It is not the intention of the writer to characterize the results as "good" or "bad," though it is probable that such value judgments are often present as assumptions.

The biographical questionnaire provided the type of information which has been the mainstay of most follow-up studies, and provided it for a far larger proportion (94.5 per cent) of the potential subjects than is usual. However, there are several factors which need to be kept in mind when using the figures and tables in this study.

The element of chance can give amazing twists to certain statistics in a group as small as this. One specific example will illustrate. Among the one hundred fifteen children in the families of the class members, there are three pairs of twins, a high proportion; all of them are boys, an unusual circumstance; and one pair of twin boys was born to every girl in the class who lives in Southern California, and to no one else in the group!

Statistics and statistical comparisons involving a small group must be handled very tentatively, and one can begin to be reasonably sure of meaning only when different organizations of data support each other.

[4] Pp. 203–4.

The same caution needs to be used in making comparisons with published studies; the fact that they are in print and include similar data does not mean that comparisons are necessarily valid. As noted earlier, only one study has been found on the high-school level; however, a few words are pertinent about the use made of the various college reports.

The most thorough study of an individual class is that of Harvard 1926, *The Life and Opinions of a College Class,* assembled and written by Cornelius DuBois and Charles J. V. Murphy on the occasion of the class's twenty-fifth reunion. The data gathered and analyzed for this study offer many tempting opportunities for comparison, some of which have been used. But a nagging doubt intrudes itself, a doubt of the comparability of a college class of 1926—"A mere whiff of the Golden Twenties, then the Crash. Turmoil was our legacy."—and a high-school class of 1938 with its very different kinds of turmoil.

The same reservations apply to the less extensive report of the Princeton Class of 1929. *The First Decade,* by Princeton 1944, is the only study (at least the only one discovered) of a particular college class which both goes into considerable detail and also represents a group of men who lived through essentially the same succession of experiences at approximately the same age as the guinea pigs. Although older groups, of course, lived through the immediate prewar, war, and postwar experiences, it is assumed that the impact varied for different age groups, according to their earlier background of experiences, the stage of their careers, and various other factors. There are certainly many college studies which the writer failed to locate. This type of study is usually privately printed and not copyrighted, so few of them are listed in the *Cumulative Book Index.* The most abundant source which was discovered for reunion books was the New York Public Library. They have dozens, or perhaps hundreds, there, but only a small percentage contain any data which are statistically handled.

The most thoroughgoing analysis of college graduates as a group in our society is *They Went to College,* by Ernest Havemann and Patricia West, published in 1952. It is a very rich source of information, and the only one so far discussed which includes women college graduates. It should be noted that, whereas Harvard and Princeton had reasonably consistent educational programs and philosophies which might be presumed to have an effect upon their graduates, the subjects of this study, selected by careful sampling techniques and questioned in 1947, represented the whole range of American colleges and all age groups. The statistics, however, are frequently broken down by sex, type of college, and age group, which helped greatly in determining comparability.

Walter B. Barbe, for his doctoral dissertation at Northwestern University, made a follow-up study of the students who graduated over a period of years from Cleveland's special classes for gifted children. One of the groups which he studied appears to resemble rather closely, both in age and ability, the gifted guinea pigs, and hence affords some valuable comparisons from a neighboring city.

The Gifted Child Grows up, by Lewis Terman and Melita Oden, is the most careful and detailed follow-up so far published. The final data for this report were gathered in 1945, twenty-five years after the beginning of the study, so the subjects are closer in age to the members of Harvard 1926 than they are to the guinea pigs. Terman's gifted children were studied at intervals down through the years; but except as this fact focused attention upon them and their needs, any special program for them or attempt to meet their needs was dependent upon the unco-ordinated action of a wide variety of home and school situations. When comparisons are made between Terman's group and the twenty-four gifted guinea pigs, a number of qualifications must be kept in mind.

1) All of Terman's gifted children had I.Q.'s of 135 or higher, whereas probably less than one-fourth of the twenty-four gifted guinea pigs ranked so high.

2) Terman's group had widely differing school programs; the guinea pigs all experienced one that was planned to stimulate them to their own best efforts and at the same time meet their needs for broad social experience and for both breadth and depth of learning.

3) Terman's group on the average is about ten years older than the guinea pigs.

Part III of this report is based upon analysis of the protocols in relation to the philosophy and purposes of the school. The full interview was given to forty-five students who had been in the school three or more years. Only the first group of fourteen questions about the school was asked of the four who had attended two years. As a preface it was explained to each one that the interview data were confidential, that we were trying to find out by a variety of questions how people were thinking and feeling and behaving to discover whether there were likenesses within the group greater than might be expected. If so, those likenesses could scarcely be explained by experiences since 1938 because the patterns since then had shown such great contrasts. Likenesses, if any, might be explained by attendance at University School, or by the selective factor which sent students there in the first place, or by influences in Columbus in the 1930's. The atmosphere in the interviews was kept as informal and as free of tension as possible.

The resulting protocols contained much richer characterological data than this particular research was able to use. Five major points from the philosophy and purposes of the school were selected for analysis: self-direction, social sensitivity, democratic living, the use of the method of intelligence, and creativity. Arrangements were made for some expert assistance in analyzing a sampling of the protocols to give the investigator help in working out the basic problems of method.[5] Heavy reliance was placed upon the work of Riesman and Adorno, though the results cannot lay claim to the level of skill and technical training which their analyses represented.

The confidential nature of the data creates a problem in reporting it. The usual methods of disguising individuals will not work where the subjects of the study are limited to a small group, all of whom know each other. As a general policy, favorable references, while

[5] Alice Seeman, former associate professor of education at Ohio State University, with advice from her husband, Melvin Seeman, a social psychologist, assisted the author.

anonymous, are to actual individuals, who may be recognized by the initiated. Actual quotations are used only with the consent of the individual concerned. Unfavorable references are handled in very general terms or disguised.

The interviews and questionnaires supplement each other. A questionnaire cannot discriminate between the person who crowds his life with strenuous activity as an escape and the person whose time is overflowing because of zestful, purposeful living. The multiple approach has been used to throw some light on and differentiate in such matters.

III

THE SETTING—THE SCHOOL PROGRAM,
THE STUDENTS, THEIR HOMES

The School Program

The University School opened in the fall of 1932 as the Eight Year Study was beginning, and was immediately included in the group of thirty high schools involved in the experiment. According to the terms of the agreement, over two hundred colleges were to accept graduates of the thirty schools during the experimental period on the basis of the schools' recommendations without regard to the usual unit or examination requirements. Curriculum planning for the new school took place in a unique atmosphere of freedom from arbitrary restriction and of challenge to use creative intelligence.

In September, 1932, the faculty, most of them strangers to each other and to Columbus, reported for a month of planning prior to the start of the fall quarter at the University on October 1. The new school, as a department of the College of Education, was to follow the quarter system of the University.

As must be true in any new school, curriculum problems were basic. Under the leadership of Rudolph Lindquist, the faculty tried to make intelligent use of their uniquely wide area of freedom to plan a curriculum in terms of a democratic philosophy and to make a schedule which would implement curriculum and general educational values. The principal limiting factors were the inevitable ones that each faculty member brought with him—habits, unanalyzed experiences, and unrecognized assumptions.

Mr. Lindquist had spent the previous year studying other university schools and assembling his faculty from a wide variety of backgrounds, geographical and educational. Perhaps the only common characteristics which they had were open-mindedness and a concern for education. A situation which required such diverse people to work and think together was enormously stimulating.

For information on the actual high-school program of the guinea pigs, there are two major contemporary sources, the students' own account in *Were We Guinea Pigs?* and the report which the faculty wrote for the Eight Year Study which is included in *Thirty Schools Tell Their Story* (pages 718–57). Quotations in this section are from the original, mimeographed report prepared by the faculty. This account is, in spots, more extensive than that printed in *Thirty Schools Tell Their Story,* but differences are generally minor.

During the seventh, eighth, and ninth grades, this group was enrolled in one of the very early core programs in the country, a program in which English, social-studies, and later, science teachers were trying to learn to see their areas in functional relationships to the problems of living. Those were the days of battles—at Progressive Education Association conferences, or conferences of the Thirty Schools, or in the pages of the journals—between correlation and integration, which at that time, of course, referred, not to interracial schools, but to the way in which subject-matter was presented (integration versus unrelated or simultaneously presented fragments) and to the thinking of children and adults (integration in contrast to logic-tight compartments). The University School took a consistent stand for integration; the subject-matter of core units came from the group analysis of the problem being studied.

> The seventh grade began with a core course in which teachers from the English, social science and the various arts areas participated. The second year the science area was included. Since then teachers in the science, social science, and English areas have usually been associated with each core, the arts specialists have helped in planning and in

many phases of the work, and arts laboratories have been available during core periods. Consideration of immediate environment in the seventh grade core has frequently emphasized the work in home economics. Varied organizations have been used. In the first year the core was more heavily staffed than it has been since that time. . . . The faculty is still experimenting with this matter of staff assignments in a core program, and with the degree and nature of the responsibility of representatives from the various areas of organized knowledge. Basic to the problem of organization is the concept of the core; and differences in organization represent, to a significant extent, differences among the faculty on that score. An analysis of these differences, and study of the core concept in terms of pupil maturation, needs, and school purposes are among the important current faculty undertakings.[1]

However, leisure reading was never tied to the core unit.

It has developed in practice that subject matter organizations begins to appear in the core. Leisure reading, for example, is carried on by the children in the elementary school; in the seventh grade, the English teacher gives guidance during core time. Book discussions are held on occasion, and near the end of the seventh or early in the eighth grade these discussion periods are scheduled regularly. Core science periods at times have been similarly scheduled in order to prevent conflict in the use of laboratories.[2]

Mathematics was a required subject during all the six years. It was developed around a set of unifying concepts essential to the problem-solving processes. Those selected for this purpose were number, measurement, relationship, operation, symbolism, and proof. It became the responsibility of the teachers in this area to strengthen and extend the growth of the concepts. Each of them was emphasized throughout the six grades and together they served as continuing threads which tended to unify the mathematics program, to relate it

[1] "The Eight Year Study: A Report of the Ohio State University School to the Commission on the Relation of School and College of the Progressive Education Association by the Faculty of the School" (Columbus, Ohio, October, 1940), pp. 13–14.
[2] *Ibid.*, p. 17.

to the core and to the other areas of knowledge. Additional aspects of the program were described in the 1940 report:

> The mathematics program has become increasingly flexible and functional. While textbooks were used during the early years, they are now used chiefly as references and the content studied is selected to a considerable extent in terms of the immediate personal and social needs of the student. Instead of solving only ready-made problems from textbooks the student is now guided in the solution of those problems that have the tang of reality for him. The mathematics classroom is a laboratory wherein the student learns to recognize the importance of accurate data. He weighs, measures, tabulates, and computes. He studies relationships and examines the implications of his data. . . .[3]

During the last two years all the students took a course based on demonstrative geometry, which was offered three hours per week for the first year and two hours per week for the second year. They examined the processes by which conclusions are reached and generalizations established. The course included both inductive and deductive procedures, and because of its continuing emphasis on the question of what constitutes proof, it came to be known as "the nature of proof."

> . . . This kind of subject matter is particularly appropriate, for the concepts considered and the ideas studied are devoid of strong emotional content. The student's native ability to think is not stifled by prejudice or bias. Under the guidance of his teacher he enters into such significant learning activities as creating and refining his own definitions, critically examining the assumptions he is willing to accept, and studying their implications. He "learns by doing" and there are potential refinements about the kind of "doing" which are helpful in developing his critical and analytical insights. He slowly becomes conscious of the fact that the so-called "laws of geometry" were not divinely revealed to some mathematical Moses in a Mount Sinai experience, but that they are the logical outcomes of the definitions and assumptions to which he himself has agreed. He learns what it means to challenge an assumption, for in the exercise of his free intellectual sovereignty he can change an assumption to suit his own

[3] *Ibid.*, pp. 17–18.

individual ideas and trace the inevitable effect of this change on the conclusions which depend on that assumption. He learns that conclusions are true only to the degree that the assumptions from which they are derived are true, and he is thus introduced to the idea of the relativity of truth.

It is recognized, however, that to study situations which involve only the idealized concepts of mathematics is to limit the extent to which the kind of thinking developed may be used. Transfer is secured best by training for transfer, and the methods of thought used so effectively in connection with geometric content are extended to situations beyond the narrow confines of mathematics. The student, for example, is asked to examine the *Declaration of Independence* and to select the assumptions which the signers of that document considered essential to democratic government. His attention is directed to the quality of argument found in political speeches, editorials, advertisements, and the like. He is asked to analyze arguments of this type, selecting the words and phrases on which the validity of the argument depends as well as the stated and unstated assumptions which are essential to the conclusions reached.[4]

The way in which this program was adapted to individual needs is illustrated by the mathematics report of a gifted tenth-grade boy.

January 28, 1936.   Mathematics report by Harold Fawcett on John Jones, 10th Grade.

John has worked steadily during the quarter and while he has not made the unusually rapid progress which distinguished his record of preceding years he has done exceedingly well. He is working independently of his grade and, to a large extent, is directing his own activity. He is now nearing the completion of his geometry and there is no question as to his comprehension and broad understanding of the subject matter he has covered. His test record is excellent and his ability to handle difficult original exercises is especially noticeable. He has keen analytical ability, is able to express his ideas concisely, and will go far in the field of mathematics. When he completes the work in geometry I shall give him a college board examination. Following that I recommend that he resume his study of advanced algebra which was interrupted last year and carry that to a completion which he can easily do before the end of the year. We can then plan together as to what would be his best program for the following year.

[4] *Ibid.*, pp. 46–47.

John is a consistent and thorough worker. I have acted only in the capacity of adviser and have done little more than discuss with him certain questions which he has raised from time to time. He is a very capable pupil.

Courses in the arts, fine arts, industrial arts, music, typing, and home economics were elective throughout the six years.

The school began with a rich elective program in the arts, but with a student body too lacking in experience to appreciate the opportunities. Many devices have been used to encourage students to broaden their interests and to experiment in new fields. Present practice requires all students to work in one or more of the arts, and entrusts the grade chairman with advising children on their schedules. These programs of arts electives are kept as flexible as is consistent with worthwhile accomplishment. A special event such as an operetta may require a complete rearrangement of many schedules until the performance is over.

To make possible an activity to include all grades and to make room within the school day for interests which are ordinarily extra-curricular, many schedule devices have been used. The one which has been most common has been the setting aside of one afternoon, freed from all regularly scheduled classes, for a program variously known as "Free Choice," "Special Electives," and "English-Arts." The groups scheduled in this time have varied widely. In many cases, interests which first appeared there have moved into and modified the content of regular classes. Others have been satisfied and disappeared, while new ones have taken their places. Certain ones remain and always appear: orchestra, dramatics, publications.

In the arts laboratories students carry on both individual and group projects. Even when special courses are organized they are set up in terms of the needs and purposes of a particular group. Typing is taught for personal use and students work at their own speed at their own undertakings. "Fine Arts" on a program means that the student at a given hour goes to the studio, where he may paint, model, tool leather, weave, work in ceramics, or engage in various other activities according to a plan which he has worked out with the teacher. The industrial arts teacher and his assistant act as consulting experts to help students develop and execute their individual plans in a shop whose facilities permit work in hot and cold metal, hand and machine woodwork, and coiling, throwing, casting, or glazing clay. Group undertakings, such as printing, radio work, and boat building may be organized under faculty sponsors.

The nature of work in music and home economics emphasizes a considerable amount of group activity. Students elect chorus or instrumental groups or arrange for instrumental lessons. Classes in home economics set up a group plan of study within which individuals develop their own plans. There is a constant demand from boys for work in this area, though the exigencies of teacher time and schedule seldom permit such groups except as special electives on one afternoon per week.[5]

Foreign languages—French, German, and Latin—were elective in the tenth through the twelfth grades. The distribution of the electives of the Class of 1938 during those grades is shown in Table 4.

TABLE 4

ELECTIVES OF THE CLASS OF 1938 IN GRADES 10, 11, AND 12

Electives	Boys (N–26)	Girls (N–24)
Industrial arts.	22	..
Fine arts.	5	13
Home economics.	..	11
Music.	9	11
Typing.	13	16
Only one art elective.	8	3
French.	16	23
Latin.	11	13
German.	6	1
No foreign language.	2	1
One year only of foreign language.	3	..
Two foreign languages.	8	13

Electives of foreign languages were heavy; only six students, or 12 per cent, failed to complete at least two years of foreign language. All students were required to elect one or more of the arts, and only eleven, or 22 per cent chose only one art area. Thirty-nine, or 78 per cent, chose two or more.

Meanwhile, in the upper grades every student continued with required work in the major areas, English, social studies, science, and

[5] *Ibid.*, pp. 21–23.

mathematics. Mathematics has already been discussed. The science program was in a state of flux. In the seventh grade it was a separate course; in the eighth and ninth it became a part of the core, and science experiences were developed from the core units. In the three upper grades it was taught as a broad-fields course. In the 1940 report the faculty wrote about science as follows:

> The science program has taken a less definite pattern than have some others, because of shifting personnel, but certain generalizations can be made. It has become increasingly concerned with meeting the needs of maturing individuals and with development of problem solving abilities and attitudes. The science experiences of the junior high school grades have become an integral part of the core program. The problems are those which present themselves in the progress of the large undertakings. . . . Whether science electives in the upper grades will continue to be taught as was the science formerly required at that level in a broad fields course, the problems studied having their origin in the backgrounds of the children, or whether the interests of more advanced students will bring more conventional organizations can only be learned through additional experience.[6]

In the social-studies field, pupil participation was very extensive. It rested on a foundation of student awareness, sophistication, and concern about the world in the days of the depression and the New Deal, the rise of Hitler in Germany, and the events of the thirties in Russia.

> The values for which the social science teachers are working are reinforced by the whole organization of the school, the relationship between pupils and teachers, and the orientation of the work in other areas. Students are encouraged by all teachers to use critically information from all kinds of sources. Books, pamphlets, periodicals, radio programs, recordings, pictures, plays, trips, interviews, and many other kinds of experiences are used as means to a fuller understanding of the immediate and larger community. While all classes make short trips in Columbus it has become a tradition for the eleventh and twelfth grades to make longer journeys to some destination selected by the class after investigation of many possibilities. Trips have been made to Detroit, New York, Washington, the T.V.A., and New

[6] *Ibid.*, p. 17.

Orleans, while Chicago, Quebec, and many other destinations have been considered. Planning and carrying out the plans for such trips are activities which have called for a high degree of practical cooperation and the results have been gratifying.

The English and foreign language programs are much more closely articulated now than formerly. Teachers of the various languages (English, French, German, and Latin) are organized as a single committee. General language is required in the ninth grade, and is a cooperative venture of the language staff. Children may elect a foreign language in the tenth grade, only with the permission of this general language faculty, who consider proficiency in the mother tongue a major factor in readiness.

From the beginning of the school the discussions of literature in English classes were based upon the books which the children had read or were reading. The books recorded by students on their English folders have come to include not only a wide range of books in English, French, and German which are usually classed as *belles lettres,* but also a great quantity not so considered. Many of these are in the fields of science, social science, and other areas. Similarly, English teachers find much of the materials for class use in the written work prepared for reports in other academic areas. Principles of organization (sentence, paragraph, and theme structure) and the varied functions of words are frequently studied in connection with written work developed in core or special area classes. All teachers carry at least part of the responsibility for teaching good usage and acceptable written form.[7]

Physical education was a required activity every day. After a physical examination, all were required to take part in some phase of the intramural-sports and physical-education program. This program provided a wide range of activities, which included something appropriate for every individual. Those who could not participate in active sports might take walks or act as timekeepers.

It is obvious that the schedule was crowded and that not every class could meet every day. Planning a division of time in terms of the all-round development of children was one of the difficult faculty

[7] *Ibid.,* pp. 18–19.

responsibilities in the series of planning meetings which ended each school year and preceded the beginning of a new one.

While many aspects of living remained competitive—the faculty, after much thought, concluded that competition was natural and could be socially desirable if properly directed—the school watched for and tried to develop the co-operative opportunities which presented themselves, particularly those in which a variety of student interests and talents could combine to achieve a result that even the most gifted could not have reached alone. Teachers also tried to help every individual to secure status in his group, to feel emotionally identified with the school, and to achieve as good results in both academic work and activities as he was capable of achieving. Of course no one believed then or believes now that such goals were fully reached.

During these years the school recognized the importance of a counseling system which was in day-to-day contact with each child as he worked alone or in his peer group, and which could deal with individual or group problems before they became acute. It is worth noting that, although the Dean's letter to the trustees in 1933 mentions "mental health," the concepts in that area were still imprecise in the early thirties, and few of the books which have since helped to clarify ideas had yet been written when this class was in high school.

The type of counseling arrangement varied from year to year during the 1932 to 1938 period. The one constant was that the whole staff was concerned with developing an effective system, and that they believed that counseling should be able to do something effective in the fields of mental health, moral values, and democratic living by using the actual experiences provided by school life.

The Class of 1938 attended high school during a time of crisis for democracy—the depression within and the rapidly rising threat from fascist and communist totalitarianism without. In that period the characteristics of democracy which were emphasized tended to be those which offered the sharpest contrasts to totalitarianism. From the point of view of today, the school's concepts of democracy itself may appear too simplified, without enough allowance for the pluralism of our society or enough tolerance for the ambiguities inherent in a society of free individuals. But at least teachers and students were searching for answers and values together.

What Sort of People Were the Guinea Pigs?

The seventh grade which entered the University School in the autumn of 1932 numbered fifty-one, twenty-seven boys and twenty-four girls. When they graduated in 1938, there were fifty-four, twenty-nine boys and twenty-five girls. Thirty-three of them were in the class through all six years, forty-seven for four or more years, and forty-eight for three or more years.

For each one there was in the graduate files at the school an individual permanent record folder in which home and test data and other individual records were preserved. In addition, the school maintained a file of carbon copies of all progress reports sent home, which were later collected in a bound volume for each reporting period.[8]

Upon graduation each student was given an individual "senior statement" which was a final progress report addressed to the student himself; carbon copies of these were bound and preserved, and several carbons were put in each individual's folder.

When examined, the records proved less complete than had been expected; and no two folders contained exactly the same kind of data. In the middle 1930's when research studies of many kinds were in progress, records which had been removed for temporary use were apparently mislaid. For example, all the bound progress reports for the first three years of the school are missing. Another cause for the lack of uniformity in records is best expressed in the words of the faculty report:

. . . The early years of the school were full of examples of duplicated functions and of other important ones which went undone because

[8] Since its beginning, the school has reported on pupil progress through letters to the parents two or three times a year instead of by report cards and grades.

they were nobody's job. This is nowhere better illustrated than in the matter of records, reports, and guidance. Gradually the location of general responsibilities has been agreed upon in practice, though particular phases are still under discussion.

At the request of the director, in the spring of 1939 an executive committee was elected by the faculty to give advice on administrative problems, while major matters of policy are discussed and decided by the whole faculty. . . .[9]

Whatever the explanation, the records of the class included four Binets of assorted dates; fifty Otis I.Q.'s [10] from the ninth grade; and from the twelfth grade, forty-four Iowa Silent Reading Tests,[11] forty-nine Henmon-Nelson Tests,[12] fifty scores for a form of the American Council on Education Psychological Examination,[13] and ten Ohio State Psychological Examinations. There were some test scores for everyone, but not the same ones. Yet it seemed important to establish some ability groups within the class. There had been some brilliant students whose later records should be compared with Terman's gifted children. Memory and the records, especially the Binet test scores, identified certain ones, but the problem of which others should be included in the same group was a difficult one.

With a tabulation of the recorded test scores, the writer approached an expert on tests and measurement of the Department of Psychology at Ohio State to ask how such miscellaneous data could be used to determine ability groups within the class. He suggested making a distribution of the available scores on each test, dividing them into fifths, or quintiles, then preparing a summary sheet showing in different columns the quintiles for each of the tests. By making such a sheet for each student, entering his score for any test in his folder at the bot-

[9] "The Eight Year Study . . . ," p. 15.
[10] Otis Self-Administering Tests of Mental Ability, Form A: Grades 4 to 9 (World Book Company, 1922). The scores were recorded, but the test forms were not preserved.
[11] Iowa Silent Reading Tests. Advanced Test: Form B (1931).
[12] Henmon-Nelson Tests of Mental Ability—Form A, High School Examination, Grades 7–12 (Houghton Mifflin Company, 1931).
[13] Psychological Examination for Grades Nine to Twelve, American Council on Education (1937).

tom of the appropriate column, and circling his quintile, one could get comparative standings. Since from two to five test scores were available for each student, it was assumed that the missing ones would be similar to the ones which were known.

He also suggested that a special effort be made to get scores on the Ohio State Psychological Examination (O.S.P.E.) which had already been in use for some years before 1938 and had been well validated. Since it is a scholastic-aptitude test required of all students enrolling at the University, the registrar's office was able to supply a large number of scores to supplement those in the folders. Scores on this test were thus available for forty-three of the fifty-four students.

The use of quintiles gave results which were reasonably consistent with faculty memories and the evidence of progress reports. In two cases in which the comparison of test ratings placed the student much higher than the teachers had thought him to be in high school, the follow-up interview revealed psychological factors which had been unsuspected earlier, and which fully accounted for the discrepancy. Parenthetically, one of the fascinating things about the follow-up study has been these illuminating insights into the events of twenty years ago.

When the quintiles were used in tabulating data on college attendance, it appeared that two or three individuals were rated far too low by this device; for example, the man placed in the fifth quintile who earned a Master's degree (see Chapter IV, pages 51–68). College attendance, on the whole, however, tended to validate the general distribution. There were, nevertheless, six cases in which the O.S.P.E., probably the most reliable single test, was significantly higher than the composite test rating, and one in which it was significantly lower. The quintiles, based on the composite test ratings, have been used with caution for these reasons, but they have been helpful.

For purposes of comparing a group of guinea pigs with Terman's gifted children, a means of selection had to be established. It was finally decided to take the top quintile plus those students whose O.S.P.E. scores were equivalent to the seventy-sixth percentile or better. This includes twenty-four students and admittedly takes in a great many who would not have qualified for Terman's group. It has the advantage of identifying roughly the outstanding individuals in a class of high ability. Some of these are a fair match for Terman's gifted children and others are competent runners-up. The remaining thirty cover the range of normal to superior with only a few in the low-normal category.

The quintiles, for all their weaknesses, were useful for many basic tabulations. Another arrangement used in some tabulations was based upon college graduation or non-graduation.

For some other purposes, it has seemed best to use the whole class as a unit. An examination of the academic competence of the group as a whole shows a spread of between 59 and 99 I.Q. points from the highest to the lowest score. It is 99 points if one uses the highest I.Q., as measured by a Binet (170 I.Q.), and the lowest one, as measured by an Otis (71 I.Q.), which is the only score that was available for one student. Of course, a comparison of these two scores, one from an individual test and the other from a group test, cannot legitimately be used. Using Otis I.Q.'s alone, the range is from 71 to 130, a 59 point difference. However, the top Otis score of 130 was earned by the same student who showed an I.Q. of 170 on an individual Binet; the Binet is almost surely more accurate. On the Otis scale, the median I.Q. was 115, and seven were below 100.

Forty-three scores were available for the Ohio State Psychological Examination, which has been found to be predictive of academic success at the University. By law, any graduate of a first-class high school in Ohio must be admitted to Ohio State. The norms used in this study were derived from the O.S.P.E. scores of the students entering at the same time as members of the Class of 1938, and the predictive reliability of the test has been studied from their college records. How this group compares with the general population of those entering college throughout the country is not known, but it is typical of high-school graduates in Ohio. The ability data are summarized in Table 5. The range on this test was from the first percentile to the ninety-ninth with the median score in the sixty-third percentile. Thirteen were below the fiftieth percentile. Eight of the eleven students for whom no

O.S.P.E. scores were available were in the top group on other tests and only two were in the bottom group, so this median is probably too low.

TABLE 5
GENERAL ABILITY GROUPINGS OF THE GUINEA PIGS

INSTRUMENT	RANGE		MEDIAN	NUMBER OF SCORES BELOW I. Q. 100 (FIFTIETH PERCENTILE)
	High	Low		
Otis Self-administering Form A................	130	71	115	7
Ohio State Psychological Examination...........	Ninety-ninth percentile	First percentile	Sixty-third percentile	13

There were six students in the group with serious reading handicaps, which in two particularly severe cases, were connected with defective vision. There were none with serious behavior problems beyond those normal for the various age levels.

From What Types of Homes Did They Come?

The class entered the University School in the fall of 1932, which, as any reader over forty well remembers, was the depth of the depression, the autumn of the Roosevelt landslide, the winter of the bread lines. What kinds of parents in that time of trial chose to send their children to a new, "progressive" school which charged tuition, even though the charges were small? Why did they make the decision?

This has been the subject of much speculation but no research; at this late date probably not much that is reliable can be learned about motives. For their book, the students gathered a certain amount of information about their homes, but nothing about their parents' reasons for choosing the school. From school records, faculty memories, and references in the interviews, some information and a few theories can be assembled.

It seems reasonable to suppose that different parents selected the school from quite dissimilar motives. Some were genuinely interested in its program and its purposes—nine families had sent a boy or girl to Laura Zirbes' Little School for one or two years before the high school opened—and were willing to go to a great deal of personal inconvenience to enable their children to attend. For example, one father commuted thirty miles to his job in a neighboring town so that his family might live near the school. Some were interested in what they believed the school would stand for, but found themselves in some disagreement with its actual operation. A few of them withdrew their children after one or more years, and the places were taken by others who were sympathetic. Sometimes the children insisted on staying, however, and sometimes the parents learned to understand the school's point of view or at least to tolerate the differences. Some parents entered their children because of the obvious failure of earlier schools to give them the individual help and understanding that they needed. It seems likely that certain ones would have preferred to send their children to one of the prestige private schools of Columbus, but finding their finances pinched by the depression, took a chance on the less expensive University School in preference to the public schools. Probably the differences in motive are not as significant as the fact that all parents had to make a conscious selection, in that no one went to the school automatically because of the district in which he lived.

The homes were scattered over metropolitan Columbus. They formed no community and had no common denominator except the school. There is no doubt that, on the whole, they represented relative comfort and economic security, though there were a few families whose financial problems were severe. By their senior year there were some students who were earning their own tuition and spending money; but as the class wrote in *Were We Guinea Pigs?*, "We have no problems of malnutrition or insufficient clothing." When the class investigated family income in 1938, they found the distribution shown in Table 6; whether the 35 per cent for whom no figures were available tended to represent a low income group or were distributed throughout the scale cannot now be determined.

The students reported that 88 per cent of their fathers and 43 per cent of their mothers had attended college or trade school, though they had not necessarily graduated. Of the fathers, 42 per cent were professional men, 34 per cent were in a trade or business, 8 per cent were in government service, and 16 per cent were deceased. Only 11 per cent of the mothers were employed; the data do not show how many of those employed were widows. Seventy-eight per cent of the families owned their own homes.

TABLE 6

INCOMES OF THE PARENTS OF THE CLASS OF 1938

Family Income in 1938 *	Number of Families †	Per Cent of the Total Number of Families *	Equivalent Income in 1956 ‡
No information....	19	35.0	....
$2,000 to $4,000....	11	19.0	$4,120 to $8,240
$4,000 to $6,000....	16	28.0	$8,240 to $12,840
$6,000 to $8,000....	6	11.5	$12,840 to $17,600
$8,000 and over....	3	6.5	$17,600 and over

* This information was taken from *Were We Guinea Pigs?*, p.6.

† The percentages used by the students in their book could not be converted into whole numbers of families, but approximations are probably accurate enough for our purposes.

‡ The figures in this column were derived from those given for a married couple with two children in "Effects of Taxes and Dollar Depreciation on Selected Gross Incomes" ("Road Maps of Industry," No. 1079), issued by the Conference Board, 460 Park Avenue, New York 22, New York, on August 31, 1956.

According to *Were We Guinea Pigs?*, about 25 per cent of the homes of the class members were broken by death or divorce. Using a combination of data from records and interviews, and memories of actual situations, the writer has attempted to classify the home situations to discover how many were the kind of warm, secure home which promotes the development of healthy personalities in children. The number of broken homes, at least in this instance, offered no clear indication, for in retrospect, a number of the one-parent homes seem to have been happy, secure, and free of tension, whereas other homes with both parents living together were quite disturbed.[14]

[14] This procedure cannot be called research because objective data were lacking; for that reason, tabulations have not been included.

The first thing which is obvious from such an examination is that the large majority were good homes by any standard and that there were no thoroughly bad homes where children were rejected, trained in antisocial behavior, or exposed to depravity. In 20 to 25 per cent of the cases, however, there were enough tensions and disturbances to create problems for a child growing up in that environment. In view of current emphasis on broken homes as a cause of children's problems, it is interesting that the percentage of children with problems in this study turned out to be almost the same as the percentage of broken homes; however, this is only an apparent correlation since half of the children with problems came from tension-filled two-parent homes.

TABLE 7

AN APPRAISAL OF THE PARENTS' POLITICAL AND SOCIAL
ATTITUDES BY THEIR CHILDREN

Political and Social Attitude	Per Cent Classified in 1937–38	Per Cent Classified in 1955
Reactionary................................	....	2.0
Conservative................................	57.0	56.0
Part liberal and part conservative..........	16.5	22.5
Liberal....................................	21.5	17.5
Radical....................................	6.0	2.0

It is interesting that the students in 1938 did not classify their parents as Republicans or Democrats. Instead they rated their parents' political beliefs as conservative, between conservative and liberal, liberal, and radical. A very similar question concerning the parents' attitudes in their high-school days was included in the 1955 questionnaire. The responses are summarized in Table 7.

Since the percentages in the second column of Table 7 add up to 101 per cent, all are probably fractionally too high. Whether the slight shifts between the 1938 and 1955 appraisals are due to changes in definition would be hard to determine. No one was uncertain in answering this question in 1955. The generally close agreement between adolescent and mature judgments is striking. Perhaps the period from

1932 to 1938 focussed attention on political attitudes with more sharpness and less ambiguity than is ordinarily true. It is possible, too, that the emphases of the school's program might have contributed to this clarity.

Religiously, the group was predominantly Protestant with a very few Catholics and one Jewish student. Although nearly three-fourths of the parents, as shown by Table 8, were church members, only a few more than half attended regularly. The proportion of children who attended is slightly, but not significantly, higher.

TABLE 8

CHURCH MEMBERSHIP AND ATTENDANCE IN HIGH SCHOOL AS
REPORTED ON THE 1955 QUESTIONNAIRE

Extent of Church Membership and Attendance	Number of Families	Per Cent
Parents belonged, and parents and child attended more or less regularly..............	23	44
Parents belonged and attended; child did not go to church regularly......................	3	6
Parents belonged but did not attend; child went regularly................................	4	8
Parents belonged, but neither they nor the child attended with any regularity..............	10	19
Neither parent belonged, but child attended....	4	8
Parents and child neither belonged nor attended.	8	15

In general, then, these students came from comfortable, upper—middle class homes which gave them support and understanding, as well as physical amenities. Finances were difficult, but not critical, in an undetermined number of cases, certainly less than one-third of the total. In about one-fourth to one-fifth of the families, there were home problems from time to time which constituted traumatic experiences for individual children; these were of the same kinds that are likely to occur in any similar group of the population in a difficult period. In most cases, though not in all, the school was aware of the difficult situations or the shattering experiences at the time, and the teachers and students did what they could to adjust their expectations and the school program. The homes were more frequently conservative than liberal, but the liberal influence was strong. In 50 per cent of the families, the parents belonged to and attended church; in 27 per cent, they belonged but did not attend; while in 23 per cent, they neither belonged nor attended. Sixty per cent of the class members attended church services during their high-schools days, and 40 per cent did not.

PART II

WHAT DO THE DATA SHOW?

IV

FURTHER EDUCATION, VOCATIONS,
INCOME, AND MILITARY SERVICE

Further Education

The University School has a student body that is heterogeneous in academic ability. The proportion of its graduates who go on to further education beyond high school has consistently been large, and that fact tends to create for all students social pressure toward college, irrespective of their academic interests, special abilities, or vocational plans. The location of the school on a corner of the University campus contributes to this tendency.

The laws of Ohio require that the state universities accept any graduate of a first-class high school who wishes to enrol. When the first senior class at University School was approaching graduation in 1935 (the tenth grade was the highest one in which a student could enrol when the school opened in 1932), the faculty faced the problem of who should be graduated. The teachers and the director decided that students who had achieved up to the level which could reasonably be expected of them should be awarded senior statements. If they were individuals who could not or should not attend college, the counseling system was trusted to help them make intelligent plans for some other next step. If this procedure failed, it was believed that the school and the University would have to let them try and learn from experience what they were able to do.

With one possible exception (a man who failed to return either questionnaire, and about whom information is scanty and unreliable), the students who graduated in 1938 entered some school for further training. In most cases, they enrolled in colleges or universities, although one began and completed a junior-college course, and four others completed a special training course for a particular vocation. Two members of the class attended college for two years, then enrolled in and completed vocational courses. Six of those who entered college decided they were not getting what they wanted and withdrew. Four failed to make good enough grades to stay in. Three girls left to

TABLE 9
COLLEGE ATTENDANCE, DEGREES, AND HONORS

Quintile	Number of Students in Quintile	Number of Students Entering College	Number of Students Graduating from a Four-Year Course	Number of Students Receiving			Number of Honors
				M.A. Degree	Ph.D. Degree	Honors	
I.........	11	11	11	5	3	8	30
II........	10	10	8	2	1	6	12
III.......	11	11	9	3	..	2	5
IV.......	11	11	5	1	..	1	2
V........	11	6	1	1	..	..	..
Total...	54	49	34	12	4	17	49

be married. Thirty-four students, or 63 per cent, completed four years of undergraduate work and received a Bachelor's degree. Twelve, or 22 per cent of the total, went on to earn M.A. degrees, and four (7.5 per cent) earned the Ph.D. degree. The distribution of these degrees by quintiles is shown in Table 9. Seventeen individuals, or 31 per cent, received one or more honors in college.

Another way to look at the scholastic data is by tabulating the records of the twenty-four class members who might well be called the "gifted guinea pigs" and comparing them with those of Terman's gifted group. (The method by which the gifted guinea pigs were selected for comparison with Terman's gifted children has been described on pages 40–44). Classifications similar to Terman's are used in Tables 10 and 11.

Study and comparison of Tables 9, 10, and 11 indicate several in-

TABLE 10

COLLEGE AND HIGH-SCHOOL RECORDS OF THE GIFTED GUINEA PIGS IN COMPARISON WITH TERMAN'S GIFTED GROUP

COLLEGE AND HIGH-SCHOOL RECORD	CLASS OF 1938 MEN (N-10)		TERMAN'S MEN (PER CENT)*	CLASS OF 1938 WOMEN (N-14)		TERMAN'S WOMEN (PER CENT)*
	Number	Per Cent		Number	Per Cent	
Graduation from college....	8	80	69.5	14	100	66.8
One to four years of college..	1	10	13.5	..	...	14.3
One year or less of college...	1	10	4.6	..	...	3.4
High-school graduation alone, or plus special training...............	..	..	12.0	..	...	14.1
High school not completed..	..	..	.4	..	...	1.4

* Percentages from Terman's *Gifted Child Grows Up*, p. 149, Table 21.

TABLE 11

HIGHER DEGREES AND HONORS OF COLLEGE GRADUATES

HIGHER DEGREES AND HONORS	CLASS OF 1938 MEN (N-8)		TERMAN'S MEN (PER CENT)*	CLASS OF 1938 WOMEN (N-14)		TERMAN'S WOMEN (PER CENT)*
	Number	Per Cent		Number	Per Cent	
One or more graduate degrees (M.A., Ph.D.)...	5	62.5	51.2	2	14.0	29.3
M.A. or M.S.............	2	25.0	10.5	2	16.0	18.2
L.L.B.................	2	25.0	14.2	...	...	.7
M.B.A.................	1	12.5	3.4	...	...	.2
Graduate engineering degree...................	1	12.5	2.5	...	...	...
Graduate degree in theology.................	1	12.5	.5	...	...	...
M.D..................	...	...	8.5	...	...	1.2
Ph.D..................	3	37.5	10.8	1	7.0	3.1
Others.................	...	...	.8	...	...	5.7
Degree with distinction or membership in college honorary.............	6	87.5	39.8	5	35.7	32.5
Phi Beta Kappa.........	3	37.5	17.2	1	7.0	19.4

* Percentages from Terman's *Gifted Child Grows Up*, p. 151, Table 22.

teresting points. The percentage of the whole University School class which graduated from college (63 per cent) is almost as large as the separate percentages for men and women in Terman's group (69.5 and 66.8 per cent respectively). The proportion of college graduates among the gifted guinea pigs is much larger than in Terman's group (80 per cent of the men and 100 per cent of the women).

The gifted men of 1938 surpassed Terman's men in almost every category shown in Table 11. A slightly larger proportion won graduate degrees. More than twice as high a proportion was elected to Phi Beta Kappa, and either graduated with distinction or was elected to college honoraries. Ph.D. degrees were earned by 37.5 per cent in contrast to 10.8 per cent of Terman's men. There were no doctors of medicine graduated from the Class of 1938, but there were higher percentages in all of the other categories of degrees into which Terman classified his subjects. Of course, the absolute numbers of guinea pigs in each category are small, so one individual makes a big difference in a percentage.

All of the gifted women of 1938 graduated from four-year colleges. Two of them (14 per cent) earned additional, graduate degrees, against 29.3 per cent of Terman's women; one of the two (7 per cent) received a Ph.D., against 3.1 per cent of Terman's women. Only one woman was elected to Phi Beta Kappa, compared with 19.4 per cent of Terman's group. The percentages winning honors and earning Master's degrees are very similar in both groups of women. Of the seven gifted guinea pigs in education, four won degrees with distinction or *cum laude,* and were elected to Pi Lambda Theta. One graduate of a liberal-arts college took her distinctions so lightly that she could remember only that she had been elected to some kind of honorary, but not which one it was since she could not find her pin.

The figures in Table 9 tend to validate the general groupings in the quintiles; however, the incidence of advanced degrees and honors in the two lower quintiles strongly suggests that the test data used in establishing the quintiles were not adequate for wholly reliable judgments on individual cases.

Table 12 contains a list of the colleges and universities which

TABLE 12
COLLEGES AND UNIVERSITIES ATTENDED, AND DEGREES WON, BY MEMBERS OF THE CLASS OF 1938

COLLEGES AND UNIVERSITIES	NUMBER OF STUDENTS ATTENDING		NUMBER OF DEGREES RECEIVED					
			Bachelor's		Master's or Equivalent		Ph.D.	
	Men	Women	Men	Women	Men	Women	Men	Women
California Institute of Technology	1	...	...	...	...	...	1	...
Colgate Rochester Divinity School	1	...	...	...	1	...	...	...
Columbia University	...	2	...	...	...	1	...	...
Columbia University Teachers College	...	1	...	...	...	1	...	...
Cornell University	3	...	2	...	...	...	1	...
Denison University	1	2	1	...	...	...	...	...
Iowa State College of Agriculture and Mechanic Arts	...	1	...	1	...	...	...	...
Massachusetts Institute of Technology	1	...	1	...	1	...	...	...
New Mexico Highlands University	1	...	...	...	1	...	...	...
Ohio State University	22	15	11	11	3	...	1	...
Ohio Wesleyan University	1	...	1	...	...	...	...	...
Radcliffe College	...	1	...	...	...	...	...	1
Sarah Lawrence College	...	1	...	1	...	...	...	...
Sweet Briar College	...	1	...	1	...	...	...	...
Swarthmore College	...	1	...	1	...	...	...	...
University of California at Los Angeles	3	...	1	...	...	...	...	...
University of Chicago	1	...	1	...	1	...	...	...
University of Michigan	1	1	...	1	1	...	...	...
Vassar College	...	1	...	1	...	...	...	...
Western Reserve University	1	...	...	...	1	...	...	...
Total	37	27	18 *	17	9	2	3	1

* One man received two Bachelor's degrees under the co-operative program between M.I.T. and selected liberal-arts colleges. The total number of men who received Bachelor's degrees is 17.

awarded one or more degrees to members of the Class of 1938. The list does not include junior colleges, special training schools, or four-year colleges which class members attended for periods of from one semester to three years without completing work for a degree. Nor does it include graduate schools at which three guinea pigs studied but did not earn degrees. The twenty institutions listed in the table awarded thirty-five Bachelor's degrees, eleven Master's degrees, and four Ph.D. degrees to members of the class. Even the most cursory examination of the table shows that Ohio State University played a large part in the totals.

TABLE 13

OTHER COLLEGES AND UNIVERSITIES, JUNIOR COLLEGES, AND
SPECIAL SCHOOLS ATTENDED BY MEMBERS OF
THE CLASS OF 1938

Four-Year Colleges and Universities (Attended three years or less)

Bennington College	New College, in Teachers College,
College of Saint Mary of the	Columbia University
Springs (Ohio)	Ohio University
Goucher College	University of Miami (Florida)
Hillsdale College	Wells College
Muskingum College	

Junior Colleges (Two-year courses completed for certificates)

Briarcliff Junior College	Stephens College

Special Schools (Offering, in most cases, a program of courses leading to a certificate)

Cincinnati College of Embalming	Kirksville College of Osteopathy
Cranbrook Academy of Art	and Surgery
Franklin University, Columbus,	Insurance school
Ohio (Practical business courses)	Office training school
	Vocational arts school

At some time or other thirty-seven (75.5 per cent) of the forty-nine guinea pigs who attended college went to Ohio State. Twenty-two of the thirty-five undergraduate degrees, or 63 per cent, were earned at Ohio State, and the remaining thirteen at twelve different institutions. Three Master's degrees and one Ph.D. degree were earned at Ohio State. Because Ohio State University is accessible and reasonable in cost, and offers liberal, business, and professional education, it is natural that it should have drawn a large number of local students. Twenty-seven members attended nineteen other colleges from which they received thirteen Bachelor's degrees, eight Master's, and three Ph.D.'s. Obviously, there is a great deal of overlapping in the totals of college attendance because people at different times went to more than one college. This becomes even more conspicuous when one looks at the nine additional four-year colleges which were attended for periods varying from one semester to three years, and the list of special schools and courses selected for well-considered reasons (Table 13). From statements in the interviews, it is apparent that three people in the class shopped around with inadequately formulated plans; but even in these cases, the interviews revealed that the various college experiences became an education in realities.

An interesting group of seven individuals, 13 per cent of the class, chose special schools suited to their needs and interests and went ahead to get certificates from junior colleges, office-training schools, Franklin University (business courses), a college of enbalming, and so on. Two of these tried college first, but gave it up after one or two years. Without exception, these individuals have found their training to be what they needed for the jobs they now hold.

Vocations

There is information concerning vocations for twenty-five of the twenty-six women. Just before the study began, the twenty-sixth one, who had an office job, married and moved to Florida. It was impossible to interview her there, and since she did not return the questionnaire, there is no reliable information about her. All of the women are now married but one. Before marriage, all but two of them had worked for a median of three years, and 65 per cent of them were interested enough in their jobs to have considered them as careers. However, only two of the women have been employed full-time continuously since marriage, one as a researcher in ethnology and linguistics and the other as a high-school dramatics teacher. Neither has children. The ethnologist is listed in both the 1957 *Directory of American Scholars* and the 1958 *Who's Who of American Women*. A third, also without children, is being tempted to return to her old job by various inducements, chiefly accommodation of her hours and vacations to those of her husband. Three of the women with children are employed part time: one helps her husband with his business, another does part-time work in testing for the local schools, and the third writes columns of local news for a nearby metropolitan newspaper. The unmarried woman is an elementary-school teacher after some years in department-store work. The other eighteen are full-time homemakers, and all but one have families of children.

TABLE 14

VOCATIONS OF THE MEN OF THE CLASS OF 1938

(N-29)

Vocation	Number
Business and sales	8
Science and engineering	8
Accounting and bookkeeping	4
Art	3
Law	2
Advertising	1
Clerical work	1
Factory work	1
Ministry	1

The vocational pattern of the men is more complex, and more difficult to tabulate. The classifications that have been used are accounting, advertising, art, business and sales, clerical work, law, ministry, science and engineering, and factory work. With one exception, the jobs fall into the various groups analyzed by C. Wright Mills in *White Collar*. The one exception is a factory job which pays more than any white-collar opening which the man could fill, so he feels "stuck with it" but rather resentful.

Table 14 shows the distribution but covers up the fascinating variety of the occupations. One of the artists has headquarters in Hollywood, and although we have little information about him, we know that his name appears in the theater news occasionally; another teaches art, has one-man shows of his paintings and sculpture from time to time, and is active among the art teachers of his state; another uses the silk-screen process to print fabrics and is establishing his own pottery. One of the accountants is an investment analyst and estate manager, and has had to acquire a knowledge of farming as well as of stocks and bonds and taxation because his duties include the management of a great many Illinois farms. One is a Certified Public Accountant, and two work in the accounting departments of business firms. The businessmen include salesmen, a food broker, a buyer for a department store, an insurance man, and a district sales manager for a calculator company. Three of the men are in independent family businesses: one is a mortician, one manufactures stained-glass windows, and one operates a seed company. The advertising man has written for the screen and for a comic strip.

The minister is executive secretary for a council of churches, and works with ministers from many different denominations, helping them work toward common values and community improvement. Several of the scientists are actually businessmen, too, since three are industrial engineers and two are in important administrative positions because of their engineering background. One of them did not graduate from college—he had three years of engineering study, and some special training and very valuable communications experience in the army in helping set up the stations which guided the planes "over the hump" from Burma to China in the Second World War. Since the war he has been too busy to bother with "trivia like degrees." Two of the scientists are doing fundamental research and teaching in colleges; another is the head of guided-missile research for a company with large government contracts. The last three men are listed in the most recent edition of *American Men of Science*.

Four of these men might have been classified as teachers: the two research scientists who are also college teachers; the artist who is also an art teacher, and the industrial engineer who teaches some evening classes in the local high school.

There are two lawyers: one manages a regional office for a title insurance company in a distant state; the other left his private practice for a time to help clean up some scandals in local government. The one man whose work is listed as clerical has such a severe visual handicap that he is classified as blind for income tax purposes. He has tried a number of vocations and has now found a position as a transcriber from Ediphone disks for one of the local divisions of government.

In general, it appears to an interested observer that these men have found work which is consistent with their level of ability and their interests. In the interview, an attempt was made to find out how their occupational situations looked to them.

Sixteen of the twenty-four for whom information is available reported that they are very happy in their work, and three more said that they like what they are doing—79 per cent who are satisfied with or enthusiastic about their work. Five of the remaining eight said their work is all right, but————. The "buts" are as various as the individuals. One person finds himself blocked for the present, but knows that the situation will work out in a few years at the most. Another finds his present office work too sedentary, and thinks he might like to be a salesman. The man with defective vision is not enthusiastic about his job, but he recognizes that this is work which he can do, and that it has taken considerable experimentation to discover it. One is earning his living by work with silk screens that is not particularly interesting, but is putting his real thought and interest into building up his pottery. Another thinks he might like something else better than what he is doing, but he does not have anything in mind.

The remaining three reported that they wanted to change. One who has had expert vocational counseling is already in the process of doing so, having taken the specialized training which was recommended; he is not yet sure how well he is going to like the results as he begins to establish himself in his new line. The second, now in a family business, would prefer selling; the chances seem good that he will find a way to follow his preference, since he seemed to be examining alternatives realistically. The third one would like "anything that paid a lot of money," but there was little indication that he would do anything about changing his job, or that he was even seriously looking for another one.

How did these men find their way to their vocations? Twelve reported that they chose their lifework in high school or even earlier; one made his decision in college before the war, and another as a result of communications experiences in the army. Nine decided after the war was over; and in many of these decisions, there seemed to be a large element of chance. Four do not know when they decided; and two are still in the process of deciding, so they are not sure what their vocations will be eventually. The one who has had vocational counseling feels very strongly that vocational guidance should be a part of college; he made a very good record in an excellent liberal-arts college, but graduated with no idea of what he wanted to do for a living. He resents this quite bitterly, but rejects the idea that high school should have done more to push him toward a decision.

Income

The section of the biographical questionnaire which asked about income was placed at the bottom of a page; and the respondents were promised that it would be detached and kept anonymous in a separate file. In the various alumni studies which have been made by college classes, far more elaborate methods were used which guaranteed anonymity, but it was hoped that this relatively simple one might be adequate. Five men and four women returned the questionnaires with the income figures omitted, but a total of forty-two guinea pigs, or 81 per cent of those turning in information, included the income figures. The responses were coded M for male or F for female, given a mark to show the number of years of post–high school education, and detached and filed separately.

Comparisons of income are easier to find than any others. If a college class includes any statistics at all in its reunion book, it reports income figures. This may be, in part, because of the apparent simplicity of handling income statistics, and also, in part, because of the popular tendency to measure success in dollars.

Comparisons of income seem plausible and are practically irresistible, but there are four major factors which prevent them from being accurate. The first is the question of whether the figures represent earned income, which is presumably related to some extent to education, or total income, which may merely indicate that a child was wise in his selection of grandparents. The second factor is the age of the earner, since earning power tends to rise, at least for the college educated, until about the age of fifty. The third is place of residence: at any given date, incomes vary from large to small cities and from town to country. The fourth factor is so complex that it has seemed wisest to avoid comparisons in which it is important: within our rapidly changing patterns of inflation and a rising standard of living, the valid comparison of income figures from different periods may require complicated statistical treatment to correct for differences in the value of the dollar and income distribution.[1]

The most thorough postwar study (1947) of income distribution among college men is by Havemann and West, in which the investigators found a median for all male college graduates of $4,689.[2] Havemann's breakdown of incomes by types of colleges, and the comparison with the Class of 1938, are shown in Table 15.

The median earned income for the men of the Class of 1938 was the same, $6,839, whether it was calculated for all of them or only for the college graduates. This is a higher figure, even when corrected to 1947 purchasing power, than Havemann found for any college group except the Ivy League. It represents the figure reached fifteen years after high-school graduation, with a war thrown in for good measure. Twenty-four of the twenty-nine men are married; none of the wives of the twenty-three men about whom full information is available is working outside the home, perhaps because all of them have children.

Three of the four married women who have no children are working full time. The unmarried woman also has a job. The three married women with children who are working part time have not been

---

[1] It is for this reason that no use has been made of the income figures collected by Terman in 1940 and 1945, nor of those gathered by Babcock in 1939, in *The U. S. College Graduate.*

[2] Ernest Havemann and Patricia West, *They Went to College* (New York: Harcourt, Brace and Company, 1952), p. 26.

included in the calculation of the median for employed women. This median, $5,000 (or $4,173 when corrected to 1947 purchasing power), is notably higher than the $2,689 found by Havemann for all college women in 1947.

TABLE 15

COMPARISON OF THE MEDIAN INCOMES OF THE CLASS OF 1938
AND SEVERAL COLLEGE GROUPS *

College Group	Earned Income in 1947
Big Three (Harvard, Yale, Princeton)...................	$7,365
Other Ivy League (Columbia, Cornell, Dartmouth, Pennsylvania)...	6,142
Seventeen technical schools.............................	5,382
Twenty famous Eastern colleges........................	5,287
Big Ten...	5,176
All other Midwest colleges.............................	4,322
All other Eastern colleges..............................	4,235
Men of University School Class of 1938...................	5,709 †
All college women in 1947.............................	2,689
Women of University School Class of 1938................	4,173 ‡

* Income figures and college groupings are taken from Havemann and West, *They Went to College*, pp. 178–79.
† In 1953, the median income of the men of the Class of 1938 was $6,839, which has been corrected to the purchasing power of 1947 for the purposes of comparison.
‡ In 1953, the median income of the women (4 individuals) of the Class of 1938 was $5,000, which has been corrected to the purchasing power of 1947 for purposes of comparison.

The median income of the husbands of the women in the class was $7,500, or $6,261 corrected to 1947 purchasing power. This figure is somewhat higher than the median income of the men of 1938, which may reflect the fact that nine of the girls married men who were four to thirteen years older than they, and therefore significantly nearer the peak of their earning power than the men of the Class of 1938.

It should be noted that Havemann's figures include college graduates from a wide range of ages. The guinea pigs are all close to the same age, about thirty-two in 1953, an age at which they can expect to increase their earning power for another fifteen or even twenty years. Since they are already earning more than the national median, the Big Ten, the "twenty famous Eastern colleges," and the "seventeen technical schools" (see Table 15), perhaps it would be interesting to make some comparisons with each of the "Big Three" (Harvard, Yale, and Princeton), using data they have assembled for reunions (see Table 16). The members of each of these groups will

TABLE 16

COMPARATIVE INCOMES FROM REUNION REPORTS

Institution and Class	Date of Report	Years out of College	Median Earned Income	Median Income Corrected to 1947 Purchasing Power
University High School, Class of 1938 (Men)...............	1953	11	$ 6,839.00	$5,709.00
Princeton, 1944................	1954	10	6,500– 7,800.00	5,405– 6,489.00
Yale, 1936....................	1951	15	9,392.50	8,080.00
Princeton, 1929...............	1949	20	10,000.00	9,478.00
Harvard, 1926 *..............	1951	25	11,549.00	9,932.00

* The Harvard figures are for total income, earned and unearned, so they are not strictly comparable; they have been included in order to have representation from that institution.

be about the same age. All figures are given first as they appear in the reunion books and then as corrected to 1947 purchasing power by the use of the cost-of-living index.[3]

The group in this table which is most nearly comparable to the guinea pigs is Princeton 1944, a class which found both its college work and the beginning of careers interrupted by the Second World War. Income brackets were used by the Princeton class to collect information, so a close comparison is impossible; in addition, the Princeton men have been out of college a shorter time than the Class of 1938. However, it may be noted that the University School group falls within the lower limits of the median Princeton bracket. The figures for Yale 1936, Princeton 1929, and Harvard 1926 show an ascending scale of earned income which seems more closely connected

[3] *The World Almanac and Book of Facts* (New York: New York World-Telegram and Sun, 1956), p. 771.

with the number of years out of college than with the institution. The Harvard study points out that "it is entirely possible, in the light of actuarial data, that as a group we have reached or are close to the peak of our earning power." [4]

An examination of all these figures can only lead to the conclusion that, in the economic sense, the guinea pigs have higher earning power than the average group. It is possible that their higher incomes are in part due to the fact that they are all employed in the city, whereas the median income for the Big Ten, for example, includes some people who farm or are employed in small towns. However, the Big Three graduates are concentrated in large metropolitan centers to at least as great an extent as the members of the Class of 1938.

Military Service

The gathering clouds of the Second World War were already showing their menace while the students were in high school. *Were We Guinea Pigs?* records some of their attempts in classes to understand the war in Spain, conflicting ideologies, and various aspects of the surge of events abroad and the tides of opinion at home. The outbreak of war in Europe came a year after they graduated—one member of the class was in Paris when Hitler marched into Poland— and the attack on Pearl Harbor during the senior year of college for those who continued their education immediately after graduation from high school. Eight of the men completed their undergraduate work before their military service, two left college to enter the service, and nine were out of school and working. In all, nineteen men saw military service. Several were rejected because of vision handicaps, and others because of health reasons, such as hernia, heart murmur, and arthritis.

In Table 17, the induction rate of the men of 1938 is compared

[4] *The Life and Opinions of a College Class* (Cambridge, Massachusetts: Harvard University Press, 1951), p. 27.

with the rates of other groups. Princeton 1944 evidently excelled the guinea pigs in physical well-being, and even Yale 1936, whose members were on the average six years older, exceeded their rate by a small margin. However, the class's rate of induction was very close to the national average. Of the women, one girl joined the WAC and others worked with the USO.

TABLE 17

PERCENTAGES OF MEN FROM SELECTED GROUPS IN THE
ARMED FORCES IN THE SECOND WORLD WAR

Group	Per Cent
National average (men aged 18–37) between November, 1940, and August, 1945	65.3 *
University School Class of 1938	65.50
Yale 1936	67.72
Princeton 1944	89.00

* Information of national average is from *Outline of Historical Background of Selective Service and Chronology* (Rev. ed.; Washington 25, D. C.: U. S. Government Printing Office, 1952), by Irving W. Hart.

Of the nineteen men in the armed forces, four were in the navy and fifteen in the army. Their record of changes in rank during their periods of service is striking (see Tables 18 and 19). Whereas 73 per cent were inducted into the army as privates, only one remained a private at the time of discharge. In the army, 53 per cent became non-commissioned officers, and 40 per cent commissioned officers; of those who joined the navy, every one had a commission by the end of war. For purposes of comparison, Terman's group was the only one which could be found which offered information on changes in rank during military service.[5]

The difference in age range is a factor which needs to be borne in mind in all comparisons between Terman's group and the guinea pigs. Most of the Class of 1938 were about twenty-four as the war ended, whereas Terman's gifted children were, on the average, ten

[5] Lewis Terman and Melita Oden, *The Gifted Child Grows Up: Twenty-five Years Follow-up of a Superior Group* (Stanford, California: Stanford University Press, 1948), pp. 353–54.

years older. A man of thirty who interrupts a career to enter the armed forces is more likely to enter officer-candidate school than a boy fresh from college. Probably the most significant thing about the percentages of changes in rank in both groups is the recognition of leadership.

TABLE 18

CHANGES IN RANK OF THE MEN OF 1938 IN THE NAVY DURING THE SECOND WORLD WAR IN COMPARISON WITH TERMAN'S GIFTED MEN

RANK	PER CENT IN EACH RANK AT INDUCTION		PER CENT IN EACH RANK AT END OF WAR OR DISCHARGE	
	Class of 1938	Terman's Group	Class of 1938	Terman's Group
Seaman	25	13.8	...	3.4
Petty officer	...	19.8	...	21.6
Cadet	25	3.4	...	...
Commissioned officer	50	62.9	100	75.0

TABLE 19

CHANGES IN RANK OF THE MEN OF 1938 IN THE ARMY DURING THE SECOND WORLD WAR IN COMPARISON WITH TERMAN'S GIFTED MEN

RANK	PER CENT IN EACH RANK AT INDUCTION		PER CENT IN EACH RANK AT END OF WAR OR DISCHARGE	
	Class of 1938	Terman's Group	Class of 1938	Terman's Group
Private	73	49.5	7	6.9
Non-commissioned officer	...	1.0	53	22.1
Officer candidate	7	3.4	...	1.0
Commissioned officer	20	46.1	40	70.0

The open-ended question concerning "unusual experiences, assignments, associations, or responsibilities" in the military-service section of the questionnaire produced few and brief responses. One man who had worked on weather forecasting for the Sudanese section of the South Atlantic plane-ferry route to the war fronts answered "none," as did another whose unit had won distinction in amphibious operations in the Pacific. One man who had been the captain of a bomber based in Britain wrote, "Shot down October, 1944." Another said, "None outside of seeing Europe and teaching for over a year at the Field Artillery School."

Six told briefly of experiences:

Spent most of the war in Casablanca. We operated the air depot there, assembling fighter aircraft, modifying bombers, and operating the supply base.

Assigned for 6 months as aide to Brigadier General Jerry V. Matejka.

Aircraft maintenance. Pacific Islands.

Served in South Pacific Theater for two years, New Caledonia, Solomons, Australia, New Guinea, Philippines.

Commanding officer for approximately 2 years of a seven-man crew aboard a 63-foot army rescue boat in Philippine Islands, Japan, and Gulf of Mexico.

Four years in China-Burma-Tibet: Supervision of communication engineering installation over entire area. [Radio signal system to guide planes "over the hump" from Burma to China.]

War experiences seem to have receded very much into the background for these men. Only one has joined a veterans' organization. Asked about special citations, decorations, and so on, one wrote, "It is rather vague at this point, but I recall some nine battle stars which had no relation to my particular activities." In the absence of data from the men themselves, the investigator can only note that, according to general information and belief, those in the armed forces and those in civilian life made larger contributions to the war effort than these modest answers indicate.

V

ESTABLISHING HOMES

Marriage

When the guinea pigs were in high school, marriage rates and birth rates in the United States had reached an all-time low. Extrapolating from the curves of vital statistics, prophets announced that the population of the country would reach its peak by 1970 and begin to decrease by 1980. There was considerable speculation as to what a declining population would mean to our economy. A large number of the guinea pigs themselves had no brothers or sisters. There was a median of two children in each home, and only one family out of the fifty-five had as many as six children.

By the time these students had taken a few steps into whatever kind of education they had chosen to follow high school, the picture had altered suddenly and fundamentally.

The 1940's were a fine decade for Cupid. The young men going off to war rushed right from the recruiting station to the marriage license bureau, or proposed to the first girl they met in the PX at their army camp, or failing that dashed home and married their old hometown sweethearts on the last furlough before going overseas. A great many women who had shown no previous interest in or attraction for men were caught up in the whirl. . . .

. . . .

Our college people were not immune to the spirit of the times; indeed, as we shall see, they were possibly more enthusiastic than anyone else.[1]

[1] Ernest Havemann and Patricia West, *They Went to College* (New York: Harcourt, Brace and Company, 1952), p. 38.

The Class of 1938 shared the tendency to earlier marriages. By the time they were twenty-four or twenty-five, as the war was ending, 55 per cent of the men and 73 per cent of the women were already married. Four of these marriages were wartime mistakes, and were quickly terminated by divorces; no children were involved. All four of these individuals have now remarried, and their second marriages give every indication of being very successful.

Since the end of the war, nine more men and eight more women have married, an additional 31 per cent of each sex. At the time of writing (1957), there are forty-nine members of the class who are married; six, one woman and five men, who have remained single; and four who have married twice. Since two men in the class married classmates, there is a present total of forty-seven marriages. How these rates compare with selected groups in the population may be seen in Table 20.

The marriage data for the guinea pigs have been compiled both for the year 1947 when they were, on the average, twenty-six years old, and for 1957 when they were about thirty-six. The 1947 figures permit comparisons with Havemann's data in which one can have considerable confidence. Whether the 1957 marriage rates may legitimately be compared with the same age group in 1947 is less certain; there was considerable fluctuation in marriage rates during the period between 1947 and 1957, though nothing to compare with the reversal of trends which took place between 1940 and 1945.

Havemann's figures point out this reversal. Before 1940 college men married at a lower rate than the generality of males, and almost half of all college women failed to marry. Between 1940 and 1947, male college graduates married at a much more rapid rate than the generality, so that by 1947, 85 per cent of the male graduates were married as against 81 per cent of the general male population. The college women did not catch up with their non-college sisters, but they gained remarkably.

The members of our group were too young to be included in the 1940 national statistics. By 1947 about the same proportion of non-college men among the guinea pigs were married (59.3 per cent) as

TABLE 20

MARRIAGE RATES OF THE CLASS OF 1938
IN COMPARISON WITH OTHER GROUPS *

GROUP	PER CENT OF MALES			PER CENT OF FEMALES		
	1940	1947	1957	1940	1947	1957
All American adults................	76.0	81.0	...	83.0	87.0	...
All American college graduates.....	71.0	85.0	...	51.0	69.0	...
All American adults under thirty...	...	55.0	...	...	75.0	...
All American college graduates under thirty....................	35.0	64.0	...	33.6	59.0	...
All American college graduates between thirty and thirty-nine years of age..........................	77.4	87.0	...	59.9	78.0	...
University School Class of 1938 college graduates...................	...	64.7	88	...	58.8	94
University School Class of 1938 non-college group...................	...	59.3	72	...	88.9	100
Terman's gifted group (in 1945, twenty to forty years of age, average thirty-five).................	69.5	84.4	...	71.6	84.2	...

* The statistics in Table 20 have been assembled from Havemann and West, *They Went to College*, pp. 39 and 62; and from Terman, *The Gifted Child Grows Up*, pp. 224–26. Terman uses the figures in Babcock's *The U. S. College Graduate* for some of his comparisons, and also the 1940 census figures; he did not have available the second set of statistics collected by *Time* in 1947, which are the basis for the Havemann book. A large part of the increase in the marriages of the gifted, reported by Terman on page 227, is actually not unique to that group, but is a phenomenon shared by all college graduates in the United States in the war years. See Havemann, pp. 38–40.

among all American males under thirty (55 per cent). Among college graduates the proportions were almost exactly the same: American college graduates under thirty, 64 per cent; University School Class of 1938 college graduates, 64.7 per cent. At the same time the women of the Class of 1938 who graduated from college were approaching the national figure almost as closely: American college women under thirty, 59 per cent; University School, 58.8 per cent. Only the non-college women from University School exceeded the national averages: all American women under thirty, 75 per cent; University School, 88.9 per cent. The comparisons of 1947 figures turn out to be reliable.

Is there any value in comparing the national figures for 1947 for those between thirty and thirty-nine years of age with the statistics for our group in 1957, when the average age was thirty-six? The parallels remain close enough to be striking. Havemann points out that in 1947 college men had married at a greater rate than the general population, 85 per cent to 81 per cent. The same relation is true for the University School men; by 1957, 88 per cent of the college graduates were married, and only 72 per cent of the non-college men. Of all American men between the ages of thirty and thirty-nine who had graduated from college, 87 per cent were married in 1947; in 1957, at approximately the same age, 88 per cent of the men of the Class of 1938 were married. Among the women, 87 per cent of all adult American women, and 78 per cent of all college women between the ages of thirty and thirty-nine, were married, in comparison with 100 per cent of the non-college members of the Class of 1938 and 94 per cent of the college women. It was already obvious ten years earlier that the marriage rate, at that time 88.9 per cent, would be high for the non-college women in this group, and by 1957 the college women had almost caught up with them.

Terman's gifted group provides an interesting comparison. His last statistics were gathered in 1945, and for comparisons he had to rely on 1940 material which antedated the wartime explosion of the marriage and birth rates. He believed that his gifted men and women were outmarrying the general population,[2] whereas actually they apparently only reflected the general trend. His women made a higher percentage of marriages (84.2 per cent) than the generality of college graduates their age (78 per cent), but not so high as the University School women graduates (94 per cent).

Many people believe that college men tend to "marry down," selecting wives with less education than they have, and that college women tend to be "choosy," a term intended to explain their lower marriage rates. To make a quick check on this, the educational levels of all class members and their spouses were tabulated (see Table 21). Three-fourths of the women, both the college graduates and the non-

[2] Lewis Terman and Melita Oden, *The Gifted Child Grows Up: Twenty-five Years Follow-up of a Superior Group* (Stanford, California: Stanford University Press, 1948), p. 227.

graduates, married college men. Nearly four out of five of the men who graduated from college have wives with degrees. A few more than half of the men who did not graduate from college married wives who had graduated. The only support in the Class of 1938 for the theories that college women are "choosy" and college men "marry down" is that the women with advanced degrees have husbands with

TABLE 21

THE EDUCATION OF THE MARRIAGE PARTNERS OF THE CLASS OF 1938

Group	Number for Whom Data Is Available	Per Cent Whose Spouses Graduated from College	Per Cent Whose Spouses Did Not Graduate from College
Men of 1938 College graduates......	14	78.5	21.5
Men of 1938 Non-college graduates..	9	55.5	44.5
Women of 1938 College graduates...	16	75.0	25.0
Women of 1938 Non-college graduates........................	8	75.0	25.0

the same degrees, whereas the men with advanced degrees have wives with B.A. degrees or less. The general educational level of the spouses is very close to that of the class members.

Divorce

The number of divorces in the Class of 1938 seem to be few, but it is difficult to discover reliable divorce statistics for large groups with which they could be compared. Each state has its own system of keeping statistics which makes it hard to assemble national figures. The Bureau of the Census counts as divorced only those individuals who have not remarried at the time they are polled. Terman encountered difficulty in finding accurate comparative figures, and his discussion of the unreliability of the statistics and the reasons therefor is very interesting.[3]

In Table 22 the few statistics on divorce which have been found

[3] Terman and Oden, *op. cit.*, pp. 228–29.

are compared. Princeton Class of 1944 is most nearly comparable to the University School group because the ages are similar. It is obvious that, unless one adopts the Bureau of the Census expedient of wiping out a divorce with a second marriage, the percentage of divorces can never decrease and is likely to increase with age.

The comparison with Princeton makes the figures for the guinea pigs look normal (4 per cent in each case). Terman's figures make both the men's and women's percentages appear low. There is no ready explanation for the wide variations among the figures in the table other than that of the general difficulties of obtaining accurate data in

TABLE 22

PERCENTAGES OF DIVORCES IN SELECTED GROUPS

Group	Date of Report	Per Cent of Men	Per Cent of Women
Terman's gifted children....., ...	1945	14.4	16.3
Princeton Class of 1944......................	1954	4.0	...
Harvard Class of 1926........................	1951	13.0	...
Yale Class of 1936 *.........................	1951	2.0	...
All male college graduates (Statistics collected by Havemann).............................	1947	5.8	...
Class of 1938................................	1956	4.0	12.0

* The figures for Yale were given in a magazine article by John Hersey, "Yale '36— Look at Them Now," *Harper's Magazine*, CCV (September, 1952). In summarizing the findings for the fifteenth reunion, Hersey did not indicate how carefully the statistics had been gathered and handled. When he quotes a figure, he notes that it is a certain percentage "of those reporting," but does not show whether the sample is typical.

this field. It is interesting to note that the three most careful statistical studies—those by Terman, Havemann, and Harvard Class of 1926 —give the highest figures. The very low figure of 2 per cent for Yale 1936 may indicate that Yale men are superior marriage partners, or it may suggest that those who were successful in their marriages responded to the request for reunion data with more enthusiasm than those who were not.

For the guinea pigs, the marriage statistics, as collected by the Bureau of the Census, would show no divorces since all have remarried and are living with the second husband or wife.

Children

Keeping a count of the children of the members of the Class of 1938 has required a large measure of co-operation from class members. The biographical questionnaires, on which children were listed, were returned in 1955. In the course of the interviews in late 1955 and early 1956, the writer discovered a number of infants who had arrived since the questionnaires had been returned, and the mails since then have brought enough birth announcements to keep one reminded that the roster is not yet complete. The present score is one hundred fifteen living children, five of whom are adopted. Five chil-

TABLE 23
FAMILY SIZE OF SELECTED GROUPS

Group	Average Age of Group	Date of Statistics	Average Number of Children Per Family
University School Class of 1938.........	36	1957	2.45
Yale Class of 1936.....................	36	1951	2.31
Harvard Class of 1926.................	46	1951	2.34
Princeton Class of 1944................	31	1954	1.80
Terman's gifted group.................	35	1945	1.52

dren died in infancy, the oldest at the age of two months; three of these were in the same family, each living less than a week. There has been no death of any child more than two months old.

Six of the fifty-five class members have not married, and two couples married within the class, so there are actually forty-seven families. Of these, five have no children. The other forty-two families range in size from one to six children, with the median a family of three.

Table 23 shows the average family size of the University School graduates in comparison with those of other groups. Excluding the five adopted children, but including the five children who died in infancy and the five childless families, the forty-seven married couples have produced an average of 2.45 children per family. This figure is very close to but larger than that for Yale Class of 1936 at the same age (2.31), and also larger than that for Harvard Class of 1926 (2.34), which at the time of the report was ten years older and presumably had almost reached its final score. Princeton Class of 1944 is far behind with 1.80, but this is doubtless because they are two years younger than the Class of 1938 and their statistics were recorded three years earlier, so that they have a five-year handicap at the age when it is likely to make the most difference. On the other hand, Terman's report on his gifted group at approximately the same age in 1945 showed that they had only 1.52 children per marriage. He quotes J. K. Folsom, an authority on the family, as estimating in 1934 that marriages must produce 2.62 live births in order to maintain the stock.[4]

There would have to be a total of eight more babies born in the forty-seven families of the Class of 1938 in order to reach this figure. It is probable that the increase in marriage rates and the sensational reduction in child mortality since 1934 make Folsom's estimate unnecessarily high, and that even without any further births the present families are sufficiently large to maintain the stock.

When the figures for the class were studied, no significant differences in family size appeared between those who had attended college and those who had not. From the first quintile of the class to the last, there was a slight decline, for the most part, in the numbers of children—first quintile, 26; second, 26; third, 23; fourth, 21; fifth, 24. (This counts twice the five children who had two guinea pigs for parents, since the father and mother in each case were in different quintiles.) The differences are irregular and are accounted for by a small number of large families and by the accidental clustering of childless families and unmarried members of the class in certain quintiles. The twenty-three gifted guinea pigs who are married average 2.6 children per family, somewhat above the whole class average of 2.45.

Studying the children of the members of the Class of 1938 was not within the scope of the follow-up, but in the course of the interviews

---

[4] Terman and Oden, *op. cit.*, p. 235. On careful examination, the figure used by Folsom proves to be a quotation from a preliminary 1930 census report which was based on an earlier study which, in turn, was based on 1920 census figures.

the writer saw ninety of the one hundred fifteen children. No abnormalities of any kind were observed. All seemed happy, healthy, well-cared for children. Comment will be made in another section on the relations between parents and children.

How Successful Are These Marriages?

The question whether the marriages of the class members are stable and happy is important to the parents and children in these homes and to the purposes of the follow-up. The questionnaires supply the information used in this section.

To draw meaning from a mass of statistical data, Havemann developed a device for judging objectively the success of a marriage about which nothing is known except certain basic facts.[5] This device has not been validated experimentally, so it is used here as tentatively as it was used by its inventor.

Each individual was assigned points according to the following scale:

Marriage: For having married and being married still—in other words never divorced and not now separated—3 points.

For being married and living with a wife (or husband) now, although divorced in the past—2 points.

For having married, but at the present time being divorced or separated—1 point.

For being a bachelor (or spinster), no points—a zero.

Children: For each child, 1 point—to a maximum of 3 points for fatherhood (or motherhood).

Home Ownership: For owning one's present home—1 point. [Havemann notes that the part of home ownership in family stability is fairly well established.]

[5] Havemann and West, *op. cit.,* p. 49.

This scale has been applied to all the members of the Class of 1938, and their scores have been tabulated and compared with those given by Havemann. The results are shown in Table 24.

Eighty-two per cent of the male college graduates among the guinea pigs had scores of 6 or 7 points, as opposed to 52 per cent for the generality of college men over forty. Of the non-college group, 66.6 per cent scored either 5 or 6 points. Havemann offers no point distribution for non-college men. Those with 2 points or less were the

TABLE 24

MARRIAGE SCORES ON HAVEMANN'S SCALE

	MEN			WOMEN		
	Have-mann's Group	University School Class of 1938		Have-mann's Group	University School Class of 1938	
POINTS	Per Cent of College Graduates over Forty	Per Cent of College Graduates (N-17)	Per Cent of Non-College Graduates (N-12)	Per Cent of College Graduates over Forty	Per Cent of College Graduates (N-17)	Per Cent of Non-College Graduates (N-9)
7..............	23	41	....	12	35	78
6..............	29	41	33.3	19	29	..
5..............	22	..	33.3	15	6	..
4..............	14	6	8.4	13	6	11
3..............	6	..	....	7	12	11
2 or less........	6	12	25.0	34	12	..

bachelors in both the college group, in which there were two, and the non-college group, in which there were three.

The University School women scored much higher than Havemann's college women over forty. Sixty-four per cent of the college graduates and 74 per cent of the non-college graduates scored 6 or 7 points, as opposed to 31 per cent for the generality. At the other end of the scale, 50 per cent of Havemann's college women had 4 points or less, whereas only 30 per cent of the college graduates and 22 per cent of the non-graduates among the guinea pigs scored as low.

Particularly interesting are the women in the guinea-pig class who did not graduate from college. More than three-fourths of them scored 7 points, the highest rank, whereas only a little more than one-third of their female classmates who graduated from college and less than one-eighth of all American college women reached this rank. One wonders if this is connected with Terman's observation that the highest incidence of marriage among his gifted women was among those who began college but did not graduate. Perhaps a simple explanation for both phenomena is that the girl who places marriage very high on her vocational list is more likely to marry early and acquire a home and children.

It should be noted that Havemann's "college graduates over forty" have a five-year or greater advantage over the guinea pigs, who may well add to their scores in the next five or ten years. Some may add points for marriage since six are still unmarried. Havemann cites statistics to show that the number of bachelors among college graduates over forty is less than half the number between the ages of thirty and thirty-nine, and nearly equal to the number for all men in the United States. They may add points for children (twenty-two marriages have fewer than the three for whom he allows points, and in fifteen of these the youngest child is two years old or younger) and for home ownership (fifteen do not own their own homes). Theoretically, these possible gains might be offset by some divorces in the next five years; the writer considers this improbable, on the basis of evidence which will be discussed, though not impossible.

If this scale is a valid measure, most of the men have fine prospects for success in family living and almost all the women have excellent ones. As Havemann points out, it is probable that anyone can find numerous criticisms of the scale. Because of the large amount of information which the writer had about each of the members of the Class of 1938, it was possible to check its reliability in specific cases. In general it seemed to work well as a rough classifying device, though many of the low-scoring marriages gave every indication of being stable and satisfying, and two which gave some indication from other evidence of being precarious rated 6 or 7 points.

Parent-Child Relationships

The data for this section are to be found in the protocols of the interviews rather than in the questionnaires. The principal questions on the interview schedule which relate to the area of parent-child relationships are the following (See Appendix C for complete schedule):

16. Do you regulate the children's TV?

21. Are you bringing up your children more strictly than you were raised, less strictly, or about the same? Can you be specific about ways in which you hope to differ from what your parents did?

22. Do you and your wife (husband) have different ideas about bringing up the children? In what specific ways are they different and how do you work that out?

27. What things do you try to instill in your children?

28. What plans and ambitions do you have for your son(s)? For your daughter(s)?

33. If you knew you had only six months to live, but could do just as you pleased during that period, how would you spend the time?

36. Do you consider your own family—you, your wife (husband), and children—as democratic? If not, who is boss? If yes, how are decisions made?

42. What kinds of recreation do you enjoy which you share with other people outside your family?

43. What kinds of recreation do you enjoy as a family group?

For Women:

50. *a*) What do you like most about being a homemaker?

51. *a*) What do you like least about being a homemaker?

For Women Who Work:

50. *c*) What difficulties do you find, if any, in combining marriage and a career?

For Men:

50. *b*) What do you like to do around the house and yard?

51. *b*) What do you do as household chores which you do not really enjoy?

52. What aspects of bringing up your children do you enjoy or find challenging?

53. What aspects of bringing up your children are just necessary routines which you do not really enjoy?

Forty-five of the forty-eight graduates of 1938 who had been in the University School for three or more years were given the full interview. Four of the forty-five who were not married and four others who were married but had no children were not asked these questions. The thirty-seven remaining protocols, which included those of seventeen men and twenty women, were analyzed under three different headings:

1. *Acceptance.* Degree to which parent accepts his children as individuals whose personalities, abilities, and interests he respects and tries to foster. Is parent planning for children in terms of offering encouragement and opportunity, or in terms of parent-determined vocational and other goals?

2. *Discipline and responsibility.* Degree to which parent is firm and consistent in discipline, insisting on children respecting rights of others, including the parents, in the home and outside. Is there evidence that parent helps children begin to participate in small decisions which concern them at an early age and to move with increasing maturity into more responsible roles?

3. *Husband-wife relationship.* Degree to which this appears congenial and stable, judging from attitudes toward home and children, shared recreational and other interests, ways of approaching areas of disagreement, and other pertinent data, including overtones of interview.

The ratings of relationships within the home made from the evidence of the protocols are shown in Table 25. Responses to the questions from the interview schedule were read as a group, and considered in relation to each other and to the rest of the protocol. Those individuals who were rated "very high" gave clear and consistent evidence of that quality. The "high" rating was used where the evidence was incomplete in some small particulars, or showed minor inconsistencies. The "some" rating will be discussed in connection with each heading, as will "little" and "very little."

Acceptance. Twenty-four of the guinea pigs showed consistent and unmistakable evidence of accepting and enjoying the personalities, abilities, and interests of their children. The behavior of nine more was

TABLE 25

RATING OF THE RELATIONS OF THIRTY-SEVEN GUINEA PIGS
WITH THEIR SPOUSES AND CHILDREN

HEADING	RATING				
	Very High	High	Some	Little	Very Little
1. Acceptance................	24	9	4	....	....
2. Discipline and responsibility.	23	9	5	....	....
3. Husband-wife relationship...	28	5	4	....	....

almost as clear and consistent on this point. All of them rejected the idea of parental plans and ambitions. Two answers to the question, "What plans and ambitions do you have for your sons?", are typical:

> I think that that is something that should be left up to them. My ambitions or plans for them might not jibe at all with what they were capable of doing or enjoyed doing.

> Well, I don't have any ambitions, except that they grow up in a normal way with reasonable happiness. I mean I am against a person or parent endeavoring to direct their youngsters into particular patterns which are of the parent's choosing. If anything, that is one thing I want to stay away from and that probably is the only thing that I do feel on the subject.

Other aspects of acceptance are shown in the following answer to the question, "What aspects of bringing up your children do you enjoy or find challenging?":

Developing curiosity, for one, interests me very much; and I try and put things in front of them that will develop a curiosity, try and get them—well, if they take a toy apart, I like to see them put it back together. Surprisingly enough, they do it most of the time, even little Larry (3 years old). One of the biggest problems, and I imagine it's a problem with any family that has more than one child, is trying to prevent the sister to sister and sister to brother scraps that come up. I haven't found an answer to that one yet.

Another remarked, "I try to be closer to my children than my parents were to me."

The four parents who were rated "some" shared most of the same attitudes and qualities of those rated "very high" and "high." In each case, however, there was some evidence of what seemed to be parental pushing toward predetermined goals, or of some parental impatience with the childishness of children.

In none of the families were there parental complaints about children, dislike or rejection of them, favoritism among the children, possessiveness toward them, or signs that the adult regarded his children as projections of himself in which to realize his own ambitions. Any of these qualities would have resulted in placing the parent in either the "little" or "very little" rating.

Discipline and responsibility. The ratings in this category (see Table 25) are very closely parallel to those for acceptance. The questions which were most productive were those about television-viewing, about the strictness with which children were being brought up, about differences between parents, and about what parents were trying to instill in their children.

The twenty-three who rated "very high" began developing responsibility in their children early and increased the area as the children grew and developed. They were firm, reasonable, and fairly consistent in discipline, and tried to work out any parental differences behind the scenes. They taught their children to respect themselves and others—and sometimes encountered problems in doing so, which they faced honestly:

Question: What things do you try to instill in your children?

Answer: Well, a respect for each other and the family and a serious-ness towards life, an interest—to get them interested in something themselves, I think, and to respect what they do. I know very often they will do something, draw something which I think is quite nice, but they seem inclined to be ashamed of it. They seem to be striving for perfection, and I sometimes worry that I'm probably the cause of it and try to figure out what I'm doing which is wrong. So that is a prob-lem along that line, to get them to like what they do and have some self-confidence in themselves.

The nine rated "high" resembled those in the highest category closely, but often did not give quite as full information about themselves and what they were doing.

Three of the five who were rated "some" were given that rating because they were not consistent. In the other cases, there were unre-solved and occasionally open differences between the parents over discipline. These were relatively minor, however; had such differences appeared serious, the individual would have been assigned a lower rating.

Ratings of "little" or "very little" would have been assigned to quarreling, dominating, or laissez-faire parents, to parents who failed in their responsibility to create a climate of values for their children, or to those who imposed upon children a rigid pattern of "right" behavior in which the child's responsibility was merely to conform. None of the guinea pigs fell in these groups.

Husband-wife relationship. As noted earlier, this investigator has neither the skill nor the data to undertake an evaluation of the mar-riages of the Class of 1938. This section merely attempts to look at the husband-wife relationship as a significant part of the family living of the children. The points examined are the relations and attitudes of the parents to child rearing and to domestic routines, the kind and extent of the interests they share, and the way in which disagreements and outside interferences are handled.

Twenty-eight were rated "very high," and five others "high." All of them appear to have worked out their compromises and their divisions of responsibility with good humor and understanding of the other's point of view. The homes are essentially democratic. These parents appear very much interested in their homes, the men as well as the women; quotations from some of the men will illustrate the range within a do-it-yourself group, which includes thirteen of the seventeen men.

Question: What do you like to do around the house and yard?

Answer: . . . Now that you mention yard—we have a common power lawn mower, a common half ownership—me and the next-door neighbor—and if I don't mow the lawn, my wife gets the opportunity, which is often. Don't care to do what we normally think of as the household chores. Mechanical things about the house I enjoy—the equipment and the breakdown in one machine or another which seem to be quite frequent. [You really *enjoy* those?] Yeah, in a maddening sort of way. I will attempt to fix anything from the television set to the clothes washer. Attempt, that is. Sometimes it works.

Question: What are your individual recreations?

Answer: No hobbies particularly. I find that there is enough handy work to be done around my own house; it keeps me pretty well occupied, what with the outside garden and repairing a leak in the faucet. I have no particular individual hobby along the line of coin collecting, which I did at one time, but I've grown away from it.

Question: What do you enjoy doing around the house and yard?

Answer: Probably complaining about the work that I have to do when I really don't mean it. Nobody thinks anything of it. But I'm a great procrastinator—at least my wife says so, but I find that all my neighbors are, too—but I enjoy working around the yard as long as I grumble about getting worked.

Question: Do you do any household chores that you really find distasteful?

Answer: No. Well, let me put it this way: there are certain household chores that have to be done, that probably just because they have to be done, we don't like to do them. They're distasteful from that standpoint, but they've got to be done, so they might as well be done and get them over with. I think that's true of anybody keeping house.

Question: What do you like to do around the house and yard?

Answer: Well, anything that has to do with buildings and grounds and maintenance I don't care too much for. If it comes to doing things around the house, the best things I like actually are—oh, I would say tinkering and putting in new electrical equipment, plumbing—things mechanical. I put in an extra thermostat upstairs so that we can turn the heat off downstairs and have the heat all go upstairs at night—automatic devices. I have a temperature recording device, automatically records the temperature every day, just for the heck of it. I don't know why. I built this heated bird bath. Or if there is something like putting in a new electrical outlet—mechanical things, I think I like to do around the house—but I don't care about washing windows or painting or things like that, or gardening—I don't care for that. I'll cut the lawn, not too frequently.

Question: What do you like to do around the house and yard?

Answer: Most anything. There are very few things I don't like to do. It's a case of finding time to do them more than liking or not liking them. [What things do you find time to do in your busy life?] Well, you mean around the house? [Yes.] Well, for example, when the house—the trim—needed repainting, we did that, and, of course, I take care of the yard, flowers. I hope to get a rose garden started this year. Up until this past summer we always had a garden out where my father lived, but with his passing I tried it one more year—it just wasn't the same. We dropped it. As far as in the house goes, I put in an intercommunication system from each of the rooms in the house, general repairs, anything like that—it has to be a pretty major item for me to have to call a repair man. I just enjoy fixing and luckily I'm fairly handy with tools, so that generally doesn't present much of a problem. [Are there any things you do around the house which you dislike doing, but do just because they're necessary chores?] Well, there probably are, but there are very few of them that would come to mind without a little study. Oh sure, for example, the sink gets clogged up. It has to be worked on, why that's a disagreeable task that has to be done, but by the same token, that's an unusual thing. Very few of the regular tasks bother me.

Four individuals were rated "some" because there seemed little evidence that their major interests, recreational and other, were shared by their marriage partners; and there was some evidence of the persistence of unresolved differences over child discipline or other family matters. None of these marriages seemed in immediate danger, though there were irritants of long standing in at least two cases. The conflicts did not appear to be causing any feelings of insecurity in the children, but the period of observation was insufficient for any certainty on that point.

Open quarrels or overt conflict of any kind would have caused an individual to be rated "little" or "very little." There were no such cases among the guinea pigs.

In each of the three classifications, acceptance, discipline and responsibility, and husband-wife relationship—which are believed to be basic to the development of healthy personalities in children—the guinea pigs appear to be outstanding parents. Four or five in each category (11, or 13.5 per cent) are distinctly less adequate than the others, but only one is in the middle group, "some," in all three classifications. Ninety-seven per cent of the class ranked "high" or "very high" in at least one of the three.

As a check on this rating procedure, the responses to direct questions were checked against the replies of the same individuals to a projective question: "If you knew you had only six months to live, but could do just as you pleased during that period, how would you spend the time?" The general distribution of the replies to the projective question are shown in Table 26.

None of the men clearly rejected their families in their plans for the last six months, though there were four cases in which it was not clear whether "travel" included the families. One woman rejected the question, and another rejected everything ("Get away from everything and everybody"), though she was quick to retract. The large majority of men and women specifically included their families in their plans. Seven women would be glad to shed housekeeping responsibilities, but not their families, and nine would go on doing just what they are doing now. About half of the men, however, have plans which would not include their present jobs, whereas only two men and two women proposed plans which were extensions of their jobs.

As was pointed out earlier, almost all of the men are employed in the kinds of jobs discussed by C. Wright Mills in *White Collar*. He speaks of what he calls "the new middle class" in the following manner:

Alienation in work means that the most alert hours of one's life are sacrificed to the making of money with which to "live." Alienation means boredom and the frustration of potentially creative effort, of the productive sides of personality. It means that while men must seek all values that matter to them outside of work, they must be serious during work. . . . Leisure time thus comes to mean an unserious freedom from the authoritarian seriousness of the job.[6]

TABLE 26

ANSWERS TO THE QUESTION "HOW WOULD YOU SPEND YOUR LAST SIX MONTHS?"

Answer	Men	Women	Total
Doing about what I am now doing..............	6	9	15
Doing the same, because I (1) have no frustrated ambitions, (2) can't think of anything else.................	2	..	2
Travel with my family to specific places...........	4	8	12
Travel to specific places (no mention of family or Job)...	4	..	4
Creative or intellectual pursuit growing out of Job...	2	2	4
Creative or intellectual pursuit interfered with by Job...	2	..	2
Get away from everything and everybody..........	..	1	1
Silly question......................................	..	1	1

It is possible that the men who did not mention their jobs subconsciously reflected this attitude to some degree, though it was expressed clearly only by one. The question was, "What emotional satisfactions do you get out of your life out of working hours?", to which he replied, "That's what I live for, with my children, my wife, my friends. Certainly the method of relaxation makes it possible to go back and be capable of doing the job you are working at."

However, in reply to the question, "What kinds of activities and experiences give you the greatest sense of personal worth and achieve-

[6] *White Collar: The American Middle Classes* (New York: Oxford University Press, 1953), p. 236.

ment?", almost all of the men mentioned some aspect of their work, among other things, so it may be dangerous to push the suggestion of alienation too far. Fully half of the men seem to see meaning in their work, and possibly all but two or three find important satisfactions in it. Clearly, almost all find their home and family relations satisfying, and in a choice between career and family for their last six months of life, would give priority to family.

The cross-check using the projective question tends to support the rating of husband-wife relationships which was based on other questions in the protocol.

VI

RELIGION AND COMMUNITY
PARTICIPATION

Religion

The University School offered no instruction in religion, no prayers or Bible readings. Questions concerning religions, our own or others, were handled as they came up in history, literature, or science classes, in discussions or units concerning values or ideologies in all parts of the school. Christmas programs explored the various ways of celebrating Christmas at different times, in different places, and in various religious groups; Protestants, Catholics, and Jews took part with equal enthusiasm.

Information about religious involvement, both in high-school days and in 1955, comes from the biographical questionnaires returned in 1955. The information sought was sufficiently simple and specific that memory over a seventeen-year period should be entirely accurate. Table 27 summarizes and compares church and Sunday-school attendance in 1955 and in the 1932–38 period.

During the time these students were in high school, only a few more than half of them attended church (60 per cent), either alone or with their parents; another 34 per cent attended seldom if at all. By 1955 the percentage with no religious involvement had dropped from 34 to 25.5 per cent. Sixty-three per cent of the class members with children were sending them to Sunday school. Only 16 per cent of the families did not send their children to Sunday school at all, though doubtless

90

TABLE 27

RELIGIOUS INVOLVEMENT OF THE CLASS OF 1938
A. *Church Attendance*

Extent of Attendance	During High School, 1932–38 (Per Cent)	In 1955 (Per Cent)
Attended church (Sunday school) more or less regularly...	60	74.5
Parents attended, but child did not.....................	6	....
Attended seldom if at all.............................	34	25.5

B. *Sunday-School Attendance of Children*
(1955)

Extent of Attendance	Number of Families (N-43)	Per Cent
Send children to Sunday school..........................	27	63
Children still too young for Sunday school..............	6	14
Children attend irregularly.............................	3	7
Do not send children to Sunday school..................	7	16

C. *Comparison of Religious Involvement
in 1932–38 and 1955*

AMOUNT OF INVOLVEMENT	PER CENT
Same amount of involvement in 1938 and 1955..............	47.0
No involvement either in 1938 or in 1955..................	11.8
More involvement in 1955 and in 1938.....................	27.5
Less involvement in 1955 than in 1938....................	13.7

some of the children who are now too young will not go when they reach the appropriate age, and those who attend irregularly may drop out. Even if these two possibilities were realized, the proportion of those attending church would still be higher than it was for the Class of 1938 in high school.

Evidently the movement toward organized religion which has been noted repeatedly in the press and magazines has had its effects within this group. Contrary to the first impression, however, the movement has not been all in the same direction. There were trends both toward

and away from the churches: 27.5 per cent reported more religious involvement than their families had when they were in high school, and
13.7 per cent reported less. Almost half (47 per cent) attended with
what appeared to be about the same amount of devotion as their
parents had, ranging from very active membership to a rather per-
functory relationship, while 11.8 per cent stayed away entirely, also
as their parents had.

There is no clear evidence that the school had much influence one
way or the other. One woman wrote on her biographical questionnaire
that the science courses searched so hard for logical explanations that
they left no room for God, and that she had needed some time to re-
gain her faith. The other members of the class were subsequently
questioned about this in the interview. No one else supported her statement, which must, then, be taken as a purely individual reaction.
Many spoke with deep appreciation of moral and ethical values in the
program, but believed that University School, as a non-parochial institution in a pluralistic society, should not assume any responsibility in
the religious area.

Community Participation

The high-school program of the guinea pigs emphasized in many
ways the community and the individual's responsibilities to it. For
one thing, much of the work in the core course and some of the work
in other classes was set up in such fashion that the school or the class
itself was a community and the work of each individual contributed to the success of a community project.[1] The book *Were We
Guinea Pigs?* was written in this way.

The school curriculum also gave more attention to community
problems, local, national, and world-wide, than was usual. The times
were full of problems, and the faculty took seriously their responsibility for developing a curriculum to help students understand their

[1] See pages 29–84 of *Were We Guinea Pigs?*, by the Class of 1938, for examples of the ways in which this method was used.

lives and times; teacher-pupil planning very frequently operated to bring community materials and problems into the classroom, though much of the basic subject-matter of traditional courses continued to be taught as a necessary background.

There was some group activity in community projects outside the school, although sponsorship by the school of such projects was on a very limited scale, in part because the homes of the students were widely scattered over the city.

All areas in the school tended to emphasize participation by pupils in planning and evaluation, the activity and responsibility of pupils, and the importance of critical thinking. There was a conscious attempt to develop in the students an understanding of and skill in democratic processes in classes, in student government, and in extra-curricular activities. There was also a conscious effort to develop individual personalities and aptitudes, and to help all students understand how such differences could be enriching if individuals were considerate and appreciative of each other. Each student was expected to achieve at his own best level, and the children learned to accept individual differences in the amount and the complexity of achievement with amazingly little self-consciousness.

In evaluating the guinea pigs' records of community responsibility and participation, including politics, in 1955–56, one is handicapped by the lack of norms. There is a general impression that Americans are "joiners"; but there is a certain amount of difference of opinion among experts as to how much joining is good and even greater differences as to the amount of participation which might legitimately be expected of a group of individuals.[2] The only study of actual adult membership in voluntary organizations which the writer was able to find was made by Wright and Hyman.[3] They found that

[2] See such works as Erich Fromm, *The Sane Society* (New York: Holt, Rinehart and Winston, Inc., 1955); Hans Gerth and C. Wright Mills, *Character and Social Structure* (New York: Harcourt, Brace and Company, 1953); and David Riesman and Nathan Glazer, *Faces in the Crowd* (New Haven: Yale University Press, 1952).

[3] Charles R. Wright and Herbert H. Hyman, "Voluntary Association Membership of American Adults: Evidence from National Sample Surveys," *American Sociological Review*, XXIII (June, 1958), 284–94.

membership in voluntary organizations was not characteristic of the majority; that it was more characteristic of whites than of Negroes, more of Jews than of Protestants, and more of Protestants than of Catholics; and that it was directly related to socioeconomic status and to urban living. The highest percentages of membership which they found will be used for comparison with the guinea pigs.

Certainly a significant feature of American life is the multiplicity and range of voluntary organizations, from the Red Cross to the White Citizens Councils, from bridge clubs to parent-teacher associations, from the Daughters of the American Revolution to the Civil Liberties Union. Whether joining them is "good" or "bad" seems to the writer to depend on the character and purposes of the individual and the organization. Playing a middle-class role in any but the largest communities or the most scattered rural districts frequently involves a commitment to certain of these—United Appeals, March of Dimes, Parent-Teacher Association, and so on. It is only when participation goes beyond the superficial that one begins to sense the purposes of the individual's participation, and the extent to which his activities are a dynamic influence in the community or an expression of the individual himself.

One thing became obvious as the data from the questionnaire (Appendix A, Question 14) and from the protocols (Appendix C, Questions 59–63) were tabulated—there seemed to be sex roles in the community participation of this group. Or possibly, the distinction is instead between the role of the gainfully employed and the role of the housewife, since the women who were employed outside the home showed patterns closer to those of the men than to those of the housewives.

There are data for twenty-seven of the men; twenty-two (81.5 per cent) participated actively in various kinds of community enterprise, whereas five took almost no part. In their study, Wright and Hyman found that only 36 per cent of the college graduates joined two or more organizations, and that 39 per cent joined none. The pattern of activity of the guinea pigs shows a concentration in business or professional organizations (Society for the Advancement of Management,

American Institute of Electrical Engineers, Institute of Radio Engineers, American Physical Society, Columbus Technical Council, bar associations, and so on) or in churches (singing in the choir, membership on the board of deacons or trustees, presidency of the men's club, solicitation for the building fund, and so on). Some participated actively in both, and all but two appeared to give major emphasis to one or the other. Three of the four employed women gave major emphasis to their participation in professional organizations; the fourth found no time for participation in anything.

Although the number of men participating in some sort of com-

TABLE 28

A. PARTICIPATION IN COMMUNITY ORGANIZATIONS BY
TWENTY-SEVEN MEN OF THE CLASS OF 1938

Type of Organization	*Per Cent*
Business	52.0
Community service (general)	44.4
Community organizations related to their families (Scouts, and so on)	15.0
Church (elective office, choir, other groups)	37.0
Social (Kiwanis, and so on; Elks, Masons; country clubs)	37.0
Patriotic (American Legion)	3.7
Self-expression, self-improvement, or hobby	11.1
No participation or almost none	18.5
Individual style in participation	26.0

B. PARTICIPATION IN COMMUNITY ORGANIZATIONS BY
TWENTY-FIVE WOMEN OF THE CLASS OF 1938

Type of Organization	*Per Cent*
Community agencies (One or more of the following: March of Dimes, Red Cross, United Appeals, Children's Hospital, P.T.A.)	80
Self-expression, self-improvement, or further education	20
Church (Sunday-school teaching, membership in other groups)	32
Social (bridge, yacht club, country club, and so on)	32
Business	16
Little or no participation	12
Individual style in participation	24

munity service was large (14), the amount of participation seemed to be slight, usually a matter of helping in some capacity with fund raising. Five of the men took much greater responsibilities than the others. Social organizations ranked low: five belonged to country clubs, two were in and one was resigning from Kiwanis, one was a member of Lions' and another of Optimists, two were Masons and another was an Elk. One is active in the Audubon Society, and one has become inactive and is withdrawing from the Sports Car Club of America. Only one of the nineteen who were eligible has joined the American Legion, which was the only veterans' organization mentioned.

The five men whose community participation seems definitely more far-reaching than that of the others are among the seven who will be described briefly because each has developed a style of participation which is individual and closely related to his abilities. Two are playing a large part in civil defense, one in radio communications, and the other in radiological defense. Both of these men have admirable backgrounds for the roles they have accepted. One of them is also an Audubon Society member who climbs to inaccessible places to band baby hawks in their nests, and writes columns about birds for the newspapers. A third man, the one minister in the group, has been extraordinarily successful in helping large groups of people to discover their common purposes and to work together in community-wide efforts to achieve them. In his case, organization of the energies of church people for the betterment of the community is his business, so our classification of activity into business, church, and community breaks down. The separation of business and community also breaks down in the case of one of the artists, a teacher, who is working very effectively, using a variety of approaches, to spread art-education opportunities through his whole area. Another who is unmarried and lives at the Y.M.C.A. participates in a variety of square-dance and folk-dance groups, helps teach beginners, and is an active Youth Hosteler—a pattern of activities well calculated to bring him the kind of contacts which he needs and to give him an effective avenue for helping others in a specialized field. Two others, both of whom are greatly interested in politics, seem to have time for and an interest in everything that goes on in the community. One of them made the following answer to the question, "Do you work for community organizations?"

> Yes, I do, and I believe in them. I probably have several reasons—and one is a charitable nature. I think we all have that. And I give well to my church. Still I only try to do my part. However, I probably have a third reason, also. I feel that charity from the heart by the people is—I probably have the feeling that maybe if I didn't, the government would take it over, and they'd force me to give it.—It occurred to me at this moment.

To summarize, one might note that the predominant pattern of the men's involvement in voluntary organizations is of business and church interests, with heavy involvement in community betterment by only a few, although an effective few. Social and fraternal organizations seem relatively unimportant. Eighteen and five-tenths per cent are involved in no voluntary groups (or almost none), 55.5 per cent follow pretty much the general pattern with endless personal variations, and 26 per cent have their own style of participation, suited to their particular situations, abilities, interests, and philosophies.

The pattern of participation of the women is dominated by the homemaker. The four who are employed full time are too small a group to have much influence on the results. As has been mentioned, three of the employed women have joined and do considerable work in their professional organizations. The pattern of 80 per cent of the women consists of quite extensive involvement in one or more of the community-service organizations plus activity in one or more of some other kind. (This contrasts with the highest figure quoted by Wright and Hyman—only 56 per cent of the women questioned in Denver who were the same age as the guinea pigs belonged to one or more community-service organizations.) In this type of organization, the women help collect funds during special campaigns, and also do the work around the year. Many of their enterprises center in the working groups of the Junior League (e.g., Children's Hospital and training courses for baby sitters), Girl Scouts, Cub Scouts, P.T.A., and so on. Only half as many (32 per cent) mentioned social organizations —a bridge club, country club, yacht club, or similar group. An equal number were working participants in church groups—as teachers of Sunday school or members of active church groups. Only three individuals, or 12 per cent, did not participate in community organizations. One of these women, and her family, had moved six times in the previous five years; now that they have come to rest on a college campus, the picture will probably change.

As with the men, the women's individual patterns of participation differed. On the whole, however, 64 per cent seemed fairly conventional, doing the things which, according to general belief, any "good citizen" would do under similar circumstances. Six of the women, or 24 per cent, seemed to show an individual style in their participation, which indicated that they were following particular interests, and were initiating or working for causes which had meaning for them, or were putting their special talents to work for good causes. Most notable, perhaps, are the achievements of two women: one has succeeded in getting crippled-children's troops into the Girls Scouts and in getting camp experience for them, and the other has worked successfully to get special classes for retarded children established in the schools of her city and is also concerned about the problems of the gifted. It should be noted that each of these women has three bright and healthy children of her own; her sympathy and concern for the handicapped was not born out of personal sorrow but rather out of a warm sense of concern for those who need help.

Since there are no established norms for participation in voluntary organizations, evaluation is difficult.[4] Apparently none of the guinea pigs is a "joiner." There is evidence in the protocols that they say no to many requests, but also that they feel responsible for accepting when they can. There is also some evidence that both sexes show leadership

[4] For purposes of comparison it can be pointed out that the upper–middle class groups studied by Wright and Hyman did not show nearly so much participation in significant community activities as the guinea pigs.

on many occasions in civilian life, as the men of the class did in the armed forces (see pages 66–67).

To find 25 per cent of a group who are participating with a style of their own, with individuality and creativeness, seems to the writer most encouraging. All of them, and a number of others who are not in that somewhat arbitrarily selected group, are finding much personal satisfaction in helping to improve their communities or lighten the load of misfortune for others.

POLITICS

The relation between voluntary organizations and the political process has not been very thoroughly explored by theoreticians. Probably, a fundamental truth was expressed by the man, quoted in the last section, who suddenly sensed in the interview that voluntary activity must meet problems or government will surely step in. Conservatives and liberals can unite on a program of treasuring spontaneous, local initiative in meeting problems.[5]

Many social psychologists and political scientists are much concerned about the poor reputation of politics and politicians in our society, and about the apparent feeling of many citizens that political activity is futile and frustrating. Certainly, the prospects for democracy depend to a significant degree upon the ability of citizens to work effectively through their political institutions, old and new, to attain the objectives that can only be reached by political means.

The data on politics, which came both from the questionnaires and from the interviews, were studied from several points of view. First, the questionnaires and protocol of each individual were analyzed to discover what shifts there had been in party alignment and political attitudes between the home in 1938 and the guinea pig in 1955.[6] For

[5] Participation in community activities and voluntary organizations, other than country clubs and college clubs, was given almost no attention in the reunion books studied, in Havemann and West, or even in Terman. This does not shake the confidence of the writer that this is an extremely important area. Wright and Hyman note that membership in organizations is connected with interest in public affairs and with voting.

[6] Of the forty-nine interviews, four were short forms and one an experimental form, so this analysis was possible for forty-four subjects.

their book *Were We Guinea Pigs?*, the students in 1937–38 classified the political attitudes of their parents; in 1955 they did so again on the questionnaires. Since these two evaluations, seventeen years apart, corresponded very closely (see Table 7, p. 45), it is assumed that they give a reasonably accurate view of the parents' conservatism, liberalism, and so on, as well as their party preferences. Each guinea pig underlined his own party preference on the questionnaire, but was not asked to rate himself on the conservative-liberal-radical scale.

The ratings of the guinea pigs as to conservative-liberal-radical atti-

TABLE 29

PARTY PREFERENCES OF FIFTY-TWO GUINEA PIGS IN
1955 AND THEIR PARENTS IN 1938

PARTY OF PARENTS IN 1938	PER CENT IN EACH PARTY	PER CENT OF GUINEA PIGS WITH EACH PARTY PREFERENCE IN 1955			
		Republican	Democrat	Independent	None
Both Republicans............	61.5	45.5	4.0	8.0	4
Both Democrats.............	13.5	4.0	9.5	....	...
Both Socialists..............	2.0	....	....	2.0	...
Both Independents...........	7.5	....	2.0	5.5	...
Mixed—Difference between parents...................	13.5	2.0	4.0	7.5	...
No data....................	2.0	....	....	....	2
Total....................	100.0	51.5	19.5	23.0	6

tudes were derived from their responses to the political questions in the interview. A description of the pattern of political attitudes characteristic of persons in each classification was prepared by the writer and modified after checking with a number of faculty members in University School and on the university campus (see Appendix D). The protocol responses which gave relevant material (Appendix C, Questions 64–78) were read as a unit, and each individual was assigned to one of the five classifications by the ineffable process through which every teacher averages incommensurable objective and subjective data to come out with a grade.

Table 29 compares the party preferences of the guinea pigs in 1955 with those of their parents in 1938, and Table 30 compares their political attitudes in 1955 with those of their parents when they were in high school.

In 1938, both parents of 61.5 per cent of the families were Republicans; in 1955, 45 per cent of their children were Republicans, 4 per cent were Democrats, 8 per cent were independents, and 4 per cent had no party preference. Fifty-one and five-tenths per cent of the guinea pigs listed themselves as Republicans in 1955.

In 1938, both parents of 13.5 per cent of the families were Democrats; in 1955, 9.5 per cent of their children were Democrats and 4 per cent were Republicans. Nineteen and five-tenths per cent of the guinea pigs listed themselves as Democrats in 1955.

The mixed families of 1938 made up 13.5 per cent of the total and were divided into almost equal numbers of Democrats, Republicans, Socialists, and independents. In 1955, their children reported themselves as 2 per cent Republicans, 4 per cent Democrats, and 7.5. per cent independents.

Among the parents, there had been 7.5 per cent independents and 2 per cent Socialists; among the graduates of 1938, there were 23 per cent independents and 6 per cent with no party interests or preferences.

The independents gained from every group except the Democrats. (Those people who labeled themselves as Independent Democrats or Independent Republicans were counted as Democrats or Republicans.) The increased percentage of independents (from 7.5 per cent to 23 per cent) was made up of guinea pigs from one in every eight of the 1938 Republican families, two-thirds of the 1938 independents, and one-half of the 1938 mixed-party families.

These proportions are significantly different from those shown in the Harvard and Princeton reunion books, in which the Republican percentages are very much higher. The percentages of guinea pigs in each party do not differ very much from Havemann's figures for northern college graduates who live in the north (Republicans, 45 per cent; Democrats, 18 per cent; independents, 37 per cent),[7] though the Class of 1938 has more Republicans, fewer independents, and 6 per cent who are refugees from the political scene, a classification ignored by the other studies.

The extent to which the guinea pigs have shifted from their family patterns may be the result of mature, critical thinking, developed by the program of University School; this seems, however, a rather idealized explanation. Other influences can be hypothesized and often documented: a revolt against the parents years ago, the influence of the spouse, certain issues of our times. The writer tends to feel that the role of the school was minor except that it tended to make the students more willing to make their own decisions.

The increasing extent to which the electorate is crossing party lines and voting on some other basis than party affiliation has been frequently remarked in recent years. Perhaps political attitudes are more important than party labels.

In Table 30, the political attitudes of the parents in 1938 have been tabulated from the 1955 questionnaire, although such a table was made by the students in 1938.[8] The two tabulations differ somewhat; it would have been preferable to use the table made by the students except that it did not identify separate families as conservative or liberal, and thus the shifts in political attitudes could not have been traced except as gross totals.

In Table 30, the most striking points are the disappearance of the radicals, the absence of a non-rational fringe (see Appendix D)—the two extreme groups—and the attrition of the conservatives. Of course, there is no reason to think that in 1938 all the children of conservative parents were conservatives; it is unlikely that many of them believed that they were at that time. But when adolescent rebellion is over, the usual tendency seems to be for the offspring to move back toward parental patterns. In the Class of 1938, however, of the 52 per cent who came from conservative homes, only one-third (18 per cent) re-

---

[7] Ernest Havemann and Patricia West, *They Went to College* (New York: Harcourt, Brace and Company, 1952), p. 112 (Chart 26).

[8] See Class of 1938, *op. cit.*, p. 5.

main conservative, one-sixth (9 per cent) have become liberals, and two out of five (20.5 per cent) take a middle-of-the-road position. Two individuals from this group, one from a background in which the parents differed in political attitudes, and one who does not describe the political attitudes of his parents, form the 8.5 per cent who either spurn politics or are so confused or ill-informed about issues that they do not seem to be able to participate effectively.

There has been significant growth in the middle-of-the-road group (40.5 per cent in 1955), the category which is most nearly

TABLE 30

POLITICAL ATTITUDES OF FORTY-FOUR GUINEA PIGS IN
1955 AND THEIR PARENTS IN 1938

ATTITUDES OF PARENTS IN 1938	PER CENT IN EACH CATEGORY	PER CENT OF GUINEA PIGS HOLDING EACH ATTITUDE			
		Conservative	Middle of the Road	Liberal	No Commitments or Attitudes
Conservative..............	52	18	20.5	9	4.5
Liberal...................	16	..	7.0	9	...
Radical..................	2	..	....	2	...
Mixed—Difference between parents.................	28	2	13.0	11	2.0
Unknown.................	2	..	....	..	2.0
Total..................	100	20	40.5	31	8.5

comparable to the mixed (difference between parents) group of 1938 (28 per cent), at the expense of both the conservatives and the liberals. In spite of their losses to the middle-of-the-road group, the number of liberals has nearly doubled through recruitment from conservative or mixed groups.

There is no way of knowing whether these shifts merely represent the trends of the times, or whether the habits of independent thinking, which the school tried to foster, have caused the guinea pigs to keep on clarifying their ideas and modifying their philosophies. It is also possible in this whole dubious field of political labeling that if others had been doing the classifying, they might have changed the results by assigning various individuals to different groups. The writer is reasonably sure, however, that no one would classify any of them as radical or as members of the non-rational fringe.

Another significant factor to study in a group of people is the degree to which they participate in politics and how well they understand the process. This inquiry required another attempt at classifying information from questionnaires and protocols and rating individuals as shown in Table 31.

The four active individuals in the first group of Table 31 were all men. One had run unsuccessfully for mayor of his city, but felt that the campaign had brought about real progress on certain issues in spite of his defeat. Another had accepted a party appointment and had

TABLE 31

POLITICAL ACTIVITY OF FORTY-FIVE MEMBERS OF THE CLASS OF 1938

Degree of Participation in Politics	Number	Per Cent
1. Takes part in regular, organized political activity........	4	8.8
2. Takes active part in campaigns on many issues...........	6	13.4
3. Votes regularly; feels responsible for knowing issues and working for some causes..............................	15	33.3
4. Does nothing but vote................................	16	35.6
5. Shuns politics.......................................	4	8.8

worked for many months at considerable personal sacrifice to bring honesty and order into a county office where scandals had been discovered. A third works actively in the local political organization, and the fourth, who finds local politics in his area unrewarding because of the overwhelming numerical superiority of the opposition party, keeps close track of affairs in Washington and writes regularly to inform key people about his views.

The guinea pigs in the second group had not been so consistently active, but had been in the thick of the fray more than once on some important issues, or had, perhaps, maintained steady pressure on an issue which they regarded as important.

The third group consisted of those who voted regularly and kept themselves relatively well informed on issues. This group merged into the fourth which was composed of people who voted, but appeared to be inadequately informed. This was a subjective judgment on the part of the investigator and was often at variance with the opinion of the respondent. An equal number of individuals in the third and fourth groups expressed themselves as dissatisfied with their own knowledge of the issues. The investigator made the judgment as to whether the individual was an informed voter on the basis of his information about political issues between elections, on the theory that the voter who waits to begin thinking about politics until the campaign is under way will find reliable information hard to come by and careful thinking hard to do.

It was easy to identify the fifth group, although there were marked

TABLE 32

POLITICAL SOPHISTICATION OF FORTY-FIVE MEMBERS
OF THE CLASS OF 1938

Level of Political Sophistication	Number	Per Cent
1. Seems to understand the nature and importance of political activity and to have an understanding of issues..........	17	38.0
2. Shows a fair level of understanding.....................	14	33.3
3. Either asserts ignorance while showing some information, or expresses naïve or contradictory opinions.............	8	17.7
4. Seems to think in stereotypes or to be very confused or to have rejected politics altogether.......................	5	11.0

differences among the four individuals, some of which are pointed out in later discussions. All were alike in rejecting politics and politicians.

Another kind of tabulation was attempted in Table 32, for which the political and allied questions in the protocols were evaluated, not in terms of attitudes or conclusions, but in terms of the individual's concepts of the political process and his grasp of issues. A comparison of answers to the question, "Who do you think runs the country now?", will illustrate what was sought.

Well, I think—I don't know. I think the government—the national government—has a strong effect. Economically, I think probably the large industry, the big corporations, actually control the economic function of the country. I think they're tempered by the government. I think if you take the big companies such as DuPont, General

Motors, General Electric, those companies, I think they run it from the economical point of view. I think it's tempered and controlled and held in check by the government.

Compare this with two other answers, one of which was simply, "Big money," and the other, "I think it runs itself."

The line between the first and second groups in Table 32 is vague and shifting. Possibly a second attempt at the same kind of "grading" would produce somewhat different results, and no two people would reach precisely the same ones. However, since no figures have been found with which they might be compared (probably cautious researchers avoid anything so subjective), these will do well enough for our investigation.

A comparison of the percentages in Tables 31 and 32 shows that the level of political sophistication appears definitely higher than the degree of active involvement in politics—61.3 per cent are in the two top groups of political sophistication as compared with 22.2 per cent who are actively involved. In his article, "Yale '36—Look at Them Now," John Hersey noted, "Lots of deploring but little political action." He does not, however, offer any figures. Nor does Zinsser, who quotes the following comment from a member of Princeton 1944, "Some of us take a hand in local politics." The evidence is widespread that political concern is greater than political involvement. There are no figures to tell whether 22.2 per cent is a high proportion of political activists, but it seems probable that it is. Certainly, the proportion of voters in the Class of 1938, 91 per cent, is far higher than in the generality of the population as shown by election figures year after year. One set of figures, cited by Jacob, corresponds fairly closely to the record of the guinea pigs:

> Scattered bits of evidence from other programs tend to support the hope that incorporating carefully designed student experience in their college education can have a considerable influence upon their values. For many years Toledo University required a course in "Effective Citizenship," which was originated by Professor O. Garfield Jones. In it every student makes a precinct survey and predicts how that precinct will vote in the next election. Part of the student's grade de-

pends on the accuracy of his prediction. A 100% canvass of graduates who had taken the course twenty years before indicated a lasting effect on their political behavior. Over 95% were registered voters and over 92% had voted in the 1950 state election. A particular factor apparently contributed to an almost perfect voting record for the classes which graduated in 1930 and 1931. As students they had participated along with faculty in a house-to-house canvass and manned the polls on election day in order to secure approval of a bond issue to buy a new campus and erect buildings for the university. Professor Jones concludes that "in the process of persuading the Toledo electorate to vote for the university bond issue in 1928, these students did an even better job of convincing themselves of the importance of voting." [9]

The investigator was especially interested in the individuals at the bottom of the scale, and in the attitudes which lay behind the behavior of those at all levels. There are four guinea pigs in the lowest group of the activity scale who shun politics, and five on the sophistication scale who are confused or reject politics.

To check on the attitudes behind the various amounts of activity and sophistication, the answers to Question 66 (Appendix C) were examined—"What kind of person do you think of when you think of a person very much interested in politics?"

There was a striking difference between the replies of all but one of the individuals who were given the lowest rating in Table 32 and the replies of all the others. Four of those who abstained from politics thought of a politician as "crooked," "foolish," "a screwball." Only one would grant him anything: "I suppose a person who is very much interested in politics must be a very aggressive, rather active person, by and large disinclined toward the arts and sciences."

Those who were rated in the top and middle classifications of the scales thought of the person interested in politics in sharply contrasting terms. "I am inclined to think of him in glowing terms. I say it with a good deal of bias, naturally." "What I would like to see would be everybody taking a very keen interest in politics, which never will be as a practical matter, probably."

[9] Philip Jacob, *Changing Values in College* (New York: Harper and Brothers, 1957), p. 97.

The middle group included those who had minor reservations: one had little respect for certain local politicians, but tried not to generalize from that experience; two others found that they were inclined to believe that politicians tended to be opportunists or were out for personal gain; one was amused to discover that although she felt that politics was a slightly dirty word, she very much admired people who were interested in public affairs.

The response was overwhelmingly (77.8 per cent) in favor of considering the person very much interested in politics as a good and useful citizen; 11.1 per cent qualified the appraisal somewhat; the other 11.1 per cent considered him a crook, a foolish person, a "screwball," or an aggressive and active person not interested in the arts or sciences.

No means as been discovered to check these percentages against the figures of any comparable sample. However, the significance of politics seems reasonably well apprehended by this group, although any teacher is always disturbed over the size of the fraction, in this case one out of every nine, who did not learn any of the things which the teacher believed were being taught.[10]

After studying the protocols, reading, and listening to many discussions of politics in a democracy, the writer is left with an unanswered question: Does democracy require the active political interest of every single citizen, or is there room for individual differences in participation? One of the guinea pigs offered his opinion:

> Me! I don't have a strong feeling that everyone must be and I don't happen to be. I have heard that democracy requires it, etc. I'd be interested in issues that are close—a school bond issue—but on larger issues where I don't feel competent and there is no easy source of reliable information, I am not the type who will dig and dig.

The final inquiry to be treated in this chapter concerns the attitude of each person toward the danger of war and his suggestions for the most promising means of avoiding it. As a group, the Class of 1938 is not particularly sanguine about the chances of avoiding war; only a

---

[10] For a more extensive analysis of political attitudes see Chapter X, "The Achievement of Purposes: Democratic Living," pages 254–59.

few believe it is inevitable, most think it probable, and a few are sure that it can be avoided. Almost three-fourths seem to sense the complexity of the factors involved and to believe that some are beyond American control.

No one, however, thought that isolation was the way to make war less likely. Six women and one man (16 per cent) had no suggestions as to what could be done; and a second group of five men and women (11 per cent) made suggestions which seemed more consistent with the theories of the causation of war which sprouted in the 1930's, following the Nye investigations and the propaganda for the Ludlow amendment, than with the realities of the contemporary world.

Thirty-four, or approximately three-fourths, put their faith in one or more of the following recommendations. (The number of times each was mentioned is given after the item.)

1. Improving understanding among peoples, chiefly through student exchange (12).

2. Improving economic well-being of the world, with major assistance by the United States (10). Adjusting our tariff and immigration laws (1), and controlling world population (1).

3. Co-operating with the United Nations and its agencies or strengthening the international organization (10). Placing some restrictions on national sovereignty (1).

4. Patience, negotiation, and compromise (5).

5. Maintaining an armed force for balance of power or retaliation (4).

6. Making people aware of the moral problem or the foolishness of war (4).

7. Turning our attention to the problems of space travel instead of war (2).

Five people offered specific suggestions for changes in our own attitudes which were difficult to fit into the above tabulation. In varying language, each of the five pointed out that we should not assume that our ways are the best for everybody, but that we should try to give respect and understanding to other peoples, and to learn from them as well as to teach them.

VII

HEALTH, RECREATION, AND ATTITUDES
TOWARD LIVING

Physical Health

One of the remarkable facts about the Class of 1938 is that, twenty years after high-school graduation, all of the members are still alive. Of course, there is a strong element of chance in that record. Many University School servicemen from earlier and succeeding classes lost their lives in the Second World War, and some of the guinea pigs had narrow escapes; for example, two of the men who were Air Corps pilots were shot down over German-occupied territory. Among the civilians, a former member of the class, who did not graduate with them, died in the crash of a commercial airliner; there may have been other deaths among former members that have not come to the writer's notice. But since the fatal illness of one of their number from leukemia in the seventh grade, death has passed by the Class of 1938 both in school and after graduation.

This does not mean that they all have had perfect health records. The proportion of men in the class rejected by Selective Service during the war was almost the same as the national figure; but since national rejections included illiterates, conscientious objectors, and psychoneurotic cases, none of which occurred in this group, the guinea pigs' rejection rate seems to indicate a higher than average proportion of physical impairment. Among the causes for rejection were eye difficulties which dated back to early childhood and which have been of continuing significance since the war, constituting a very serious limiting factor for one man and a problem for a number of other graduates of both sexes.

Other health problems have been serious at times. There have been three major automobile accidents, one of which necessitated plastic surgery. One woman has suffered two brain concussions; seven people reported appendectomies; two have had spinal fusions; and there have been one or two instances of a variety of other troubles. In general, these people have made complete recovery and now consider themselves in good health.

TABLE 33

SELF-RATINGS OF HEALTH BY TERMAN'S GIFTED CHILDREN, IN 1940, AND THE CLASS OF 1938, IN 1955

Self-Rating of Health	Per Cent of Terman's Men * (N-700)	Per Cent of Men of the Class of 1938 (N-27)	Per Cent of Terman's Women * (N-563)	Per Cent of Women of the Class of 1938 (N-25)
Very good.............	52.3	52.0	44.7	64
Good.................	38.6	40.6	39.0	32
Fair..................	7.3	....	12.8	..
Poor.................	1.0	3.7	3.2	4
Very poor............	0.9	3.7	0.5	..

* The figures for Terman's gifted children were taken from *The Gifted Child Grows Up*, p. 91.

Three individuals have severe health problems of long duration. One man has had very serious trouble with arthritis of the spine (rheumatoid spondylitis) and other complications which have necessitated long periods of treatment and numerous leaves of absence from his job; he has not married, largely because of uncertainty about his health. One woman has also had some serious difficulty with arthritis, but treatments and a move to a more favorable climate have resulted in remarkable improvement. The third person had been critically ill with bulbar polio; he has recovered sufficiently to return to his work, although the aftereffects still curtail his activity.

Table 33 contains the health ratings which fifty-two of the guinea pigs assigned to themselves and the comparison with the health ratings of Terman's gifted children at approximately the same age. (The age range within Terman's group is much greater.) Considering the small number of subjects in our group and all the imponderables which enter into self-rating, it is remarkable how close the two sets of figures are. This is particularly true for the men in both groups. The women in the guinea-pig group rated their health significantly higher than Terman's women: all but one of them considered their health very good or good. Terman points out that there are no comparable health statistics for other groups, but that it is clear from the table that ill health is relatively rare among his subjects. This is equally true for the entire Class of 1938, and not merely for the gifted group from the class.

Mental Health

Terman made careful studies of the mental health of fourteen hundred men and women in his group, some in 1940, others in 1945, and some in both, and assigned ratings of (1) satisfactory; (2) some maladjustment; and (3) serious maladjustment (a) without psychosis, and (b) with psychosis. The kinds of data available to Terman were closely comparable to those used in this study, and he gives both descriptions and illustrations of his classifications.[1]

The investigator attempted to apply Terman's classifications to the guinea pigs, but encountered too many problems which demanded psychological insights beyond her area of competence. When such small numbers are involved, a few individuals moved from one classification to another cause a startling shift in percentages. Without expert advice and assistance—none was available—comparisons with Terman's data could not be made with any confidence.

There are, however, a few points about the mental health of this group which can be established. The data for these conclusions were derived from the 1955 questionnaires (Appendix A, Question 6b).

[1] Lewis Terman and Melita Oden, *The Gifted Child Grows Up: Twenty-five Years Follow-up of a Superior Group* (Stanford, California: Stanford University Press, 1948), pp. 99–104.

Though the questionnaire information is essentially the result of self-rating, there is every reason to believe, from the overt and covert evidence of the subsequent interviews, that the data are candid and accurate, with certain reservations which will be noted.

More than two-thirds (thirty-five individuals) felt that they had encountered no problems sufficient to merit mention; one other said, "the usual amount," but listed no treatment and rated his present condition as "satisfactory." Sixteen named emotional disturbances—worry, nervousness, special anxiety; in three cases, the major problem was that of the spouse, and in another, that of the parents. Seven of the sixteen sought individual or group psychotherapy; two reported improvement, and all of the others believed their difficulties had been satisfactorily worked out. In two cases, medical treatment had also helped. Seven others of the sixteen reported that their worries or special anxieties had disappeared as they solved the problems which had caused the condition.

Five of the fifty-two guinea pigs about whom there was information reported that they had learned to live with the problems which had caused the difficulties. In four of the five cases, the problem was relatively permanent—physical limitations, "in-law" attitudes—and learning to live with the problem appeared to be the most promising solution. In one case, the situation causing the problem was permanent —the arrival of twin sons in a family—but by the time of the interview, the mother's nervousness had disappeared and the babies were a fascination and delight to her. In one sense, this problem should be considered solved, since the essense of the difficulty was its newness rather than its continuing nature.

It should be noted that this kind of self-rating does not yield percentages of well-adjusted and maladjusted men and women. The chances are strong that the basically well-adjusted will be the ones who are able to recognize their problems, who know what help they need in solving them, and who seek out help. The genuinely maladjusted are more likely to be found among those who deny having any problems. For example, both of the individuals in the class who appear to the investigator to be relatively maladjusted reported no emotional problems, whereas four others with a lesser degree of maladjustment reported their anxieties and what they were doing or had done about them. A denial of problems is not in itself evidence of maladjustment, of course; in the large majority of cases, the individuals reporting no problems appear to be on a very even keel emotionally.

No member of the class is psychotic or has been a patient at a mental hospital. One had some brief difficulties as a result of an overdosage of cortisone when the drug was new and not well understood, but this is a chemical not a psychological phenomenon.

Avocational Interests

What people do with their free time is generally regarded as an important index to character, personality, and general adjustment. With the shortening of working hours which is common in our day (it is more significant for manual workers than for other groups), the use of free time is meriting and receiving added attention. When the guinea pigs were in high school, the faculty was concerned with trying to help children develop a wide range of interests. The purpose of the program was not to teach specific leisure-time activities, though there was some of that, but rather to give support and encouragement to the individual's own spontaneous interests.

The extent to which the adult patterns of leisure-time activity are political or involve community participation has been discussed in Chapter VI. This section is concerned with purely recreational activities. The material for it comes from three main sources: from the questionnaire, (1) a self-rating of interests in twelve different fields, and (2) a request for specific information about principle avocational interests (Appendix A, Question 9); and from the interview, (3) probing about recreational activities and interests, and another self-rating of interests.

With Terman's permission, the form for self-rating of interest which he used in his study was incorporated in the questionnaire.[2]

[2] Terman and Oden, op. cit., p. 407 and p. 209 (tabulations).

Twelve fields were listed: travel, outdoor sports, religion, mechanics, social life, literature, music, art, science, politics, domestic arts, and pets. Each person was asked to check the degree of his interest in each category on a line marked at equal intervals "very much," "more than average," "average," "slight," and "none."

By using the same method of scoring employed by Terman, it was

TABLE 34

SELF-RATINGS OF INTEREST IN TWELVE FIELDS BY TERMAN'S GIFTED CHILDREN, IN 1940, AND THE CLASS OF 1938, IN 1955

FIELD OF INTEREST	RATINGS OF MEN			RATINGS OF WOMEN		
	Terman's Gifted (N-693)	Gifted of the Class of 1938 (N-10)	Other Members of the Class of 1938 (N-17)	Terman's Gifted (N-554)	Gifted of the Class of 1938 (N-14)	Other Members of the Class of 1938 (N-11)
Travel........	2.1	2.9	2.2	2.0	1.6	1.8
Outdoor sports......	2.5	2.8	1.6	2.9	2.2	3.2
Religion.....	3.7	2.7	2.6	3.5	2.5	2.6
Mechanics....	2.9	2.3	2.9	4.1	4.2	4.7
Social life....	2.9	2.6	3.1	2.7	2.4	2.4
Literature....	2.5	3.3	3.0	1.9	1.9	2.3
Music........	2.5	3.2	2.7	2.1	1.6	2.6
Art..........	3.1	3.5	3.6	2.6	2.0	3.0
Science.......	2.3	2.3	2.9	2.9	3.0	4.1
Politics......	2.6	3.2	3.0	2.9	2.1	3.1
Domestic arts.	3.6	3.5	3.5	2.6	2.1	1.8
Pets.........	3.2	3.6	3.3	2.9	3.1	2.3
Average....	2.8	3.0	3.9	2.8	2.4	2.8

possible to get data for comparison in a field in which general standards are non-existent and comparisons hard to find. A check at "very much" was counted as 1, at "average" as 3, and at "none" as 5. (As in golf, the lower your score, the higher your rating.) The tabulation of this data is given in Table 34. To facilitate comparison, the Class of 1938 is divided into four groups: the ten men who were selected for comparison with Terman's gifted men (see pages 40–41 for means of selection), the seventeen other men in the class, the fourteen women who were selected for comparison with Terman's gifted women, and

TABLE 35

FIELDS OF INTEREST WHICH RECEIVED THE HIGHEST AND LOWEST RATINGS FROM TERMAN'S GIFTED CHILDREN AND THE CLASS OF 1938

	RATINGS OF MEN			RATINGS OF WOMEN		
	Terman's Gifted (N-693)	Gifted of the Class of 1938 (N-10)	Other Members of the Class of 1938 (N-17)	Terman's Gifted (N-554)	Gifted of the Class of 1938 (N-14)	Other Members of the Class of 1938 (N-11)
High—2.5 or Less						
	Travel 2.1	Mechanics 2.3	Outdoor sports 1.6	Literature 1.9	Travel 1.6	Travel 1.8
	Science 2.3	Science 2.3	Travel 2.2	Travel 2.0	Music 1.6	Domestic arts 1.8
	Outdoor sports 2.5			Music 2.1	Literature 1.9	Literature 2.3
	Literature 2.5				Art 2.0	Pets 2.3
	Music 2.5				Politics 2.1	Social life 2.4
					Domestic arts 2.1	
					Outdoor sports 2.2	
					Social life 2.4	
					Religion 2.5	
Low—3.5 or More						
	Domestic arts 3.6	Art 3.5	Domestic arts 3.5	Religion 3.5	Mechanics 4.2	Mechanics 4.7
	Religion 3.7	Domestic arts 3.5	Art 3.6	Mechanics 4.1		
		Pets 3.6				

the eleven other women. Averaging the ratings in each field of interest for each group gave the figures in Table 34.

Table 34 presents a complicated picture. It may be simplified by considering all ratings of 2.5 or less, high; and those of 3.5 or more, low. Interests which are neither high nor low may be considered average. Table 35 shows the highs and lows of all groups.

The gifted men of 1938 expressed the same degree of interest in science as Terman's men (2.3). They also expressed an equally high interest in mechanics (2.3), which was an average interest in Terman's group (2.9). Terman's gifted men had high interest in travel (2.1), outdoor sports (2.5), literature (2.5), and music (2.5), all of which were average for the University School gifted men (2.9, 2.8, 3.3, and 3.2 respectively). The two high-ranking interests for the rest of the University School men were outdoor sports and travel.

The men in all groups expressed a low interest in domestic arts. Terman's men also showed a low interest in religion (3.7), which was rated 2.7 by the gifted men of 1938 and 2.6 by the others. The University School men expressed low interest in art (3.5 and 3.6 respectively), and the gifted men of the group were little interested in pets (3.6).

The cultural side of life as expressed in music, literature, and the arts had high interest for Terman's group, but did not rank high with the University School men. Terman's information was collected in 1940, and that from the guinea pigs in 1955. How much significance, if any, the difference in dates has, the writer does not know. The two groups were about the same age when the data were collected, but the information from the guinea pigs is fifteen years and two wars later than that from Terman's group.

Among the women, interest in literature, travel, and music is high for both Terman's women and the University School gifted women; the University School gifted women also expressed interest in art, politics, domestic arts, outdoor sports, social life, and religion, all of which elicited only average interest from Terman's gifted women, except for religion which received a low rating (3.5). The rest of the women in the Class of 1938 shared interests in travel and literature with the gifted groups, and interests in social life and domestic arts with the gifted from University School. They added only an interest in pets.

All of the groups of women rated mechanics very low among their interests. Whereas Terman's gifted women rated religion low, it is of high interest to the University School gifted women and of a relatively high average interest to the rest.

A few interesting generalizations emerge from these comparisons. The men in the guinea-pig class have fewer strong interests than Terman's men, or than the women in the class. The women among the guinea pigs, however, have more and stronger interests than Terman's group. The strong interest of the University School men in mechanics may be related to their heavy election of courses in the industrial-arts area in high school (22 out of 26 elected industrial arts). The interest of the women in domestic arts and in the arts, which is stronger than that of the men or of Terman's women, may also be related to high-school electives, though these are only surmises.

The fact that religion enlists relatively higher interest among the guinea pigs than among Terman's group may be due to the differences between the years 1940 and 1955, a period during which nationwide interest in organized religion increased markedly.

PRINCIPAL AVOCATIONAL INTERESTS

A partially open-ended question followed the rating of interests in the twelve fields (Appendix A, Question 9 a):

9 b. Be as specific as you can in a few sentences about what sorts of things you do as your principal avocational interest. (Collecting particular kinds of records, participating in chorus or orchestra, climbing mountains, or whatever.)

Forty-eight of the fifty-two questionnaires gave the specific information requested. The answers varied greatly in detail, but added much to the picture of the individual. It was interesting to note the number of answers that fell outside the apparently inclusive twelve categories of the list in Table 34. The descriptions varied in length from one word—"fishing," "mechanics"—to two hundred fifty word pictures. Among the interests which did not fit neatly into any of the twelve fields were gardening and various home-maintenance projects, which were mentioned by sixteen individuals. Camping, hiking, sailing, fishing, bird watching, and Youth Hosteling would probably be considered outdoor sports, in the same class as swimming, water skiing, winter sports, tennis, horseback riding, and golf, which were mentioned by twenty different people. But how should one classify square dancing and folk dancing, chess, bridge, bowling, fencing, color photography, model railroading, and amateur theatricals? And in what category can one place the theatre addict in the New York area whose husband shares her addiction so completely that they try to attend all Broadway openings, and eat dinner at a different foreign restaurant each time?

During the interviews, the investigator attempted to probe about avocational activities and interests. Part of the preparation for any interview was a review of the data contained in the questionnaire of the person being interviewed. This permitted the interviewer to bring out fuller information about questions to which the written responses had been intriguing in what they suggested but did not develop. The responses added depth and variety to the picture of avocational interests, and confirmed the impression that each individual had developed his own patterns in his own terms.

It is tempting to quote extensively from the questionnaires and the protocols to show the verve with which these people responded, but perhaps one of a quieter tone from one of the very productive intellectuals will suffice to round out the picture.

Playing bridge and drinking sherry with my neighbors—my wife claims this way of living can't be described, but can only be understood by being experienced.

Recreational interests need to be considered as a part of the whole pattern of an individual's living. It is clear that the guinea pigs have healthy interests and enthusiasms; since their recreational patterns are highly individual, the chances are strong that the patterns serve their needs. From the evidence available, it appears that there is no one who is bored with his leisure, or wonders what to do with his time, or involves himself in a frenzy of activities in an attempt to get away from himself.

Attitudes toward Living

The interview schedule included a great many questions dealing with values. Although Part III of this report is the section basically concerned with questions of values in the protocols, certain aspects of attitudes are pertinent at this point. Health, physical and mental, and recreational interests are a part of living, as are the subjects treated in earlier chapters. But the force which gives them all cohesion and significance is the individual's concept of successful living, and his feeling about himself in relation to his concept of success.

Some of the questions on the interview schedule (Appendix C) were concerned directly or indirectly with ambition, the importance of happiness, the importance of money, the factors which make for success, and satisfaction or dissatisfaction with the present age. All the answers to these questions in each protocol were read in relation to each other to determine the attitudes of the individual, and then the individuals were compared with each other to determine likenesses and trends.

The attitude toward the importance of money was judged principally from the answers to two questions:

56. If you had to choose between very interesting work at low pay and uninteresting work at very high pay, which would you choose?

58. What do you think is most important in your future—money, fame, the respect of your community, something else, or don't you know?

The responses were studied in the light of the whole protocol, and supplementary information was gathered wherever it appeared.

These men and women tended to resemble each other in their attitudes toward money. Thirty-seven (or 82 per cent) were realistic and recognized that a certain amount of money was necessary to maintain their standard of living and educate their children, but beyond that amount the acquisition of money was counted less significant than doing interesting or valuable work or achieving some significant purpose. Even for the eight (or 18 per cent) who, in varying degrees, rated money high as a measure of success, it was not the only measure.

These attitudes may be commoner in America today than in any previous period. Careful observers of social change are noting that the upper-middle class today enjoys most of the advantages which used to be reserved to the upper class. Whether a random group of the population with the same socioeconomic background as the guinea pigs would have as casual an attitude toward financial success, however, is extremely doubtful.

There were three questions about ambition in the interview schedule:

90. Is ambition something you admire in other people?

91. Do you wish you had more ambition yourself? How often?

92. Do you think that, on the whole, ambitious people have happier lives than unambitious ones?

Sixteen, or 36 per cent, said they admired it in others; and twenty-six, or 57 per cent, gave it qualified admiration—"If in the fulfillment of their ambitions, they step all over everybody they come in contact with, well, I think it's ugly, I think it's vicious. On the other hand, if it forms the quiet background for a life of good work, I think it's meritorious, I think it's wonderful." Three others identified ambition with overaggressiveness and deplored it.

All seemed quite relaxed about their own amounts of ambition. Some felt they would get more done if they had a little more, but in only one case did an individual seem disturbed about it. Most believed that they had about the right amount. As one person said, "Ambition tempered with realism about oneself can lead to a very happy life."

The replies to Question 58, "What do you think is most important in your future—money, fame, the respect of your community, something else, or don't you know?", offered a cross-check on these attitudes. As the members of the class looked into the future, the most important things seemed quite diverse at first, although they were actually quite consistent with the attitudes toward money and ambition. The respect of the community and self-respect rank high; they were mentioned by more than a third. Nearly as many, equally divided between men and women, said that their family life was the most important thing to them. Others named social and cultural usefulness, the satisfaction of accomplishment, participation in helping family and community grow, and enjoyment of life each day as it comes. Two of the men looked forward to a moderate amount of fame, and one woman wanted to leave something behind when she dies. Four mentioned advancement in jobs or in income as the chief thing in their futures, and two others hoped for a little more money as a minor goal among other major ones. Three people were unable or unwilling to answer.

Several questions in the schedule asked about happiness:

57. What do you think is most important in life: (a) trying to make the world a better place; (b) happiness; (c) making other people happy; (d) living according to your religion?

92. Do you think that, on the whole, ambitious people have happier lives than unambitious ones?

93. Do you personally care very much about happiness, or do you think other things in life are more important?

Slightly more than half (twenty-three, or 52 per cent) believed that happiness is a by-product, a point of view expressed with clarity in two quotations, one from a man, the second from a woman.

Well, I think as a goal, happiness is a dubious one. I think you get an awful lot of happiness as a by-product of what you're doing and it comes along. I don't pursue happiness too much except maybe when I want an ice-cream cone or I want to go hunting once in a while. I find this great fun. Otherwise, I don't spend much time pursuing it.

Well, I think there are a lot of things in life that are more important than a person's happiness, so that if you didn't have happiness and couldn't quite get it, you could still do other things that were important. And probably in doing them you would discover that you were happy, even though you didn't think you could be.

A group of three persons believed that happiness is just one of the important things, but not the most important. Another individual substituted "satisfaction and self-realization" for happiness. These four seem rather close to the majority attitude, as does one other who said that happiness is important but means very different things.

The remaining seventeen, or 38 per cent, feel that happiness, either personal or family, is the transcendant goal. One who rated money high, put "happiness above money or anything else." Another said, "When you are not happy, nothing else is important." Still another believed that "we are really striving for happiness and think other things will help.". Since it is reasonably clear from other data that the concept of happiness which these individuals have is a warm, family-community concept with a balance of work, community-service, and wholesome recreation, their responses are not as hedonistic as they at first appear.

No comparative studies have been found to indicate whether these attitudes are typical for a group of upper–middle class men and women in their mid-thirties. The thirties are, of course, generally a time of great vigor and promise, and perhaps the peak period of optimism. Making all allowance for such factors, however, it seems that this group is unusually confident as they face life. They believe that an individual is responsible for what becomes of him (Appendix C, Question 96), although they recognize that the pressures of events and circumstances limit or overrule that responsibility at times. Eighty-five per cent of them believed that they were already getting, or stood a very good chance of getting, what they wanted out of life (Appendix C, Question 95), 13 per cent thought they had about an average chance, and one individual could not respond because he did not know what he wanted.

On one point, a comparison is available, though it cannot be pushed very far because of the difference in the phrasing of the questions. The tenth reunion book of Princeton Class of 1944, *The First Decade,* which was reprinted in part in *This Week Magazine,* reports as follows on attitudes toward our age:

> More than half the class admits that they would have preferred a more tranquil decade to the vexatious one we actually got, but 34 per cent accept the chills and vapors of the cold war cheerfully. Almost everyone seems sure we can do a better job than our fathers' generation—or at least as good a job—in building a better world.[3]

TABLE 36

RESPONSES TO THE QUESTION "WOULD YOU PREFER TO LIVE
IN SOME OTHER AGE?"

RESPONSE	MEN (N-23)		WOMEN (N-22)	
	Number	Per Cent	Number	Per Cent
Satisfied with this age...............	13	56.6	11	50.0
Enthusiastic about this age..........	5	21.7	8	36.4
Would prefer the future.............	4	17.0	3	13.6
Would prefer the past...............	1	4.7	..	....

The guinea pigs were asked, "If you had your choice as to when you would be born, would you have preferred to live in some other age than this? Which one?" (Appendix C, Question 31). The responses are grouped in Table 36.

Among the men, 56.6 per cent were satisfied with this age. Some gave no explanation. Others offered varying reasons for their opinions.

> . . . I think I would get along just as well now—probably better than I would have in some other age.

> . . . I don't know what the future holds, and I don't think I would want to be born particularly in the past. I don't think there is that much difference in the time we have to be on this planet.

[3] William K. Zinsser, "The Class of '44 Today," *This Week Magazine* (*New York Herald Tribune,* Sec. 7), June 6, 1954.

I think this is an exciting time to live in. I'd just as soon not live in a time when so many wars are going on, although it would be hard to find a time when there wasn't war. But the problem of war bothers me a great deal.

I think we have a pretty good age. We have it—all the problems and everything. We can look only back to the past, but I'm glad in some cases I wasn't there.

. . . I certainly wouldn't wish to have been born in any different age than this. I think this has been a terrifically difficult era in which to have lived and to live, because we probably have just as many problems, nationally and internationally, as we have ever had, possibly more. As far as material benefits are concerned, we certainly have more to be thankful for today than we've ever had, economically, in terms of—of our welfare, both health and recreational facilities. I think the twentieth century has certainly been remarkable for the increases in longevity of life and other things. No, I wouldn't have any preference other than the present era. Of course, I can't speak about the future.

Five of the men, or 21.7 per cent, were enthusiastic about living in this age. One quotation will serve to illustrate.

You know, my father used to say that he was one of the luckiest men that ever lived because within his lifetime the human race made more progress than they had in all the years until he was born, and he was right; and I think we're going to do it again in the next fifty years, so I would choose to be born right now.

Four others, 17 per cent, wished that they might have been born in some future age.

With the provision that all my family and friends could be transported to that other age with me, I think possibly in a future age, possibly the one my son is coming into. [Curious to see how it all comes out?] Yes, but I know that when he is my age, he will be doing the same thing—wondering what's going to follow him.

The one who preferred the past believed that he would have liked to have been born a hundred years ago, but gave no explanation.

The women expressed themselves in much the same terms as the men, though one gave a feminine point of view.

> . . . I often miss what we think was the glamour of adventuring, even though there were discomforts involved in the time of Queen Elizabeth and the coming to the new world and all. I sometimes think I would have liked the adventure, but being a woman, I probably wouldn't have gotten much of that anyway. But I'm fairly satisfied.

Several other comments expressed satisfaction and enthusiasm for our age, and interest in the future:

> . . . I take what I have. I taught my children that fences were something they could play *within* not barriers that they couldn't go *beyond*.
>
> . . . I think the age is fascinating and challenging.
>
> . . . I think this is a fascinating time to be living. If anything, perhaps a little bit later because I want to see what's going to happen.

Whether these high percentages of guinea pigs who accept our age with all its uncertainties can legitimately be compared with the 34 per cent of Princeton Class of 1944 who cheerfully "accept the chills and vapors of the cold war" is not clear from the evidence.

VIII

THE USE OF COMMUNICATION MEDIA

By Lou L. LaBrant

The Study of Language at University School

Whereas communication is an integral part of every course and of almost every human activity, certain aspects of the study of language (reading, writing, speaking, and listening) emphasize language as such, and so are considered specifically in this chapter. As will be noted later, the quality of writing and speaking are difficult-to-impossible to evaluate: only limited aspects will be considered. The uses of listening as applied to radio and television are also discussed only briefly for two reasons: in 1932–38, there was relatively little emphasis on the use of these media by the school; and data on their use by educated adults are meager.

Although this chapter will describe the English program, it should be noted that throughout the school emphasis was placed on individualized critical reading, that in all academic subject-areas papers were written frequently, and that much of the so-called English work went on in unified studies or core courses.

Certain aspects of the language development of the class, as presented in three published documents, have been considered. First, in the book which has previously been cited, *Thirty Schools Tell Their Story*. Second, in the book written by the class of 1938, *Were We*

127

Guinea Pigs? [1] Since no teacher either directed the organization or corrected copy for the students, and since every member contributed material and also assisted in proofing galleys, it is apparent that the book itself serves as an initial evaluation of writing. The publisher, Henry Holt and Company, Inc., carefully refrained from correcting or amending the copy sent in by the students. To assure themselves that the work was entirely written by students, the company sent an editor who spent time observing and discussing the writing with the class.

The third study of the class was an evaluation of their reading. This study was based on an analysis of three years of individual reading records. It was first submitted in 1937 as a Master's dissertation in library science at Columbia University by Frieda M. Heller. The study was entitled, "An Evaluation of Free Reading in Grades Seven, Eight, and Nine." It was later incorporated in a larger study by Lou L. LaBrant and Miss Heller, and published by Ohio State University.[2] At the time of the original study, which was based on reading in the three junior–high school years, the class numbered fifty-nine. About 80 per cent of this class was included in the graduating class of 1938.

The English program was very simple in outline; complexity resulted from its highly individualized aspects. Briefly, the program may be described as follows.

Believing that the chief aims of the literature (reading) program were to improve taste, step by step, and to set up reading habits, units were developed in terms of the students' growth rather than in a predetermined logical order. Each student was expected to maintain throughout the six years an individual program of reading. His reading was recorded in a permanent file, and reviewed in conference with the English teacher at frequent intervals. Since the whole school made heavy demands on reading time, all books except textbooks were listed and considered in planning the student's work. Thus it might happen that in a drama unit in English, he would read French plays

---

[1] New York: Henry Holt and Company, Inc., 1938.

[2] *An Evaluation of Free Reading in Grades Seven to Twelve Inclusive* ("Contributions in Education," No. 4 [Columbus Ohio: Ohio State University Press, 1939]).

both in English translation and in French, enriching two courses at once. Selections for biography were often made to suit science or social-studies courses.

In class discussion, criteria were set up for judging a student's progress and resulted in considerable emphasis on variety in type of book, nationality of author or scene, and time of writing or setting. A student might, however, become interested in studying a particular author, and read a half-dozen of his books, and books or articles about him.

Class units were set up in terms of the criteria and of the maturity of the readers. Thus there were units on how to read fiction, drama, poetry, biography, magazines, and newspapers. Magazines and newspapers were, of course, widely used in other courses, particularly in social studies.

A description of the reading program was included in the evaluation of reading published in 1939. That report, which will be quoted, is likely to be more accurate than any account made now, which would have to be based on recollection.

The free reading program at the University School is based upon the belief that it is the function of the school to offer experiences designed to develop active, thinking citizens, who are freed through lack of emotional blocking and contradictory beliefs, to use their intelligence creatively, and who are accustomed to using that creative intelligence in solving the problems which they meet. Education is thus conceived of as a continuous process, in no way limited to school life. School living is only one phase of experience, which is continuous throughout the waking day, and throughout life. That is, experience is not divided into two kinds, school and home living, nor is schooling thought of as preparation for life. It is life. Such a concept is basic to reading fostered by the school. The following principles are accepted:

1. The culture of the modern world includes reading as an important factor for youth and for adults; it is an intrinsic factor in our present way of living.

2. Through this factor the individual multiplies his contacts with other individuals and with groups.

3. Individuals vary greatly in needs and interests, and hence are best served by a diversity of books and reading materials; they also

vary greatly in abilities and hence proceed at varying rates and with varying degrees of understanding.

4. It becomes the function of the school to provide for experience in reading as a factor in an expanding understanding of society. Just as the teacher is responsible for guidance into social or quantitative understandings, so he is responsible for guidance into experience through books. This guidance always considers the growing needs and interests of the student, and consequently cannot depend upon a formal pre-arrangement of materials.

The evaluation program must hence be an examination of the process rather than a testing on the basis of external or logical standards. It is the belief of the writers that reading in the school should not only extend the reader's experience, but should increasingly be a means by which he recognizes and attempts to solve both personal and group problems. Answers to the following questions, therefore, seem essential to a study of the reading program in University School:

1. To what extent has reading proved a factor in the student's life pattern; i.e., is it integrated with his varied interests?

2. Which of these interests, if any, has reading helped to extend and intensify?

3. Does the reading give evidence of being varied according to individual needs, interests, and abilities?

4. Is there evidence that the reading has met criteria developed by the students themselves; i.e., has guidance actually recognized individual and group needs and interests? is reading purposeful?

No outlined or pre-determined course in English was set up for either of the two classes [The two groups which were the subjects of the study.] Pupils in the seventh and eighth grades had, until the final two months of the latter grade, no regular days for book discussions. In the spring of their eighth grade an informal class was set up to meet once a week. During the ninth year the English periods were increased to two one-hour discussions a week, but half this time was devoted to writing. Classes above this met regularly to discuss books and other reading. The reading program is thus seen to be an extension and intensification, more and more deliberately planned and criticized by the student, of the personal or leisure reading developed in the grades, plus the reading growing out of interests and problems raised not only in organized classes in science, mathematics, and social studies, but in out-of-school experience.[3]

[3] *Ibid.*, pp. 2–3.

Work in social science and science called for frequent reports and panel discussions. During the first three years, the teacher of English worked with teachers of those subjects in a "core" course; and consequently, most of the formal oral English was centered on the reports and panels just mentioned. Often during the remaining three years, the teacher of English assisted with the writing and presentation of reports in these other subjects. Within the English class, there were frequent discussions and some formal presentation of individual or small-group studies.

Throughout the six years, the students wrote regularly. Reports in science and social studies were carefully criticized, sometimes by the teachers in those areas and sometimes by the teacher of English. Work in other areas, particularly the study of the nature of proof in mathematics and analysis of propaganda in social studies, probably had their effect on the students' care in using language. For the seventh through the ninth grades, the English teacher carried the major responsibility for supervising writing in all areas. In addition, throughout the six years each student wrote a paper approximately every other week, presenting some personal experience—description, narrative (real or imagined), verse, statement of opinion or doubt. These papers were read by the teacher, discussed by the class, and revised until the mechanics were correct and further revision for clarity and organization seemed unprofitable. When this final stage was reached, the paper was initialed by the instructor, and, along with previous drafts, filed in the student's personal folder.

A word should be said about the formal teaching of grammar, punctuation, and usage. Punctuation and usage were taught directly, in connection with actual writing or speech. Corrections of oral errors were usually given in private. In general, the level of usage in the class was fairly good, and students politely refrained from embarrassing their friends by public correction. The teacher usually made his correction through a note or a brief private suggestion.

By 1932 dissatisfaction with the formal, Latinized grammar previously taught in our schools had become general among those who were informed in this field; but the new studies of English structure were just well under way. In consequence, the faculty believed that instruction in grammar should be directly related to the writing of the students, and in general it was so restricted. This led to some insecurity on the part of the students, who felt that they were "getting no grammar." Without the usual ritual of parts of speech and types of clauses, they did not recognize that the grammar of their sentences was actually being discussed and improved. Since most college-level courses in English used placement tests including grammatical terms, it is not strange that many of the guinea pigs complain of a lack of training in grammar. It is probably unfortunate that they were not given more security through the use of terms which might have reassured them. On entering college, they found a range of understanding among freshman instructors, some of whom also felt that the use of technical terms was essential. With the materials available today, the problem could have been met in an interesting and still sound manner.

The class of 1938 included discussions of the cinema and radio in its consideration of news, opinion, and drama. Some time was given in both English and social studies to a critical examination of newsreels. It was not, however, until the German invasion of Poland in 1939 that the American public became accustomed to radio as a chief source of more than local news, or that listening took on a major role in public affairs. Moreover, not until some time after most of the present class had completed college did television develop as a household instrument. In consequence, the uses of these media by the Class of 1938 may be attributed to general attitudes, but not to specific emphases of the program during their high-school years.

Difficulties in Evaluation

Any evaluation or description of the speaking, listening (including viewing), reading, and writing habits of an adult individual or group is extremely difficult. Although studies of speaking and writing structures have been made by linguists, they are limited in number and are concerned with general principles for the spoken or written language as a whole. Studies of adult vocabularies, which at first were thought to be manageable, have not been accomplished. Studies of reading habits usually consist of polls, with few general questions, or of records of library use. Lists of books which have been reported by readers are sometimes, although not as a rule, broken down into general classes; but save for a few outmoded studies, there has been no attempt to classify these books as to value or maturity of approach. A brief examination of factors relevant to the amount and type of reading accomplished by an individual will illustrate the difficulty of language analysis.

Any individual varies in his use of reading from day to day and from month to month. Seasonal differences are known to publishers, as the phrase "summer reading" suggests.

The age of the individual is highly important. For example, a woman with young children may be expected to have less time for concentrated reading than one whose children are grown or nearly so; and the content of her reading may be directed toward child rearing or books appropriate for children. A young man in the professions or a businessman frequently has a burden of self-education which precludes use of reading time for imaginative literature.

The specific occupation of the individual is a factor. In many professions, there are heavy pressures for keeping informed in one's field, especially in fields in which the materials are changing rapidly. In science, for example, keeping informed probably calls for the use of periodicals rather than books. A case could probably be made for periodicals as the chief reading matter also in the field of sociology and in many business areas. Consequently, a man who reads many hours a week might report that he was "not reading any book."

Radio, television, and the cinema are probably changing reading uses and needs for both books and periodicals. A balance has not as yet been achieved by many, and we are still ignorant as to what constitutes a "good program." Since the programs offered differ widely from area to area, the balance achieved by each individual must be evaluated in terms of the local situation. It is obvious that, where available, good commentators may displace newspaper comment to a degree, and screen drama may substitute for a certain amount of legitimate theater and light fiction.

Financial limitations may determine selection of both books and magazines, and hence choices may not represent preferences. Books of verse and drama are expensive and less widely distributed through libraries than popular fiction. Some of the more literate magazines assume the reader's ability to purchase many books, to travel, and to attend the theatre and opera.

The study which follows was made with the limitations, or complications, which have been mentioned, in mind. In general, the analysis will attempt to do the following: (1) To compare the activities (achievements) of the Class of 1938, in 1955, with the professed aims of the school when the members were students; (2) To compare the language activities of the class in 1955 with their activities while in school; (3) To compare, when possible, the activities of the class with similar activities of groups which have previously been studied; and (4) To offer other investigators the limited data which a study of fifty persons provides.

Source Material: The Questionnaire

Before reading the analysis which is to follow, the reader may find it helpful to read through the section of the questionnaire on the uses of communication media (see Appendix B). Cross-checks will be noted. Some overlappings not obvious to those designing the questionnaire are also to be found, and have sometimes clarified and may sometimes have confused the data. Three major areas were explored by the questionnaire: reading of books and periodicals; use of writing; use of radio, television, and the cinema. The list of questions was drawn up by a former instructor of English in the school and submitted to other staff members and to several members of the class, who suggested changes.

The long general questionnaire was sent out some weeks before the one on communication media was mailed. Unfortunately, this caused some confusion about the second, communication questionnaire, and only forty full replies were received. These were supplemented, as has been stated, by materials secured either by presenting parts of the communication questions orally, or by derivations from the taped interviews. Through these substitute devices, a considerable number of answers were accumulated for ten other persons. Thus there are at least partial data for fifty of the fifty-five class members and full data for forty. In examining the findings, the reader will note some variation in the number of persons whose replies are considered, and should remember that this is because ten of the replies were only partly complete.

An analysis of the responses to questions regarding the use of language skills follows. The reader will find that the headings have been derived from the questionnaire.

Sources of News and Social and Political Opinion

Many aspects of language use are interdependent. The reading of newspapers and other written opinion is closely related to the use of news and commentator broadcasts. The first sections of the questionnaire dealt with such sources. The use of radio and of television was not differentiated, since for the purposes of the analysis such a distinction seemed useless.

The replies of all fifty were complete on these two questions concerning sources of news and opinion. Although the questionnaire made a distinction between them (news and opinion), it was pointed out by one respondent that newspapers offer opinion as well as news; other respondents combined replies or indicated by duplication that they did not differentiate among sources for the two. Replies concerning the use of the media for information and for opinion are therefore combined.

Newspapers

All fifty respondents reported using one or more daily papers. Forty-eight named the papers; one reported "headlines only," a response in accord with the serious vision handicap of this individual; another replied "local papers." Since this person is a resident of Columbus, Ohio, it was assumed that he referred to the three local dailies. The responses are given in Table 37.

Although it is to be expected that a group of high-school graduates would each read a daily paper, it is interesting that thirty-six of the fifty (72 per cent) read two or more.

TABLE 37

SOURCES OF NEWS AND OPINION—DAILY NEWSPAPERS

Number of Newspapers Read	Number of Persons Reporting
1	14 (includes one who also reads the Sunday *New York Times*)
2	20 (includes two who also read the Sunday *New York Times*)
3	11
4	5

Of the thirty-six subscribing for or using two or more dailies, fifteen listed the *New York Times;* one of those who read only one daily also read the Sunday *New York Times,* although it is not his local paper; two others specified that in addition to local dailies they read the Sunday *New York Times;* one subscribed for the *Christian Science Monitor;* two reported the *New York Herald Tribune.* Discounting overlapping, we find that nineteen of the fifty class members make use of one of the three generally recognized major newspapers from outside their own city. Comparable figures are not available, but the proportion is obviously high, even for college graduates.

Five of the twenty-four men from whom reports were received subscribed for the *Wall Street Journal* and two for *Barron's National Financial Weekly.*

Other Periodicals

On the questionnaire and in some of the interviews, it was asked that magazines used for further sources of news and opinion be listed. Of the fifty who responded, six named no magazines for news or opinion. It should be noted, however, that under Question C ("For what magazines do you subscribe?") a number listed magazines which

TABLE 38

SOURCES OF NEWS AND OPINION—MAGAZINES

Name of Magazine	Number of Persons Reporting
Atlantic Monthly	2
Business Week	4
Cue	1
Electrical World	1
Changing Times: The Kiplinger Magazine	1
Life	20
Methodist Federation for Social Action	1
Newsweek	12
New Yorker	4
Reader's Digest	4
Saturday Evening Post	2
Social Questions Bulletin	1
Time	21
U. S. News and World Report	5
Total	79

probably do contribute to knowledge of current events and opinion about them. For example, only two mentioned the *Saturday Evening Post* as contributory, although nine reported subscribing for it. Comparisons could also be made for the *Atlantic Monthly,* the *New Yorker,* and the *Reader's Digest.*

As might be anticipated, *Life, Time,* and *Newsweek* led the list with 53 of the 79 subscriptions reported as sources of news and opinion. The magazines used as sources and the number of persons reporting each one are given in Table 38.

A comparison of the list in Table 38 with the answers to Question C suggests that those who find these sources useful do not necessarily subscribe themselves. It may be supposed that they use copies found in offices, clubs, and so on.

Radio and Television

Radio or television or both were indicated as useful sources of information and opinion by forty of the fifty class members who provided data. Four indicated that they found no value in these media,

TABLE 39

SOURCES OF NEWS AND OPINION—RADIO AND
TELEVISION PROGRAMS IN 1955

Name or Type of Program	Number of Persons Reporting
Discussion programs, "town meetings," panels	9
Douglas Edwards	7
Chet Long	12
Edward R. Murrow—News (13) and "See It Now" (3)	16
Special broadcasts by political leaders and other officials	3
John Cameron Swayze	8
Lowell Thomas	5

and four answered by checking sources other than radio or television. One noted that he made use of radio and television "very seldom"; and another said "I'm afraid I do not spend much time on these things." Ten individuals may therefore be assumed to find little value in these sources, and forty to use them. Thirty-eight of the forty mentioned special programs or individual broadcasters and commentators. Thirty-six different programs were mentioned. Programs which were named or described three or more times are listed in Table 39.

Questions about further sources of information and opinion yielded little beyond the data which has already been given.

Comparable data are not available; but apparently, the following generalizations are justified. Class members make adequate use of newspapers: 72 per cent use two or more as sources of information and opinion. The news broadcasters to whom they listen would probably be accepted as among the better-informed and more dependable men in such work. The periodicals used by the class as sources of news and information are, in general, conservative, large subscription newspapers and magazines.

THE USE OF MAGAZINES

Information concerning subscriptions to and the use of magazines was received from fifty class members, either on the questionnaires or in the interviews. Of the fifty, only one reported that he neither subscribed for nor read magazines. No explanation was offered for this somewhat unusual response. The individual is not a non-reader, for he named two books he was reading at the time of his interview and he subscribes for two daily papers. The report by a second member of only one subscription is easily explained by the fact that he has a vision handicap and must limit his reading.

The forty-nine persons who do use magazines subscribed for a total of 129 different periodicals (302 subscriptions). Over two-thirds of the periodicals (87, or 67.4 per cent) have only one subscriber in the group. Twenty-one others are subscribed for by only two each. The distribution of subscriptions appear in Table 40.

Only five magazines are subscribed for by ten or more individuals, and only one (*Life*) by half of those reporting. The numbers of those subscribing to these five are shown in Table 41. In view of the fact that 108 of the 129 titles that were reported are subscribed for by no more than two of the fifty class members, it appears that the use of periodicals by this group is highly individualized.

The total number of subscriptions was 302, not counting the report of one person who wrote "Technical journals related to radio not named." There is an average of six magazines per individual. The distribution of subscriptions among the fifty members of the class is given in Table 42.

TABLE 40
DISTRIBUTION OF MAGAZINE SUBSCRIPTIONS

Number of Subscribers for Each Magazine	Number of Magazines
1	87
2	21
3–5	12
6–10	5
11–20	1
21–30	3
Total number of magazines	129

TABLE 41
MAGAZINES HAVING TEN OR MORE SUBSCRIBERS

Magazine	Number of Subscribers
Better Homes and Gardens	10
Life	27
New Yorker	12
Reader's Digest	22
Time	22

TABLE 42
DISTRIBUTION OF MAGAZINE SUBSCRIPTIONS AMONG CLASS MEMBERS

Number of Magazine Subscriptions	Number of Class Members
0	1
1–5	29
6–10	14
11–15	6

W. O. Covert in a study of 1841 graduates of six high schools in Lee County, Iowa, reported on the reading and use of magazines. He did not indicate how many of his group attended or finished college. Apparently, his group subscribed for fewer and less demanding periodicals than the guinea-pig group, but his report is not definite on this point.

> Six out of seven of the graduates subscribed to newspapers six years after graduation and most subscribed to magazines, mainly in the popular type or the women's magazines. *Reader's Digest* is the most popular . . . to which two-fifths of the graduates subscribed. *Life* magazine has half the number of subscribers that the *Reader's Digest* has and other magazines follow in much smaller numbers. . . .[4]

TABLE 43

GENERAL TYPES OF MAGAZINE SUBSCRIPTIONS

Type of Magazine	Number of Subscriptions
Professional or closely related to business	54
News	38
For parents or children	12
For women	35
Fraternity	3
General	160
Total	302

It is interesting that Covert's figure for *Reader's Digest* subscriptions—two-fifths—is exactly the figure for the present class (twenty-two out of fifty-five), though it must be remembered that we have no report from five of the total number of class members. Apparently, however, his graduates subscribe for relatively few other magazines, whereas for the present class the twenty-two subscriptions for *Reader's Digest* are a small part of the total.

[4] W. O. Covert, "High-School Graduates after Six Years," *Bulletin of the National Association of Secondary School Principals*, XXXIV (January, 1950), 278.

Further classification of the magazines was attempted. In some instances, it was difficult to make a distinction between professional periodicals and ones of general interest. For example, *Theatre Arts* may be considered a general, cultural periodical, suited to family use; or it may be used as professional matter by a teacher of drama. Usually no difficulty was found, and the few uncertainties make little difference in the totals. The source for the classification is found in Appendix E.

Class members also reported that they read occasionally 58 periodicals for which they did not subscribe. They are listed, together with the number mentioning them, in Appendix E, Section II. Most of them are likely to be found in barbershops, beauty parlors, doctors' offices, and clubs. A few are obviously associated with individual businesses.

The analysis of reports from those in the highest quintile of the intelligence rating (see pages 39–40 for means of selection) showed no marked deviation from the general pattern save that they averaged eight subscriptions instead of six, the average for the total group. Seven of the eleven guinea pigs in the highest quintile subscribed for the *New Yorker*.

Somewhat surprising in view of the general quality and range of the magazine list is the infrequent mention of such magazines as *Atlantic Monthly, Harper's Magazine, The Reporter, Saturday Review,* and *Scientific American*. The total number of times these five were mentioned, including reports of "read occasionally," amounted to only 12. Neither *The Nation* nor the *New Republic* was mentioned. No one reported the *Bulletin of the Atomic Scientists*. None of the so-called little magazines appeared. Only one individual listed a foreign newspaper or magazine.

Only limited conclusions can be drawn concerning the use made of periodicals by the class because comparable data are not available. The following generalizations are, however, offered.

1. The class of 1938 makes much use of periodicals, averaging subscriptions to six magazines per individual. (The range for the fifty members is zero to fourteen.)

2. Selection is highly individualized; only five of the 129 titles appeared ten or more times.

3. More than fifty professional or business periodicals were named, pointing up the reading demands of many vocations.

4. Magazines for general reading, although greatly varied, indicated no unusual interests in literary or social issues.

5. Women reported more subscriptions than men did.

THE READING OF BOOKS

Six items on the communication questionnaire (D., E., F., G., H., and I.) inquired about the reading of books. The findings are reported here, but comparative data are limited and standards of any kind are lacking. Obviously, the nature and amount of reading done by an adult must vary with his business or profession and with the demands of his personal life. As mentioned previously, a young mother may find it necessary to read books about child growth and books written for children. One father in the Class of 1938 said that he had to choose between personal reading and time spent with his children; he chose the latter. A professional man may have a heavy demand—as do several in the class—for the reading of research in his field, much of which appears in periodicals. We have, consequently, no measure of what an educated adult ought to be reading, and emphases will differ from critic to critic.

The school program for the Class of 1938 emphasized the following aims for each student:

a) Ability to deal with varied types of reading matter (essay, novel, history, drama, science, poetry, biography, political analysis). In order to meet this aim, all departments of the school co-operated, and reading was to a considerable degree the concern of all faculty. The teachers of English took a major responsibility, and kept a record of all reading except that in textbooks.

b) Ability to read with discrimination, that is, critically.

c) Familiarity with a number of books varied as to subject-matter, nationality of author, date of writing, date of setting, area of setting, and type.

d) Acceptance of responsibility for maintaining a reading program: each student had to help plan his own reading and was responsible for keeping it going without constant (daily or weekly) checking.

e) Familiarity with selection guides (reviews, library facilities, book-store displays, and so on).

f) Selection of reading matter in terms of individual need and special interest. "Need" included the student's academic needs, such as difficulty with specific types of material or demands for wider understanding in social studies, science, or other areas.

Relatively few studies have been made of adult reading, and those which have been published have generally dealt with gross numbers of books read. Waples and Tyler attempted to measure "maturity" of reading by relating the books which had been read to the education of the readers; [5] but their studies were completed before the Class of 1938 entered high school, and thus do not include most of the books reported by the guinea pigs in 1955.

In 1950, *Publishers' Weekly* discussed adult reading as follows, basing its comment on a Gallup poll:

> According to the American Institute of Public Opinion, mass education and a high degree of literacy in the United States apparently had little effect on this low percentage; i.e., 79 per cent of Americans answered "No" to the question "Are you now reading any books or novels?" In the American survey the results were analyzed according to degree of education of the individual respondent. This showed that nearly half of all persons who have had college training were reading some book, but only 12 per cent of persons who have had only grade school training, and 23 per cent of those with only high school education were reading books. . . . [6]

The report continued with the following short table of percentages of responses to the question, "Are you now reading any books or novels?," separated according to the degree of education of the respondent.[7]

[5] Douglas Waples and Ralph Tyler, *What People Want to Read About* (Chicago: University of Chicago Press, 1931).

[6] "Booksellers Consider Their Rent and How to Cope with It," *Publishers' Weekly*, CLVII (February 11, 1950), 893.

[7] *Ibid.*

	Yes	No
College	48	52
High School	23	77
Grade School	12	88

Asheim, in a contribution to the more recent report, *Adult Reading,* published by the National Society for the Study of Education, gave the following summary:

> . . . In cross-section polls of the population the question is frequently asked, "Are you reading a book now?" or "Have you read a book within the past month?" The percentage of persons who answer "No" to such questions consistently hovers around the same figure, as shown in the following tabulation:
>
> Study A (1950)........79 per cent
> Study B (1949)........79 per cent
> Study C (1948)........74 per cent
> Study D (1948)........70 per cent [8]

Asheim also reported in the same chapter that "women read more than men." He did not cite his authority, but certainly this conclusion agrees with the findings of the present study.

Joseph Wood Krutch, writing in the *Saturday Review* in 1957, also quoted a Gallup poll.

> . . . According to the results of a survey recently published by the American Institute of Public Opinion 61 per cent of those interviewed had not read a book during the past year. Comparison with a similar study made two years ago in other English-speaking countries produces these figures: In England 55 per cent of the population reads books; in Australia 34 per cent; in Canada 31 per cent; in the United States 17. . . . [9]

The magazine *Fortune* and the Research Institute of America studied the reading habits of executive groups and discovered that

[8] Lester Asheim, "What Do Adults Read?," in *Adult Reading: Fifty-fifth Yearbook of the National Society for the Study of Education,* edited by Nelson B. Henry (Chicago: University of Chicago Press, 1956), LV, Part II, pp. 5–28. Copyright 1956 by the University of Chicago Press.

[9] Krutch, "Dialogue on Americans," *Saturday Review,* XL (May 18, 1957), 32.

"on the basis of spot sampling in several corporations and its interviews, *Fortune* would guess that [not more than] 20 per cent of executives might read as many as a dozen books a year dealing with general subjects." [10]

Covert, in his study of Iowa high-school graduates, reported that 64 per cent of the graduates had read three or more books for recreation during the six months preceding the study. Women read somewhat more than men, but there were only small differences between the graduates of the different ranks in their classes, and between those with academic or vocational majors. [11]

Zinsser, in his report on Princeton Class of '44 in *This Week Magazine,* made the following statement:

. . . Sixteen per cent say they read no books, 62 per cent read one or two a month, 15 per cent read four or five, and a few read more. Spare time obviously goes into other pursuits. . . . [12]

Henry C. Link and Harry Arthur Hope, in an investigation sponsored by the Book Manufacturers Institute, made a study of reading and book-buying habits, and published their findings in 1946. [13] Their study was based on a careful sampling which took into consideration the type of setting (cities were classed according to size, and location in rural or non-farm area), and the economic status, education, and sex of the respondents. Using an elaborate interview-questionnaire, they secured data which they presented to publishers and manufacturers of books.

The findings of Link and Hope agree fairly well with those of other investigators. They defined "active readers" as "those who read a book yesterday or within the past month." Active readers constituted 50 per cent of our population, and accounted for 94 per cent

[10] Duncan Norton-Taylor, "Why Don't Businessmen Read Books?," *Fortune,* LXIX (May, 1954), 117.

[11] Covert, *op. cit.,* p. 278.

[12] William K. Zinsser, "The Class of '44 Today," *This Week Magazine* (*New York Herald Tribune,* Sec. 7), June 6, 1954.

[13] Link and Hope, *People and Books* (New York: Book Industry Committee, Book Manufacturers Institute, 1946).

of all books read. They found also that 21 per cent of the population, "those who read a book yesterday," read 70 per cent of all books reported.

Link and Hope also classified their data in terms of educational level. Concerning the influence of educational level, they find that 71 per cent of college graduates and 51 per cent of high-school graduates are active readers. Their study also attempted a rough measure of types of books read. Those materials will be considered later. It is interesting to note, however, that since these investigators sampled a population beginning with persons fifteen years of age, they consequently included high-school graduates still in college.

The data quoted leave several questions untouched. Granted that people in the United States read fewer books per capita than do citizens in five other nations, to what extent is this difference explained by a greater use of periodicals, radio, motion pictures, and television? That is, to what extent is the reading of a book per se a mark of a high level of literacy? To what extent, for example, are the three new media substitutes for light fiction and for the reading of drama? Of what quality are the books read by the groups polled? Does the 30 per cent of Americans who read (see figure for Study D in the statement by Asheim, page 145) consist of readers of fiction, of political discussion, of science? The Link-Hope study contains a rough breakdown of types of reading but the trends are not clear. There is evidence that best-seller lists in the United States have increasingly included non-fiction. To what degree is this shift attributable to the reading of the whole 30 per cent? To what degree does it represent a shift in emphasis for the highly literate only? To what extent does it measure improvement in level?

Asheim wisely makes the following comment:

> Another popular, but dubious, generalization is frequently voiced: Non-fiction tends to be more "important" than fiction. Here again such a generalization is only occasionally true; *The Power of Positive Thinking* is not a more serious work than *The Brothers Karamazov*. . . . If closer analysis of these shifts from fiction to non-fiction should reveal that people are reading less Melville and Tolstoy and

more books on how to play Scrabble and Canasta, we should have to revise our assumption that the trend from fiction to non-fiction is a trend toward more serious reading.[14]

Such questions as the foregoing make comparisons of numbers and percentages of less significance than might be assumed at first consideration. The present study will, however, offer comparative numbers and percentages; it will also include lists of books read for possible comparison and analysis by the reader.

TABLE 44

NUMBER OF BOOKS BEING READ BY THE CLASS OF 1938
AT THE TIME OF THE STUDY IN 1955

NUMBER OF BOOKS NAMED *	NUMBER REPORTING			PER CENT
	Men	Women	Total	
0............................	12	1	13	26
1............................	1	9	10	
2............................	5	2	7	
4............................	5	5	10	74
3............................	1	2	3	
5............................	1	1	2	
6............................	1	2	3	
7............................	..	2	2	
Total...................	26	24	50	100

* Total number of books named, 107.

Question F of the communication questionnaire (Appendix B) asked the respondent to "name, if any, a book or books you are reading or have been reading within the past month. Please do not limit your reply to books of importance or high literary quality." Replies seem comparable to some of the data just cited. Table 44 gives the responses to this question. Compared with findings of other studies, the Class of 1938 makes a very good report.

For so small a group, it is probably fair to mention that two members have had serious vision handicaps since infancy, so that for them the reading of print is necessarily kept to a minimum. One reads only

[14] Asheim, *op. cit.*, p. 11.

newspapers and magazines; the other reports limiting his newspaper reading "to headlines only."

The Gallup poll of 1950 found only 48 per cent of the college graduates reading books,[15] whereas the Class of 1938, regardless of level of training, had 74 per cent of its members reporting from one to seven books currently being read.

Study A reported by Asheim (page 145) does not differentiate according to educational level. Only 21 per cent of that group were reading books in 1950. (This figure was obtained by subtracting from 100 the percentage given by Asheim for those not reading books.) Krutch mentioned a similar figure in the article from the *Saturday Review* which has been cited, although his figure represents not only those who were not reading at the time of the survey, but also those who "had not read a book during the past year."

The Link-Hope study offers comparable data. Its active readers, those "who are reading or have read a book within a month," constituted 71 per cent of the college graduates and 51 per cent of the high-school graduates.[16] The Class of 1938 shows a higher percentage, 74 per cent for the combined group of graduates of college and high school.

When the active readers in the Class of 1938 (74 per cent) are considered according to sex and academic status, we find that of the high-school graduates, 35 per cent of the men and 100 per cent of the women are active; and of the college graduates, 64 per cent of the men and 95 per cent of the women are active. The groups are obviously too small to make percentages significant, but it is interesting to note that the most active group is the women who did not complete college work.

Zinsser in reporting on Princeton Class of '44 found that 16 per cent were reading no books. This is a better record than that made by the total group of men in the Class of 1938, 46 per cent of whom were not reading books. However, among the college men in the class for whom we have reports (sixteen), there is only one (6 per cent) who

---

[15] *Publishers' Weekly*, CLVII (February 11, 1950), 893.
[16] Link and Hope, *op. cit.*, pp. 55–56.

considers himself to be reading no book and only three (20 per cent) who read less than one book a month.

Appendix F lists the books which were reported as being read or just completed when the questionnaire was filled out. Ninety titles, with their authors, appear on the list. Four additional titles could not be fully identified. Three others, which were not included in the list, were merely indicated by topic. Of the titles that were reported, eight were named by two persons, and one by four. The other eighty-two books had but one reader each, marked evidence that members of the Class of 1938 were independent in their selection.

Forty individuals—twenty-one men and nineteen women—offered

TABLE 45

ESTIMATES OF BOOKS READ ANNUALLY

ESTIMATE OF BOOKS READ	NUMBER REPORTING		
	Men	Women	Total
None.........................	3	..	3
Less than 10..................	7	4	11
10–19........................	6	6	12
20–29........................	2	1	3
30–39........................	1	3	4
40–49........................	..	1	1
50–99........................	1	2	3
100–150......................	1	2	3
Total..................	21	19	40

estimates of the number of books read in a year. One other merely said "very few, mostly references, not complete reading." Another (obviously a wide reader as indicated by other answers) found the question as to whether a book was read somewhat "condescending" and offered no estimate. Two of those responding said they had not included plays. Estimates from the forty appear in Table 45. A comparison with numbers of active readers, as given in Table 44, may seem to show a contradiction. In that table, thirteen of the fifty are reported as not reading a book at the time of the questionnaire. However, only three of the thirteen reported "none" for the year's estimate. Seven of them were among those in Table 45 who estimated their annual reading as less than ten books. For three others, we have no estimates, although one of them in a later comment indicated considerable reading (perhaps fifteen to thirty books) undertaken at his wife's suggestion.

According to the estimates, the women read about three times as many books as the men, or a ratio of 33 to 13. Again it might be mentioned that of the twenty-one men reporting, two (or almost 10 per cent) had vision handicaps. However, there are ten (48 per cent), including these two, who read less than one book a month. For the group of forty as a whole, only fourteen, or 36 per cent, fall into this category. Stated positively, 64 per cent of the total number who reported read more than ten books a year (approximately one a month). This figure is decidedly higher than any of those in the reports cited, whether for college or high-school graduates.

Five (roughly 25 per cent) of the men read over twenty books a year. This compares favorably with *Fortune*'s estimate that not more than 20 per cent of the executives read "as many as a dozen."

Eleven men read between ten and fifty-nine books. This is 52 per cent, noticeably higher than the estimates for the combined high-school and college groups reported by Gallup, Asheim, or Link and Hope.

The study reported by William K. Zinsser dealt with a highly selective group, the Princeton Class of 1944. Fourteen male college graduates from the University School Class of 1938 reported on reading. Comparisons follow:

GROUP	PER CENT
Princeton '44—no books *	16
Men of '38—one or two books a year	21
Princeton '44—one or two books a month	62
Men of '38—one to three books a month	50
Princeton '44—four, five, or more books a month	22
Men of '38—four or five books a month	21

* Figures for Princeton Class of '44 are reported by Zinsser, in "The Class of '44 Today," *This Week Magazine* (*New York Herald Tribune*, Sec. 7), June 6, 1954.

The numbers are too small to make percentages significant, but there are marked likenesses. The figures seem to favor the Princeton class slightly; since the original study of the Class of 1944 was privately distributed, details are not available.

The writer feels from careful examination of the reports that the estimates of reading are unreliable for many individuals. Repeatedly, the members of the Class of 1938 gave qualifying words— "about," "I guess"—or a range of possibilities, such as "ten or twenty," "100–150," and so forth. For several, the estimates seemed very low in contrast to the individuals' current reading, their lists of planned reading, or other indications. There was considerable evidence that the amount of reading varied greatly from week to week as the result of professional pressures, home responsibilities, availability of books, and so forth. It is easily possible that little credence should be given to annual estimates. One further factor seemed to operate. Throughout the high-school course, the students recorded their reading of books, and also indicated any incomplete reading, and anticipated conference-discussion of books that had been finished. There seemed to be some feeling in 1957 that similar care should be used in the present report, and answers and estimates were frequently qualified. It is possible that the former student-teacher relationship tended to make these men and women avoid any possible exaggeration of their accomplishments.

Obviously, the number of books that are read is in itself an inadequate indication of reading values, since "book" may include the trivial as well as the significant. For this reason, Appendix F lists books which were being read and Appendix G, the books which had been significant in the past experience of class members. In a further effort to discover emphases, class members were asked to check the types of books included in their estimates of yearly consumption. Table 46 summarizes responses of the forty who filled out the questionnaires.

It should be noted that most of those who replied checked several areas (an average of approximately three areas for each individual), and that hence the total number of responses is greater than forty.

Although only one checked "religion," four reported Norman Vincent Peale's *Power of Positive Thinking* as current reading. Whether they considered this a minor excursion, or read for some purpose other than "religion," is not clear. Biography and fiction interested almost equal numbers. It is interesting also that professional reading was reported by one-third of the men (seven out of twenty-one) and by an almost equal proportion of women (six out of nineteen).

It has been reported from time to time that a surprising number of Americans, when asked to name books they would like to read, are

TABLE 46

AREAS OF EMPHASIS IN YEARLY READING

AREA	NUMBER REPORTING		
	Men (N-21)	Women (N-19)	Total
Professional..........................	7	6	13
Fiction (including mysteries)..........	12 (3)	16	28
Poetry...............................	2	6 *	8
Travel...............................	6	11	17
Political discussion...................	5	5	10
Biography............................	7	16	23
History..............................	2	..	2
Geography and geology...............	1	1	2
Psychology and sociology.............	..	1	1
Religion.............................	..	1	1

* Two persons qualified their answers by saying "very little."

unable to do so. Often such a negative response has been interpreted as an indication of no interest in books. The questionnaire sent to the Class of 1938 included such a question. Replies, however, came from only twenty-seven of the fifty for whom some data were secured. (It should be remembered that ten of the fifty were questioned orally, and were therefore not asked the full set of questionnaire items.)

Of the twenty-seven who responded to the question, only eighteen named a particular title. Others gave such answers as the following: "I hope to read all of the Great Books" (this from an excellent reader); "Not exactly"; "There are so many"; "I haven't time to tuck away actual titles" (from a woman who reported reading several books at the time of the questioning); "Biography and fiction." Three merely indicated that they preferred history. One noted his great preference for books in a given art field and his intention of purchasing and reading new books in that area.

Among those who named specific books were several who were not, at the time, reading; in contrast, ten who were reading, including some of the most active readers in the group, left the question unanswered.

If this group is at all typical, it appears that many good readers know only vaguely—not well enough to risk writing them down—the names of books they desire or intend to read. In contrast, some persons who do very little reading can name books they would like—or think they would like—to read. The responses from this group throw some doubt on the value of this commonly used question, even when, as in the present study, those questioned have the opportunity to check their replies. It seems doubtful that the Class of 1938 would have made many usable responses if the question had been given orally. Not one of the replies secured orally contained any definite names of books. The list of books that were named is not included, since it represents only eighteen persons.

Books Which Were Significant to the Reader

In a further effort to find some indication of reading level, respondents were asked to name a half-dozen books, read within the past ten years, which had seemed significant to them. Forty-six responded, through either the questionnaire or the interview, and named 132 books, fewer than had been requested. Fifteen of the books were mentioned by more than one person; six, by three or more—a total of 158 mentions, or about four per person. The books mentioned three or more times were *The Sea around Us,* by Rachel Carson; *Peace of Mind,* by Joshua L. Liebman; *Cry the Beloved Country,* by Alan Paton; *The Fountainhead,* by Ayn Rand; *War and Peace* by Leo Tolstoy; and *The Caine Mutiny,* by Herman Wouk.

Criteria for judging the list are not available, but it is presented for examination in Appendix G. While perhaps twenty of the titles might be considered light reading, the list as a whole represents—in the judgment of the writer—a considerable body of stimulating reading.

All but four of the forty-two who replied reported private libraries of more than one hundred books.

Several generalizations concerning the reading of books by the Class of 1938 seem fair:

1. The amount of reading exceeds markedly that of comparable groups as reported in other research studies, with one exception. The exception is Princeton Class of 1944, which reported as much, or possibly more, reading of books than the men in the Class of 1938 who graduated from college.

2. The women in the class read about three times as many books as the men. Non-readers among the men greatly outnumbered the women non-readers.

3. The reading of books, like that of magazines, is highly individualized and does not reflect mass pressures.

The Second Generation

Question M on the communication questionnaire (Appendix B) asked, "If you have children, indicate what you are attempting to do with their reading attitudes and habits, and the methods (if any) you are using." It was felt that this question might give some clues as to the individual's own feelings about the importance of reading, and might also show whether he felt that the kind of emphasis made by the University School should be continued. Replies were greatly varied in form, and included varying amounts of detail. Often they were difficult to organize. For obvious reasons, it was decided to consider the replies of the men and the women separately.

Replies were received from twenty women, fifteen of whom have children of an age to be interested in reading. The other five have no children or have infants too young to be given books for entertainment. All of the fifteen made definite replies concerning what they were doing about their children's reading. Only two mentioned serious problems concerned with reading skills; one implied that the difficulty has ended, the other that it was continuing. Another mentioned that her sons were "not eager readers," although they were apparently competent enough.

Ten of the women mentioned specifically reading to or with their children. Six said that they attempted to show the children by parental attitudes, discussions, and example that reading is a happy and rewarding experience. Eight reported encouraging individual selection in terms of interests or age levels. Twelve pictured in considerable detail family experiences of reading with the children, going to the library with them, helping the children develop personal libraries, and other methods of making reading an integral part of the family life. Three gave no such account, although of course failure to answer the question may not be sound evidence that no efforts are made.

Returns were received from twenty-one of the men. Four have no children; four others reported that their children were "too young." It should be noted, however, that in two cases, the children who were "too young" were as old as some to whom other members of the class were reading. The remaining thirteen fathers with children old enough to be of interest in this study all explained as fully as did the mothers what was being done to encourage the reading of their children. Eight described different efforts to make the reading scene a family affair: listening to the child, reading to the child, setting an example, and encouraging individual selection either at home (as with the two-year-old who selects her picture book each evening) or at the library. Two mentioned specifically suggesting to the child that books are enjoyable; three believed the child should be surrounded with good books; and three took trips to the public library. One merely discussed a problem of his child's reading skill, but indicated that the difficulty has been overcome. In general, it may be said that all of the thirteen fathers seemed to accept responsibility for reading habits as a part of family living.

It seems fair to compare the attitudes of the twenty-eight parents with the program of University School, which emphasized an abundance of books, freedom of selection, pleasure in reading, and discussion of reading.

The Effect of College on Reading Habits

A question which obviously arises in considering the adult reading habits of this group is what are the relative roles of high-school and college experiences in producing the habits and attitudes reported. The question is important, not only as it aids in judging the effectiveness of the University School program, but also as it throws light on the responsibility toward reading of American education. The analysis which follows concerns both aspects of this question.

Question K, which followed ten others that were concerned with the individual's reading, writing, and listening habits, dealt with the effect of college on reading: "If you attended college, please state effect of college on your reading and other related habits." It is interesting to note that the inclusion of this question came at the suggestion of several members of the class.

Of those returning the questionnaires, thirty-eight had a year or more of college. The reader should note that previous discussion of "college men" and "college women" has referred to college graduates. In examining the effect of college on reading, however, it seemed fair to include all those who attended college, since it is usual for some work in English to be offered in the first year. The responses are of interest as they throw light on the role of University School and perhaps on the larger question of the age at which reading habits become relatively fixed.

Although the replies are not always sharply classifiable, they are here treated under six headings: (a) no response, (b) college negative to reading, (c) college responsible for narrowing reading—channeling it, (d) college confirmed high-school habits, (e) college made some specific contribution, and (f) college influence impossible to define. Pertinent quotations will be given under each heading.

Of the thirty-eight class members who went to college and sent in reports on reading, five failed to reply to Question K. It would seem fair to infer that this group was able to see no effect of college on their reading, and hence their replies are by implication negative. It should be noted that all five answered other questions concerning reading.

Ten stated categorically that college either did not improve or actually checked personal reading. Quotations follow:

> Didn't want to see a book for months after I graduated. [This person now reports enjoying reading aloud, recently reading *Don Quixote,* and "always working on one or more books."]

> It had a negative effect on my reading habits.

> College had little or no effect on my reading habits.

> I was unaware of any effect.

> No effect. [This individual also reports the enjoyment of oral reading, and various other strong reading interests.]

> Pressure and demand to do professional reading reduced general reading to a minimum.

> Emphasis on technical studies, with practically no "literary" work did not open any avenues for outside interests.

> . . . College had virtually no effect although I received some stimulus from literature courses. High school and seminary had far more influence.

> No effect I know of.

> Technical undergraduate college did little to create a desire to read. [This man, who had been an honor student at a great eastern university, reported elsewhere "no real desire to do much reading of books."]

Eight reported a narrowing of interest, chiefly into business or professional channels. Quotations follow:

> Lost my taste and time for fiction.

> Not much time during college for pleasure reading. Due to art courses am more apt to read related books.

> . . . To condense reading . . . get thought by skipping much descriptive material. Don't know whether this is good or bad.

My reading has been increasingly directed towards professional interests. . . . But my first two years at university . . . I did some very good reading in classics . . . .

Reading narrowed to technical books and magazines connected with profession.

Switched away from so much fiction. [Apparently this statement concerned only college years, since this person's report elsewhere named chiefly fiction.]

I learned to read faster.

Did lot of reading in college because of course requirements. Have done very little (except professional) since, however.

Five said specifically that college merely confirmed habits established in high school. Their statements follow:

My reading habits were established long before college . . . . Possibly it broadened my background.

Merely confirmed the reading habits already developed.

My reading habits were well established before college. I don't feel college changed them particularly.

I don't think any appreciable effect; i.e., no habits . . . that weren't already formed.

I don't believe my reading habits changed at all.

Nine were able to give some positive credit to college work. In reading their statements, however, note should be taken of their use of such words as "increased," "regulated," "added," "continued," and "broadened." Quotations from the nine follow:

My reading habits were fairly good by the time I got to college, but I found I wasn't reading fast enough.

Not to be uninformed or prejudiced [was a desire intensified by college].

Regulated it . . . as ancient literature courses keep one pretty busy. [It is not clear whether this was suggested as a helpful effect or not.]

Short story [course added new interest].

Was most influenced by Max Geisman and Esther Raushenbush.

[Learned] to confine reading to things most interesting . . . and to get maximum from what I read.

. . . Desire to continue cultural interests.

Broadened fields of interest and increased reading speed.

Enormously increased my enjoyment of reading. Some of the credit . . . is due to the University School . . . .

One person reported that he could not differentiate among the influences.

Although the reports of only thirty-eight persons do not permit generalizing, the total effect of the reports is somewhat startling. Five refused to mention the effect of college—or at least did not mention it although asked; ten found the influence negative; nine reported that it channeled their reading into business and professional fields; and five said merely that it did not disturb established patterns. Ten indicated some improvement in speed, skills, or breadth of interests, but only three of this group seemed markedly affected. One individual, who did not attempt to specify effects, gave evidence in answers to other questions of interests much wider than were indicated by high-school records.

WRITING

The faculty of University School held it important that every student should acquire skill in writing to such an extent that he could give expression to his feelings as well as to his more objective experiences. They also believed that students should know how to present ideas and information found through reading. The teachers of English were given primary responsibility for seeing that such skills were developed, but production of clear and conventionally correct writing was accepted as the responsibility of the entire faculty. The program, as developed, was marked by the following general characteristics.

Writing was taught primarily through writing. Very little time was spent on presenting abstract rules of organization, sentence structure, or punctuation. Instead, these matters were taught through application to an abundance of actual writing and rewriting. All papers had to be presented in legible form, criticized by the teacher (usually the teacher of English), and, when necessary, rewritten for permanent filing. Thus, when the class was graduated, the school had complete folders of the students' work—not only final copies, but intermediate drafts—in all subjects. The teaching of formal grammar, it should be mentioned, was delayed until just before graduation, except for the occasions in which the use of grammatical terms and principles became essential to the understanding of actual writing problems. As previously stated, principles of grammar were taught both to the students individually and to the entire class, and opportunities for writing were frequent.

During the first three years (grades seven, eight, and nine), much writing was done in connection with the core program.[17] Each unit of study required from each student a relatively formal paper which had to meet the standards set by the teacher of English. It was usual for such papers to be presented first in a rough draft, and then to be corrected and rewritten at least once. Frequently, rewriting had to be repeated.

In the three upper grades, work in the subject-matter areas proceeded more independently, but frequently the teacher of English was asked to assist with the work of organizing papers, handling bibliographies, and commenting on final results in other areas. Some papers presented in social studies, for example, were made a part of the work in English. The teacher of English also assisted in the direction of papers on the nature of proof in the mathematics courses.

In addition to the foregoing, a regular program of personal writing was continuous. Approximately every two weeks, each student prepared a paper, presented it to the class, and received criticism from both students and the teacher of English. A final corrected draft was

[17] The core program is described in Chapter III. Its chief characteristics were unit organization, individual projects, combining of subject-matter areas, and instruction by a group of teachers.

eventually filed. These personal papers used a variety of forms—informal essay, simple narrative of an actual event, imaginative story, verse.

During the twelfth year, as has been mentioned, the class wrote *Were We Guinea Pigs?*, which was published by Henry Holt and Company in 1938, within a month after the class graduated from high school. The book offers, therefore, the first opportunity for evaluation of the writing ability of the class.

Responses to the questionnaire and interview disclosed that by 1955 sixteen of the fifty-five class members had had material published, and a seventeenth had the manuscript of a novel in the hands of a possible publisher. The published writing and editorial work of the class members were as follows:

Five major, classified technical reports; articles in physics journals and other scientific publications.

Material for a technical paper (with co-authors).

Research and other work with husband on books.

Long list of articles in highly specialized field.

Food articles for *New York Herald Tribune* (editing and preparing copy for *This Week Magazine*).

Screen comedies, radio and television shows, comic strips, and so on.

Technical reports in special science field; copy for popular lectures in chemistry; newspaper column on birds.

Articles in classified technical field; editor of page in special journal in the field.

Published letters, dealing with political and social events, to editors of various newspapers and journals, including *Life* magazine.

Newspaper articles on mental retardation and the needs of the mentally retarded.

Collaboration with husband on technical article.

Editor of house organ; research and writing for Army Engineers publication.

Preparation of patent copy; articles for technical publications.

Correspondent for metropolitan paper, with by-line.

Novel (not published).

Scripts for movies.

One class member reported, "I have written incomplete essays and stories ever since U. School days. Another plan is to get a typewriter and complete a few efforts."

Another said, "There are others means of communication which I am surprised not to find in your questionnaire—letter writing—I am conscious of trying to keep them (my letters) from being humdrum diaries of personal experiences and children's accomplishments."

When it is considered that of the fifty-five class members two are professional artists, who therefore express themselves primarily through these media (painting and ceramics), a total of seventeen out of the remaining fifty-three is a large proportion to have expressed themselves in writing, approximately one in three.

Generalizations are unsafe when data are complicated as they are in a study of reading, writing, and listening habits. It seems fair to conclude, however, that the reading of the Class of 1938 is sufficiently superior to warrant consideration. The writing activities of class members appear to be similarly superior. Their use of other media is difficult to evaluate because we lack comparable data.

To what degree the program in English is responsible for the behavior of the class members cannot be established, but a considerable effect seems probable. Which elements are more effective cannot be established, for the reading program included several factors: individualized reading, attention to selection, responsibility by students for their own progress; interest of the instructors in individual students. The widely diversified reading by class members, whether of books or periodicals, suggests that individualizing the high-school program has led to continued individualized reading. There seems to be evidence that whatever the source, habits formed before high-school graduation tend to persevere.

The writing program, with its emphasis on writing rather than on drill or learning about grammatical structure in the abstract, seems to have produced an unusual number of persons who write for publication.

The data which have been collected on the use of the legitimate theatre, drama, moving pictures, radio, television, and other communication media can be evaluated only when other groups have been studied.

The emphasis which the class members placed, in bringing up their children, on regular reading habits, on the selection of books, and on the personal needs for books points to acceptance, conscious or not, of basic principles used in the school.

Of late, much criticism has been directed toward so-called progressive education. The University School would undoubtedly be classed as "progressive" since it emphasized group undertakings, but with individualized assignments; critical thinking rather than memorization; and student participation in the responsibility for planning. It did not, however, assume that student planning meant proceeding in terms of whim or pleasure. The English program, moreover, placed prime emphasis on writing rather than on analysis of sentences, drills, or abstract grammar. Correction was in terms of individual need in a specific situation. In reading, more time and attention were given to planning and evaluating individual reading than to group discussion of particular pieces. Students were urged to read literature rather than to learn about periods and movements which they must take on faith. In view of these conditions, the findings of this study seem especially significant at the present moment

IX

ATTITUDES TOWARD THE SCHOOL
PROGRAM

The Research Instruments

In the preliminary stages of the follow-up the plans for the biographical questionnaire contained a great many questions about the
individual's reactions to various phases of his high-school experience.
The list grew very long, and with it grew doubts about the possibility of getting reliable information in this way. On the suggestion of
the class member who had been editor of *Were We Guinea Pigs?*, all
the specific queries about the school program were removed from the
questionnaire and an initial, indirect approach was substituted. The last
page of the questionnaire (Appendix A) invited spontaneous responses to several very general questions which it was hoped would
give significant leads for further investigation.

15. Write at as great length as you wish on any or all of the questions
below:

a) Do you feel *now* that the things we emphasized at University School actually were the important things, the things which
should have been stressed?

b) Do you feel that your University School experience has had
any significant bearing, positive or negative, on your over-all capacity to *enjoy* life (as contrasted with your ability to do particular
things)?

c) Are there particular experiences since you left high school which have been so challenging to you or so rewarding that you want to tell about them?

d) Are there particular values in living that you have come to prize very highly or particular causes that you watch for opportunities to further? If so, do you want to tell about them?

TABLE 47

RESPONSES TO THE QUESTION "WERE THE THINGS
EMPHASIZED AT UNIVERSITY SCHOOL THE
IMPORTANT THINGS?"

Response	Number	Per Cent
No.....................................	3	8.3
Yes and No............................	12	33.3
Yes...................................	21	58.4
Specifics given........................	29	80.6

TABLE 48

RESPONSES TO THE QUESTION "DID YOUR UNIVERSITY
SCHOOL EXPERIENCE HAVE ANY SIGNIFICANT BEARING,
POSITIVE OR NEGATIVE, ON YOUR CAPACITY TO ENJOY
LIFE?"

Response	Number	Per Cent
Negative bearing......................	1	5.5
No significant bearing.................	3	16.7
"Yes and no," or "maybe".............	2	11.1
Positive bearing.......................	12	66.7
Specifics given........................	11	61.0

Of the fifty-two who returned questionnaires, forty-one, or 79 per cent, answered one or more of the questions. The largest number, thirty-six, or 69.2 per cent, replied to the first, eighteen (34.6 per cent) and sixteen (31 per cent) to the second and third, and only nine (17 per cent) to the fourth. It was intended that all of the responses would be used principally for the construction of questions for the short first section of the interview schedule which was to be concerned with the school program. Actually, only sections *a* and *b* were used for this purpose, since *c* and *d* were covered in the longer section of the schedule which dealt with many aspects of living. Tabulations of the questionnaire responses to *a* and *b* are shown in Tables 47 and 48.

The specific responses given by twenty-nine people, noted in Table 47, and by eleven, in Table 48, were positive in some cases, negative in others. Whenever such reactions seemed to be opposed to each other, they were juxtaposed in the interview questions (see Appendix C, Group I), and all the respondents were invited to comment.

3. Tolerance for minorities was mentioned by one student as something learned at school; others mentioned respect for individuals, that you were not forced to conform, that you learned to accept yourselves. One thought this might have been overdone in the direction of too much individualism. What is your opinion?

5. Some mentioned "learning without drudgery," "enjoying learning," acquiring the attitudes and skills which have fostered later learning. Others felt they should have been compelled to learn more things, that some things should have been "rammed down our throats." What is your attitude?

6. One said that for him the school overstressed the intellectual; another said that it understressed the intellectual. Many commented that they learned to get along with others, but a few felt that human relations was a neglected area. What is your opinion?

Criticisms of subject-matter gaps, which were made by a number of individuals, were grouped together and placed at the beginning in Question 1 to show that negative as well as positive comments were acceptable and worthy of consideration.

1. Various people mentioned inadequacy of factual knowledge. Can you recall situations when you were handicapped by not knowing something which others seemed to know and you felt the school should have taught you in grammar, spelling, geography, history, science, famous quotations—all of which were mentioned—or any other?

Criticisms offered by only one or a few people were included, as were favorable comments coming spontaneously from one or many individuals, and all were submitted to everyone for comment.

2. One mentioned the understressing of traditional American values and an overemphasis on change, as though change were good in it-

self, another the development of a world picture with no room for God or faith. Were you, or have you become, aware of such tendencies?

8. A number of people felt that there was not enough "disciplined learning" in the school. Can you look back and say where you felt you got this, and where you felt that you needed more than you got?

4. Many people mentioned values derived from Nature of Proof. Can you recall a specific instance when you used methods learned in this course, or can you trace any habits of thinking to it?

7. A number of people felt that one outcome of the program should be "the ability to think for yourself." Do you agree that this is something for which the school was working? Can you explain what makes you think you do or do not have this ability? Is it related to self-confidence?

10. Do you have any feeling now about how well or how badly the balance between co-operation and competition in the school prepared you for competition and co-operation as you met them later?

13. A number of people felt as they looked back that they wasted a good deal of time in high school. Do you feel that you wasted much time? If so, was that just a part of the process of growing up, or do you feel that the faculty should have done something about it?

There were three questions included by the investigator without any specific leads from the questionnaires.

9. Do you have any feeling now that integration of subjects gave you any more habit of seeing relationships than most of the people you go around with?

11. The faculty talked a great deal among themselves about trying to make the school an experience in democratic living and about helping you to verbalize about democracy from your experience. Were you aware of that at the time and has it been of any value to you later?

12. Of course the process of growing up and assuming adult responsibilities brings some changes or at least redefinitions of our standards and our values. Were any of these changes sudden enough or drastic enough so that you were aware of them? Can you be specific about what they were and what brought them about?

The final question was included in order to permit each respondent to give his own emphases and to add anything which seemed important to him that had been missed in earlier questions.

> 14. Of course you know the school as a human institution must have changed, but since you do not know just what the changes are, assume it is still just as you knew it. Tell the faculty what things about it were particularly valuable and should be conserved and what parts were weak and should be improved.

Specific questions about the English and social-studies programs were omitted deliberately in order to avoid any danger that the interview might be thought of as an invitation to "polish apples"—the investigator had been one of the class's social-studies teachers, and the members of the class all knew that Miss LaBrant, their English teacher, was intimately associated with the follow-up.

Attitudes toward Subject-Matter

In view of current criticisms of education for lack of content and for failure to meet the needs of the gifted, it is interesting to examine the responses of the guinea pigs to questions about inadequacies of factual knowledge, the relative importance of interest in a subject as opposed to "having it rammed down our throats," the adequacy of the school program in terms of "disciplined learning" (see Chapter III for a description of the high-school program), and whether the intellectual was overstressed, understressed, or given the right emphasis.

The responses of forty-seven members of the class to these questions are shown in Table 49. (Forty-nine class members were interviewed, but the two first interviews were held before the questions about the school program had been added to the schedule.) The data were originally tabulated so that not only the men's and women's responses could be compared, but also the responses of the gifted guinea pigs (see Chapter III for the method by which they were selected) and the rest of the class. The reader should keep in mind that the later academic records of the twenty-four gifted students of the Class of 1938 excelled those of Terman's gifted children in almost every respect (see Chapter IV), although Terman's group was far more selective in terms of ability. Where no significant differences appeared between the reactions of the men and the women, the two sexes were combined in the final tabulations.

TABLE 49

RESPONSES TO QUESTIONS ON ATTITUDES TOWARD SUBJECT-MATTER IN THE SCHOOL PROGRAM

Question	Response	Per Cent of the Gifted (N-23)	Per Cent of the Rest of the Class (N-24)
1	No inadequacy of factual knowledge...........	48.0	13.0
	Difficulty with grammar......................	26.0	38.0
	Difficulty with spelling......................	17.4	26.0
	Inadequate or unsatisfactory science training.....	26.0	9.0
	Difficulty with history or geography...........	9.0	26.0
	Difficulty with miscellaneous other areas........	17.4	18.0
5	More things should have been rammed down our throats..................................	4.0	8.0
	Interest is important, but so is drill and drudgery	22.0	46.0
	Enjoying learning is most important...........	74.0	46.0
8	Got the "disciplined learning" I needed.........	57.0	56.5
	Got "disciplined learning" in some areas; needed more in others............................	43.0	43.5
6	School overstressed the intellectual..............	10.0	15.0 *
	Right balance................................	84.2	85.0
	Understressed the intellectual...................	5.3	5.0 *

* One individual believed it was overstressed for some and understressed for others.

Among the gifted guinea pigs, 48 per cent felt no inadequacy in factual knowledge. One of this group pointed out that in college he skipped the first semester of English and history on the basis of placement tests; another, that he skipped most of the first year. Those who mentioned deficiencies seemed fairly relaxed about them. One person failed the grammar section of his college English placement test, but got an *A* in the course. Five others had some grammar troubles, either in placement tests or in foreign-language courses, but only one of them seemed to feel strongly about it. (See discussions of grammar in Chapters III and VIII.) Two considered their spelling poor, but believed it came from something in their make-up which the school couldn't remedy. Six expressed some dissatisfaction with their high-school science, half of them because they hadn't developed an interest in it; however, one noted that he nevertheless had passed the science placement tests for engineering college. Two felt that their knowledge of history and dates was sketchy. One criticized the teaching of Latin; one wished he could recognize more famous quotations, another that she could read faster, and another that she could memorize more readily.

What are the attitudes of the other half of the class, the less academically gifted? Do their opinions in general agree with the gifted group? A quick look at the later educational records of the two groups, as can be seen in Tables 9, 10, and 11 (Chapter IV), will help to focus on some significant differences in post–high school experience.

All members of the Class of 1938, with one possible exception about whom information is scanty, either started college or enrolled in junior college, office-training school, or some specialized course. Since the group now being considered is the lower half of the class, in academic rating, it is to be anticipated that they would have had more subject-matter problems than the upper half as they went on to other schools, although, since the class median is high, only a few would be expected to have had severe academic difficulties. It is possible that some of those who did not complete the courses they began might be tempted to blame deficiencies in their high-school preparation for their failure to finish.

From a careful examination of the protocols, the investigator concludes that there is such a tendency, but that it is slight. It is confined to a few individuals, and is not consistently present even in these cases. As in the responses of the gifted, six in the lower half of the class mention trouble with grammar in college placement tests or college-level courses in English or a foreign language; two are having trouble helping their children with grammar homework; and one is bothered because she can't hold up her end of a grammatical argument with her husband, though she knows her English usage is correct. Two think they lack background in science, but suspect lack of interest or application. Half a dozen feel a more or less inadequate knowledge of geography or history, but suspect the same reasons.

The major difference between the two groups seems to be that the less academically gifted find subject-matter harder to master. The only area in which they encountered less difficulty than the gifted was in science. More of the gifted, however, pursued science, whereas the less gifted tended to avoid it after high school.

The question about the importance in learning of interest as opposed to drill and compulsion brought out some differences between the two halves of the class. Among the gifted, only one believed that more information and skills should have been "rammed down our throats" because people should "get used to life's drudgery." This person was the only member of the gifted group who failed in college. Of the others in the group, three-fourths took the point of view well expressed by a man in the following statement:

> I rather believe that in life in general if you don't have the desire to learn or do a thing that you are not going to do it. Perhaps a good place to start with life's tendencies is in the high school, and not ram things down your throat, but try to create the desire for the person to pick them out himself.

The other one-fourth felt that, although interest is a major factor in learning, "students should learn to see some drudgery as necessary to worth-while goals," or that individuals differ so much that no general prescription will hold. But they rejected "ramming." One noted that requiring some exploration of unfamiliar areas is necessary and is not "ramming"; others that some tools must be learned, but that the learning of them should not hamper free thinking.

The less academically gifted half of the class divided about evenly on the question of the importance of interest: almost half considered the enjoyment of learning as of most importance, whereas an equal number thought they might have accomplished more with a larger amount of pushing. Three others noted that "ramming" doesn't result in real learning: "I don't think you're going to get any place with it, because I've tried to ram it down my own daughter's throat at night in spelling or arithmetic, and it just doesn't work."

A fourth member of this group gave the following response:

Well, I've thought about that question—whether I might have been a better writer if they had put me in a closet or something, forced me to write more. On the other hand, when I think about my attitude toward school work before I went to University School—some of this was told me by my parents, I don't think I remember it all myself, but from what I think I remember and from what I've been told— I *hated* school, literally *hated* school before going over to University School. I don't think I would ever have gotten through if I hadn't found something I liked very well which happened to be art, and it gave me a purpose for doing things that I'm still very grateful for.

Sometimes I wonder if I could have learned more English if I was forced to, but somehow I think I wouldn't have. I think I would just have become more antagonistic toward school—I think it is sort of a quirk in my own self—but if you could go back and experiment, I'd be sort of curious to know what would happen if I was forced to do certain things.

The question on "disciplined learning" revealed no differences between the two groups. About 57 per cent of each group felt they got the "disciplined learning" they needed; 43 per cent believed they got it in some areas but needed more in other areas. The same individual who thought learning should be rammed down people's throats so they would be used to life's drudgery believed in addition that there is a need for the kind of discipline that will teach people to take orders and work *for* a group. At the opposite extreme are three who consider "disciplined learning" unimportant (one called it "hogwash"). A woman remarked, "I got satisfaction out of showing (in college) I could do as well as those brought up on 'disciplined learning.'"

One man who felt he needed more disciplined learning in science said, "I remember doing one lengthy experiment or project which I thought at the time was going to measure the electrochemical series, but actually measured something rather different and more complicated, namely the resistance of strong solutions of electrolytes." Whether an experiment remembered and analyzed so well after twenty years can be regarded as one which went wrong is open to argument. One could make a strong case for the learning which took place as a result of this experience, though the question as to the role of the teacher is not clear.

Others who felt they had gotten the disciplined learning they needed, made the following comments: "There must be some, but I don't agree with it for its own sake"; "Using your own initiative with

TABLE 50

Is the Course "Nature of Proof" Remembered and Used?

Group	Men of the Class of 1938		Women of the Class of 1938	
	Per Cent Who Do Not Remember or Use Course	Per Cent Who Remember and Use Course	Per Cent Who Do Not Remember or Use Course	Per Cent Who Remember and Use Course
Gifted Group (N-23)...	..	100	8	92
Rest of Class (N-24)....	23	77	40	60

guidance gave enough 'discipline' "; "We learned the methods and to know the tools." The remaining replies mentioned places in the program in which they remembered it, and offered suggestions of places in which they felt there should have been more.

The question concerning the necessity of more "disciplined learning" aroused favorable comments from some about more compulsion to get work done, more thorough learning of skills, and less time for personal and individual interests.

In regard to the amount of stress on the intellectual which had existed, most of the class (85 per cent of both groups) believed it had been about right. Three in the gifted group who are undoubtedly intellectuals dissented: one felt that it had been understressed; and two, that they had been permitted, though not necessarily encouraged, to overstress it. From the perspective of twenty years, it seems quite possible that everybody was right.

Another aspect of attitudes toward subject-matter in the University School program is interesting enough for separate treatment. The mathematics course for the Junior and Senior years was demonstrative geometry with emphasis on the question of what constitutes proof. This course, called "Nature of Proof," was mentioned several times in the questionnaire responses, so one of the questions in the interview schedule (Question 4) asked about it. The replies are given in Table 50. Although this course has for all four groups in the Class of 1938 a score of relevance which should be highly gratifying to any teacher, the logical processes which were taught in it were meaningful to a greater number of the gifted group than the rest of the class, and to more of the men than the women. The level of enthusiasm was great in all groups; the illustrations that were reported of the present situations in which it is used were extremely varied but all significant. It is striking that the lowest percentage of "remembered and used" is 60.

The Teaching of Values in the Program

In the responses to the questions concerned with values, the slight differences between the two halves of the class and between the sexes disappear in most cases. Hence, except in the responses to Question 9, in which differences appear between the gifted and the rest of the group, the whole class will be considered as a unit throughout the rest of this chapter. Since the level of agreement is high, special attention is paid to statements of minority opinion. Table 51 summarizes the responses to questions concerning values.

The question about the underemphasis on traditional American values and the overemphasis on change (Question 2) was raised by one individual who has always maintained a clear and consistent con-

TABLE 51
RESPONSES TO QUESTIONS ON THE INFLUENCE OF THE SCHOOL PROGRAM ON VALUES

Question	Response	Per Cent of the Class (N-47)
2	Understressed traditional American values and overemphasized change...	2.0
	Gave balanced emphasis on traditional values and change....	86.0
	[Individual reactions that were hard to classify.]............	12.0
	Tendency to encourage the development of a world picture with no room for God or faith........................	2.0
	Disagree that the program had the above tendency..........	98.0
3	School successfully promoted tolerance for minorities........	86.7
	Find myself holding intolerant attitudes today..............	13.3
	Too much individualism (various specific examples cited).....	14.6
	Promoting individualism is one of the strong points of the school..	85.4
6	Learned to get along with other people....................	88.4
	Learned it, but more at home than at school...............	2.3
	Human relations a neglected area at school.................	9.3
7	School tried to teach people to think for themselves.........	100.0
	Objective was achieved to a certain degree.................	96.0
	Objective was not achieved...............................	4.0
10	Somewhat handicapped in meeting competition.............	24.0
	Have felt no handicap in meeting competition...............	76.0
11	Understanding of democracy has been of service............	51.0
	The understanding of democracy has possibly been useful.....	23.4
	Have seen no use for it, or am very doubtful...............	19.2
	Aware of emphasis in school, but do not use it now.........	6.4
13	Feel I wasted a good deal of time in high school............	56.9
	Do not feel that I wasted time in high school..............	42.1

TABLE 51—*Continued*

Question	Response	Per Cent of the Gifted	Per Cent of the Rest of the Class	Per Cent of the Whole Class
9	Feel now that integrated courses encouraged habit of seeing relationships....................	82.6	30.5	56.5
	Do not see any effect............	....	39.0	19.5
	Am not sure whether or not there has been any effect.............	17.4	30.5	24.0

servative position on social and political issues. Though no one directly agreed with his statement, some backhanded support for it came from several persons: "Yes, I think so, but I'm all for it. We had to learn to think instead of accepting things by rote." "I certainly characterized the school as being biased on the liberal side, using terms as objective not emotional words; no room for a good, solid Republican, though there were a number there." "Well, 'traditional American values,' as I remember so well from Nature of Proof, is, after all, a stereotype; and I hardly know how to react to that. I think it has very little meaning. I would have to know what these values are and then react in terms of a better definition. This is a semantic problem." Such responses amounted to 12 per cent of the total.

The 86 per cent who felt that the school gave a balanced emphasis can be fairly adequately represented by the following comment: "We were growing up in a time when change—a sort of revolution—was beyond beginning, it was really in the end of the first quarter. We would have been very ignorant not to have noticed it.—We were in it and living with it and recognizing it as a fact."

The reactions to the second part of Question 2—whether University School encouraged the development of a world picture without room for God or faith—was overwhelmingly negative. Some stressed the moral and spiritual values they found in the program, others the responsibility of the home for religious education. Although the problem appears to have troubled only one student in this high-school class, it is a persistent one in groups of adolescents, wherever individuals are trying to build the different parts of their experience into a coherent whole. Why it was not more important here is not clear.

Those who agreed in responses to Questions 3 and 6 appear to define the values encouraged by the school in very similar terms. In the case of Question 3, there are individuals who differ: "I'm still intolerant of minority groups, and I try to fight it and overcome it; but I don't think that was developed in high school. I think that was much farther back in my outside environment, because high school had so little to do with forming ideas, philosophies, and inhibitions that it didn't mean anything. My prejudices may have been leveled off to some degree, but they still appear, crop up."

One interpreted the inquiry about respect for individuals in its hierarchical aspect: "I respect my superiors I work with, and my parents. I think that's gotten into me good. I think the army helps you out that way too, drills that into you a little more."

In the minority of seven who felt there was too much individualism, six cited relatively small examples from their own experience in which they had felt they were put too much "on their own." Only one said, "In all probability there was too much stress on individualism. After all we do have to conform to a certain degree when we get out in life."

The responses of a small group of five, which held that human relations (Question 6) was a neglected area, were even more diverse. One believed that he needed more of a push than he got; one said that he didn't pay much attention to human relations in school, but now thought it important; another wished he had learned to be more persuasive; and another felt that he had missed some aspects of social development because the University School was not a neighborhood school.

The respondents agreed unanimously in answering Question 7 that the school tried to teach people to think for themselves; and 96 per cent believed the objective was reached to a significant degree. Of the two who disagreed, one said, "I was always in doubt no matter what I did and I still am. I never know where I stand." The other felt

that certain teachers, though not all, believed that students were thinking only when they reached the same conclusions as the teacher.

The illustrations of "thinking for yourself" which were offered by
the members of the class show that individuals vary greatly in the
amount and kind of independent thinking that they do, but they also
tend to support the conclusion that these are thinking people. As one
person said, "To the extent that one does, I think I do."

Most of the Class of 1938 felt that their ability to think for themselves was fairly closely related to their self-confidence, the two rein-
forcing each other. A few doubted this, one remarking thoughtfully,
"Thinking for yourself breeds its tensions, too, because it will push
you often toward nonconformity in so far as conforming means accepting rather pat and glib answers. You take the risk of setting
yourself emotionally apart from a group every time you think for yourself. On the other hand, I suppose it contributes somewhat to self-
confidence, to assurance."

Class members were questioned about whether they felt that
the integration of subjects in their core and broad-field courses had
given them the habit of looking for relationships to a greater extent
than most of the people they knew now seemed to possess (Question 9). This is one of the very few questions where the answers of
the gifted were conspicuously different: 82.6 per cent believed that it
had, as against only 30.5 per cent of the rest of the class. As one of the
gifted remarked, "I'm good at this, anyway," which is probably the
main cause of the difference. Another contributing factor may be the
tendency of the gifted to have a greater awareness of many aspects
of the educational process.

The question about the balance between competition and co-operation in the school program (Question 10) produced a great many interesting comments. Nearly a quarter of the class felt they had been
handicapped by a lack of competition, but half of these mentioned
only college grades or the taking of examinations as their problems.
The other handicaps mentioned are varied and individual, and except in one case, minor. The one individual who has felt seriously
handicapped made the following report: "I thought I was being

trained not to compete with someone else but to compete with myself. That's my own idea. But it didn't train me to compete with the outside world or with anyone. I was practically a lamb as far as competition was concerned. I didn't strive or struggle with anyone."

The three-quarters who did not feel handicapped explained their attitudes in various ways: the world is really much more co-operative than competitive; in school you were competing with yourself to do the best job you could; meeting competition has presented no problems; one can learn to meet competition without being taught. Quoting several replies may make various attitudes clearer.

> The only competition we lacked was that afforded by letter grades.— There was *plenty* of competition to do jobs capably, to make a good presentation of an individual core-course investigation. This would seem to me stronger than competition on the basis of numerical standing for better grades. I have felt no inadequacy in competition since high school.

> I find competition very challenging. I like it. I wouldn't give you a hoot to do anything if there wasn't some competition involved, not because you want to win but because it's fun to compete in a friendly sort of way.

> I think co-operation was certainly stressed and I think it was well done.—My few instances of competitive endeavors, whether it be in athletics or in scholastic work, were dismal flops, and such things, to one who doesn't have self-confidence, are not conducive to instilling a desire or making you more competitive. You've got to have success somewhere along the line before—I think you can grind a man down through a series of failures till he becomes just a pulp almost, a cattail waving in the breeze.

> That [competition vs. co-operation] is one of the biggest questions—not to myself—but it didn't prepare me for marrying someone who is used to competition, and for the relationship of those two people in raising children, living in present-day suburbia. How are you going to teach them to meet it, or not to meet it, or what do you tell them?

The question as to whether the understanding of democracy, acquired at the school by means of experience followed by verbalization, had been of service in later life (Question 11) was considered thoughtfully, but many of the respondents found difficulty in answering it. Only a trifle more than half were sure that their understanding had been useful, and another quarter felt that it was possible. The other quarter were unaware of any effect.

Probably, the reason for some of the hesitation is expressed in this quotation:

> It seems to me a hard question to answer because I think the concept of democracy in our whole society has changed so much. I think it was awfully important to think about it at the time, and good that we did; but I think at the University School today, probably, the thinking about it is quite different, and rightly so. I think that maybe we tended to oversimplify, but I think that people generally did, in the '30's, oversimplify the problems of democracy.

Since the overwhelming majority of answers to the question about democracy were very temperate or even tepid in their tone and only a handful expressed real enthusiasm, the writer cannot resist including one of the responses which combines a temperate tone with a gratifying tribute to the school:

> So many things enter into a person's maturing processes that it's hard to single out the exact point at which the academic career was modified. It does seem to me, however, that this was the most significant factor in my high-school education. Social studies were tremendously exciting to me, and this was one of the most important factors, the sense of the importance of democracy. Throughout the experience, there was the consciousness of a dynamic world in flux, which we certainly had contact with through our teachers and such guidance as we had studying current events. And I don't know where the passion for democracy as a way of life had its genesis in my own life, but I truly feel it had tremendous stimulus in the high-school atmosphere, and much beyond that which I had in my college experience, much beyond.

In approaching the question of whether or not they had wasted time in school (Question 13), the respondents were apparently more or less evenly divided; a few more felt that time had been wasted (56.9 per cent) than believed it had not been (42.1 per cent). In fact, there were only five people (14 per cent) who recalled that they had always been awfully busy, and at the other extreme, about the same number who believed that they had wasted time and that something should have been done about it. All the rest expressed tolerance for the time-wasting of adolescents: "You can't spend all your time trying to improve yourself when you are in high school. Some of it should be 'wasted.'" "Time can be 'wasted' very profitably in growing up." The most adequate exposition of what seemed to be the attitude of more than half the class was expressed by the father of four children:

> In dealing with youngsters, it seems to me that sometimes we just don't give them time in which to grow. I mean they have to learn how to evaluate life, experience life in terms of their own thinking, and if we're constantly pressing upon them things which we feel are required that they do, and particularly giving them time limits with which to work, we're not going to give them time to develop their own philosophy of life and acquire a sense of values that can really be called their own, that will stick by them in terms of their own emergencies later on.

In response to Question 12, about one-third of the class reported that, since graduation, they had met one or more major crises which had required some fundamental revision of attitudes or rethinking of values. The evidence indicates, and the individuals believe, that all have been dealt with successfully and have resulted in personal growth.

The Views of the Graduates on the Strengths and Weaknesses of the School Program

ANALYSIS BY THE RESEARCHER

Question 14 was the last in the first section of the interview schedule: "Of course you know that the school as a human institution must have changed, but since you do not know just what the changes are, assume that it is still just as you knew it. Tell the faculty what things about it were particularly valuable and should be conserved, and what parts were weak and should be improved." The importance of including this kind of open-ended summary question was not apparent to the interviewer at the beginning, so it was added only after nine of the forty-nine interviews had already been completed. The advantage of the summary was that it permitted each respondent to give his own over-all evaluation, emphasizing points, positive or negative, which he felt were important, whether or not they had been touched upon in earlier questions.

The protocol responses varied greatly in the amount of detail, and the spontaneous expression of the various individuals made each response so different from all of the others that they were hard to tabulate except in quite broad classifications. A summary of the tabulations is found in Table 52, "Values in the School Program Which

TABLE 52
VALUES IN THE SCHOOL PROGRAM WHICH SHOULD BE CONSERVED

Value	Per Cent Listing Each Value
Warmth and human atmosphere	55.0
Learning as discovery	42.5
Concern of school for individuals	20.0
Co-operative work in learning	20.0
Trips	15.0
Quality of faculty	10.0
Miscellaneous: moral and ethical standards, exposure to culture, high quality library	12.5
Courses and areas praised:	
Reading, literature, and composition	20.0
Nature of Proof and the mathematics program	30.0
Social studies	17.5
French	5.0
The arts—music, industrial arts, fine arts, home economics	27.5
Physical education, especially the intramural program	15.0

Should Be Conserved," and in Table 53, "Suggestions for Improvement of the School Program."

The value of the program mentioned most frequently was, in general terms, "warmth and human atmosphere." The specific answers which were grouped under this heading were the following: friendly relations of the students with each other and with the teachers; the homelike feeling of the school; the school was living as well as learning; there was freedom, but the abuse of freedom was handled in a firm but friendly manner; the classes were small, the atmosphere informal; and students were helping make traditions. More than half of

TABLE 53

SUGGESTIONS FOR IMPROVEMENT OF THE SCHOOL PROGRAM

Suggestion	Per Cent Giving Each Suggestion
Not enough geography	7.5
Chronological history weak	10.0
Social studies a little too liberal	2.5
Not enough grammar	22.5
Spelling weak	10.0
Miscellaneous: not enough writing *required*, not taught to read fast enough, needed three R's	7.5
Foreign languages weak	5.0
Science courses not stimulating, or inadequate in some way	15.0
More conventional mathematics preferred	5.0
More use of traditional learning	5.0
More cramming for students who needed it	10.0
More help with study skills and use of time	7.5
A dozen specific suggestions, each one made by one person	30.0

the respondents (55 per cent) mentioned something in this area. It is significant that the responses were not directly suggested by any of the earlier questions, but were offered spontaneously.

The second classification, "learning as discovery," was used to group such items as the following: keep the thrill of learning in the program; continue to let students find out things for themselves, and show initiative with responsibility in their learning; keep on teaching them to think and to plan and to make decisions; encourage their interests even more. Nearly half (42.5 per cent) mentioned one of these.

About one-fifth of the class valued highly the concern of the school for individuals, its success in helping the brilliant, and its emphasis on each student working at his own best level. An equal number emphasized the values of co-operative procedures in learning in various ways—working democratically, using committees, joint ventures, unit teaching. Although only 15 per cent mentioned the importance of long and short trips, and 10 per cent the critical importance of a highly qualified faculty, the individuals making these points made them very strongly.

Particular courses and subject-matter areas shared in the commendation; it seems probable that individuals praised the aspects of the work which had stimulated their interests. Typing was not mentioned, although 58 per cent of the class members had elected it at some stage, most had done well in it, and nobody criticized it. Science received no praise, although 27.8 per cent of the boys were interested enough to follow some phase of it in college and as a career. Many explained that they were sure that several faculty changes accounted for the weaknesses in science. Those areas were named which seemed to be remembered with real enthusiasm. Probably not too much attention should be paid to the percentages praising particular areas, though again Nature of Proof ranks high. More than one-third of the women who had elected home economics in high school gave glowing testimonials to its later value to them, though this figure is buried in the general commendation given to the varied aspects of the arts program.

The suggestions for improving the program, summarized in Table 53, are clustered almost entirely around subject-matter fields, and in most cases, represent small minorities of the class. Only five were named by 10 per cent or more—grammar, science, history, spelling, and study skills. The list of a dozen suggestions, mentioned at the end of the table, includes courses in shorthand and in art and music appreciation, better vocational guidance, smoother transition from the sixth to the seventh grade, interscholastic competition for girls in physical education, earlier differentiation of courses according to ability, more careful checking on students who leave class for the rest room, and changes in the situation that "permitted some students to be intellectual snobs." Some of these suggestions for improvement, though not all, were soundly based; the situations have been considered by the faculty in the years since 1938, and modifications have been introduced to meet them.

As the protocols were read and the questions about the school analyzed, especially Question 14, the writer attempted to assign the responses to categories representing the degree of enthusiasm for the whole school experience and the extent to which the suggestions made

TABLE 54

DEGREE OF ENTHUSIASM FOR THE SCHOOL EXPERIENCE

Degree of Enthusiasm	Number of Students in Each Category (N-40)	Per Cent
Great enthusiasm, coupled with suggestions quite consistent with the school's philosophy and purposes.............	13	32.5
Enthusiasm, and no suggestions for improvement...........	2	5.0
Enthusiasm, plus suggestions which, in the main, are consistent with the school's philosophy and purposes.........	20	50.0
Tempered enthusiasm, and suggestions which, in some cases, disagree with certain fundamentals in the program........	3	7.5
Mostly criticism representing fundamental disagreement with the philosophy and purposes, but no regret at having attended the school....................................	2	5.0

for improvement were consistent with the philosophy and purposes of the school. The result is admittedly subjective, and it is offered in those terms in Table 54.

None of the nine who were interviewed before Question 14 was added to the interview schedule showed negative attitudes toward the school which would place them with the 5 per cent who were mostly critical; this judgment is based upon the entire interview, rather than on the one specific response. The evidence for the three who returned questionnaires but were not interviewed is not sufficient to support any conclusions.

The attitudes of the three persons who did not return questionnaires are presumed on the whole to be negative, however. One man expressed considerable resentment toward the school in the course of a telephone conversation, and since he had been in the class five years, the conclusion is inescapable that the school failed to reach him. The other two were a part of the program for a relatively short time, one for two years and one for a year and a half; their failure to co-operate may show a lack of identification or outright rejection or mere impatience with questionnaires.

If these three are considered a dissident group and are added to the 5 per cent who are mostly critical, the whole class (fifty-five individuals) may be divided into three broad categories as follows:

More or less dissatisfied or uninterested ...... 9.0 per cent
Inadequate information to judge satisfaction.. 5.5 per cent
Enthusiastic (to a mild degree in a few cases,
    to a very great degree in most cases) ......85.5 per cent

As a further check upon present attitudes toward the school program, a letter was sent to all members of the class, inviting volunteers to work on analyzing Question 14. Nine individuals offered to work, but because of unavoidable delays in beginning the job, three found themselves too involved in other activities to participate.

The last section of this chapter, then, is the work of six men and women, whose homes are scattered from coast to coast. Each was furnished with the tabulations of responses to the first thirteen questions of the protocols and with the complete answers to Question 14; the answers were unidentified except for the sex of the respondent. The method of handling this mass of data was left entirely to the committee of former guinea pigs. The chairman was told in general terms how the researcher had analyzed the responses, but the committee worked out its own methods to meet the exigencies of its widely scattered membership.

The aspects of the school program to be studied were agreed upon by correspondence. Each member worked on some particular aspect, studying it through all the responses, writing it up, and forwarding it to the chairman. The separate contributions were edited only by the chairman of the committee; the researcher has done no editing of this section. It seems most illuminating to allow these two independent analyses of the same data to stand side by side.

ANALYSIS BY A COMMITTEE OF THE CLASS

In this section we are considering what the guinea pigs now think of their experience at the University School. It is based on our answers to the following question which was the last of a group of fourteen questions asked during the personal interviews.

14. Obviously you know that the school must have changed since you were there. But since you haven't been around, you don't know how it has changed. If you were giving advice to the faculty, what things do you feel, on the basis of your experience, you would like to see improved, and what values would you like to see conserved?

The responses have been studied by a group of six former guinea pigs, now pushing forty, and in every case surrounded and almost overwhelmed by a younger generation—some by their own offspring and others by their students. Thus we find ourselves looking back at our own secondary education and forward to that of our children.

The writers would like to point out that this question came at the end of a long series concerning the school program. In many cases, the responses to the previous thirteen questions had been overwhelmingly favorable (learned to get along with other people—88.4 per cent; have felt no handicap in meeting competition—76 per cent; school tried to teach people to think for themselves, and this objective was achieved—96 per cent). Therefore, there may have been a tendency in answering this last question to accentuate the negative. In fact, the way the question is phrased is an invitation to be critical. No self-respecting guinea pig would ever pass up a chance for "giving advice to the faculty" or admit that a situation ever existed that couldn't be improved upon.

One of our contributing editors has this to say:

Some of the comments in this report seemed to be well thought out and carefully considered replies to the question. Others (including my own) were somewhat "off the cuff" or "top of the head" in tone and merely touched lightly on various aspects of the school life and curriculum. I, personally, can think of a number of things I would add were I interviewed again. We were not asked specifically about any particular subject (I think this was intentional), and at this point I can think of quite a few questions to which I'd like the answers before I'd attempt to draw any conclusions.

Admitting the subjective and perhaps inadequate nature of the responses, we will proceed to discuss them but will not attempt to deal in percentages nor to suggest anything more than very tentative conclusions.

Nature of Proof was one of the courses most frequently mentioned by name. Over half of the men and one-third of the women interviewed mentioned it—most of them with great enthusiasm. We already know from Question 4, "Is the course 'Nature of Proof' remembered and used?", that four-fifths of the class felt that this course had been of particular value. Some typical comments: "I think Nature of Proof was one of the finest courses I ever had," "My imagination was captured," "I felt Nature of Proof was one of the strongest phases of the University School program." Only a very few "felt a lack—didn't quite grasp the type we had." The fact that after twenty years the responses to Nature of Proof are so favorable is particularly interesting because at that time it was a very radical departure from the traditional way of teaching mathematics.

There were only a few references to science, although in answering Question 1 about one-fifth indicated that they felt they didn't learn enough science. It is possible that there would have been more comment had the same question been posed in these post-Sputnik days.

It is clear that of those commenting on science, all, to a greater or lesser degree, felt that their scientific education at the University

School left something to be desired. It is interesting that the women's reactions were more detailed and constructive. The men said either, "I didn't think that I had a good enough grounding in chemistry and other sciences," or, "I would like to have had, and would like to have someone else have, a little more fundamental training in science." The women, on the other hand, suggested that

> it would be awfully nice if there were some kind of course devised, in which things could be taught which didn't involve the laboratory, but did involve the kinds of science which would fit into a woman's life; electricity, appliances, and basic principles of physics which one can do without too complicated laboratory techniques.

Another woman commented that "I think it's possible that with a different approach my imagination might have been captured. I know that it was in geometry." This woman seemed to be saying that had science been taught as imaginatively as geometry she would have derived much more from the course. Another suggestion was that the laboratory experiments might be simplified so as to illustrate the method or theory, instead of emphasizing every detail and perhaps giving the impression that the experiments were an end in themselves.

One of our six contributors to this section comments:

> I can well remember science courses at the University School and how they were taught. I can think of nothing, except for the wonderful laboratory equipment with which we had to work, in the whole science curriculum that varied from the courses that were given at other high schools. Yet only a few people commented on this phase of their education and all of the comments were derogatory. Contrast this reaction with the host of references to the benefits received from Nature of Proof, core course, and related social studies, all of which represented significant departures from the usual manner of presentation. Here we find an area which was presented in the usual manner and twenty years later it is virtually ignored. These people who were pointing toward scientific careers were given all the tools that they needed—witness the complete dearth of any but the most general criticism concerning science, and most of that by girls. I seem to remember some students taking much extra work in science in order to

prepare themselves for college, and these scientists today seem to be doing well in their fields. Those people who had no interest in science found nothing at the University School to kindle or awaken their scientific spirit. But, if science had been presented in the manner that Nature of Proof was taught, then it is possible that several of us would have had our lives changed.

Eight of the men from this class are now in scientific fields. They are following careers in pure research, applied research, teaching, engineering, and industry. So our editor's comment, that not everyone found the preparation in science inadequate, is quite true.

Comments on the language program fell into two quite different groups—those who were most enthusiastic about the program as a whole, and those who felt there was a weakness in grammar and spelling. In answering Question 1, about a third had indicated some trouble with grammar, and a smaller group had confessed to being poor spellers. It would be interesting to know how a comparable but traditionally educated group would rate themselves in these areas.

One student said:

Grammar was the weakest. Literature and drama were marvelous and couldn't be improved upon . . . more emphasis on the basic principles of English and more drill in spelling. If they're still doing it the same way, there's going to be an awful lot of kids that are going to get in college and flounder around just like I did.

Another negative comment: "I think the English department was weak in that we got very little grammar structure. That was the point that actually was the weakest of the whole program." One student felt that if the faculty had planned a little more carefully and checked their standards of student achievement against other schools' standards, they might have come up with procedures capable of helping individual students meet their individual weaknesses.

Some of these guinea pigs assume responsibility for their weaknesses, and even twenty years later are willing to state: "And in English, it's probably my own fault that I didn't learn fundamentals. Now, that may not have been the faculty's fault at all. It may have been my own." Another woman says, "For me, the languages were not as successful as some of the other areas, but that may have been my lack rather than the school's way of teaching." Still another comments in this vein: "I've already mentioned reading skills and spelling, but I feel that spelling is my own lack of ability and type of mind."

The comments on the total language program were much more favorable:

Taught us to read the papers and to analyze what we read and to find out the source. The way they taught us fact-finding is very valuable. It's not so much what facts you retain from school, it's your attitude on how to find out . . . techniques of finding out what to read and what to look for, how to use libraries and how to use books and so on.

The individual reading program was emphasized as having been of value. The thrill of learning and the thinking through of problems creatively was remembered as part of the language curriculum. To quote one student in her feeling for the language curriculum, "I thought the French was excellent . . . when I got to college my French was perfectly adequate. I could meet anybody who had been to any private school all over the country. I could compete, which I wasn't used to doing." This same woman felt that the integration of foreign languages and music was unique and successful.

Another of our ex-student editors comments:

I feel that some of these criticisms are due to the times. The same type of criticism is being made of schools throughout the country be they traditional or progressive. Parents as well as educators are clamoring for the schools to get busy and teach children the basic skills of reading, writing, and arithmetic with little thought for the development of the natural desires to learn and develop interests. From the comments in response to this question, I would say that most of us thought that our experiences at the University School were highly successful and were pleased even today with our background education. On the other hand, the suggestions for improvement were a direct contradiction to the basic philosophy of the University School. This contradiction is a very disappointing one to me. It is disappointing because we as a group are unwilling to stand behind a basic way of learning. This writer believes wholeheartedly in the University School's philosophy and is carrying it out in spite of our desires to go to the moon.

It might be added that some of the criticism may be due not only to the times but also to the age of our aging guinea pigs. Perhaps the P.T.A.–oriented parents of elementary-school children tend to be conservative on the subjects of spelling and grammar.

Among the twenty-three who commented on some phase of the social-science program, only seven had any negative criticism to make. As one might expect from the guinea-pig class, we did not completely agree even in our disagreement. Three of the women felt that the social-science program was weak in geography. One commented that she had later had a course at the university in geography in which she had learned very elementary things—"I felt rather naive." Another felt that she was weak in geography and that possibly she should have been pushed a little harder.

Two women felt that American history was slighted. One said that "many Americans are extremely lacking in knowing very much at all about their forefathers and American history," while people from foreign countries far outshine us in knowledge of their own country's history. Another student had no complaint about American history but felt that European and ancient history had been neglected. This woman suggested that there should be "more time in lectures and examinations to make sure people learned the material and . . . you would want to stress the social situation." One person felt that a little more formal history would have helped. Another stated that while he enjoyed the social-science classes and felt that he got something from them, because of the method of study where one person studied one phase of the subject while others studied another aspect, he feels he knows ". . . quite a bit about one phase of a subject and very little about others."

On the positive side, one woman felt that the areas most beneficial to her were social science and literature. She said, "Because I got a lot out of them I think they were beautifully handled, the core course and all the rest of them were just wonderful. . . . I think the whole emphasis on each student planning how to work was very valuable . . . ." There were many other favorable comments: "I thought the social-studies program really came out with something very definite. . . . I think that now you can get into political discussions, you can get into groups . . . I've never felt inadequate in any way as far as social studies go." Another student says, "I like the idea of setting up a problem and tying in the other things such as history, geography, political science. I think that is all good. I think if you see relationships . . . you get a better picture." And from yet another: ". . . for instance . . . social-science class where we all got together as a group to pick out a specific subject that we wanted to study, broke it down to definite categories . . . and then . . . chose the type of things we wanted to study and were given the freedom to compile a thesis on that particular thing."

A number of people mentioned the class trips as having been of particular value. "The trips were important, and I hope they're still having them." "Oh, the Senior trip by all means! I think that did more to help us get acquainted with each other, as a matter of fact, as well as New York . . . ." ". . . The life together and the trips we took I think were good."

Favorable comments on the social sciences outnumbered critical comments by more than two to one.

Four women commented on the home-economics program, all of them favorably: "One of the areas that I found particularly valuable was our home-economics course, and in a way it was sort of living rather than just learning how to do this and that." "And I said nothing about my home-economics course which has stood me in good stead for so long." "It was a marvelous program."

There seemed to be no doubt in the minds of the guinea pigs that the school had an unusually fine, understanding, well-trained, and hard-working group of teachers. The following comments are typical: "To me, one of the most important things was the faculty. I think the way we were taught wouldn't be possible with the ordinary faculty." "I liked the relationship between the teachers and the students." ". . . They treated the students as though they had some intelligence."

"You poor people spent so long on all of us as individuals." "I had the sense of friendship and support which I needed." "The advantage we had in University School, I think, was mainly due to the excellent teaching staff." "The key to the school is the faculty. Without the faculty, the principles would fall down."

Math, social studies, and home economics were the fields most often mentioned as having outstanding teachers. The only part of the program which seemed to bring out a negative response regarding teaching was that of science. Here it was allowed, however, that the problem was probably caused by the turnover in the staff.

One of the women summed up what seems to be the general attitude in her statement:

Of course I'm not familiar with the school as it is now. Perhaps the curriculum is the same . . . . But to me, the important thing . . . was not only the curriculum or the things you were taught and the ways in which you were taught, but . . . the people, the individual personalities with whom you had intimate contact for a matter of six years. Here again, a lot of people probably didn't need ideals or personalities to whom they could attach themselves, or want to gain something personally from observation or trying to be like them. Finding out how they thought, listening to them . . . to me that was terribly important. That's something that . . . the school today can't have because the people aren't there. I don't think they will ever be as fine.

And one of our editors comments;

I could go on quoting and summarizing the attitudes of the class to their teachers, but it would begin to sound like one of those repetitive eulogies presented dutifully by a class president at graduation. In the case of the University School, the apparent love and the friendship are genuine.

The teaching methods were also commented on frequently and favorably. One student says, "It's not so much what facts you retain from school, it's your attitude on how to find out what you want to find out." Others commented on the importance of "learning to think

rather than just memorize," "helping the students to root for themselves, to seek out the facts and draw their own conclusions," "the
feeling we had that we had some choice about our education," "the
atmosphere of freedom—college was relatively flat in contrast."

It is the comments like these which go to the heart of the discussion.
We recall not so much what we learned as how we learned it—which
means remembering a lot. We remember the pleasures of literary in-
dulgence ("I enjoyed reading, and I think that started at the University
School. I like to read still."). Most of all we know that we can think
for ourselves because that is what we were taught to do. One of the
men sums it up with: "I think that they taught me to make my own
decisions, and I think that . . . today I make the right ones."

We would like to quote the response of one of the women at some
length to give an idea of the variety of things that were remembered:

> Well I think that very definitely the co-operative ventures . . . the
> things like how we made our house a home, and working together
> . . . on the Christmas assemblies—I don't care what it is—but I
> think that is essential. And being able to get along together too, ac-
> cepting people for what they are, and not because they happen to be
> smarter than you are or for another religion, or anything of that kind.
> Although as I look back on it, possibly you made *intellectual* snobs
> out of some of us. Now if there is some way of avoiding that, I think
> it would be worth while. The main value, I think, is the fact that we
> were exposed to culture. I mean to the cultured—not culture in the
> lady-soprano sense—but we were exposed to an awful lot of things,
> and they never shoved it down our throats. Remember, they used to
> let us go down to the shows, and that was a big thing, really, as I look
> back, it was wonderful in my career. And I know people [who] went
> to those plays and got an interest in the theater that under traditional
> circumstances would have been lacking the rest of their lives. I think
> that is a very important thing. . . . I liked the relationship between
> the teachers and students. That definitely should be maintained. And
> I liked the willingness to change a situation. At that time, of course,
> we were making our own traditions, and we weren't tied to them.
> . . . I think of the things I did in high school which I had no talent
> for at all, but just loved. The painting. Where else would I have ever
> had the chance to do some of those things. . . . I had no talent, and
> yet the very fact that I was allowed—I loved that, and I understand

art today, I think, better because I participated in it, although I never would paint now.

The tone of these comments, which runs through most of the responses like a refrain, makes one feel that the group as a whole still approves of the essential values stressed at the University School. Although some may be temporarily stampeded by the "Why Johnny Can't Read" school, it looks as if the majority of them do value the basic aims of progressive education and want them for their children. As one of our editors says:

The public school my children attend has adopted lots of the techniques of progressive education but has missed some of the main points—group planning, self-direction, and integration of subject-matter. When the class studies Spain, in geography, the children learn Spanish songs and Spanish dances (which is good, I think), but the children don't have any idea why they're studying Spain. And next week it may be Sweden (perhaps its alphabetical) or Japan. At the University School when we studied Transportation we certainly knew why—and it was only chosen after much investigation, committee reports, and voting. At our local school while studying Spain in geography, the class is on song birds in science. Every one has to choose a particular bird and write a report (also borrowed from progressive education), but even to a fourth grader this combination of subjects doesn't make sense. And of course they miss out on that wonderful feeling of participation that we had.

The over-all impression that one has in reading over the responses to this question is of a widely varied group of people, bent on being individual, for the most part seriously interested in the problems of education, and well pleased with, although not complacent about, their own education at the University School.

PART III

PURPOSES OF THE UNIVERSITY SCHOOL: VALUES AND ATTITUDES

X

THE ACHIEVEMENT OF PURPOSES

Analysis of the Protocols

From the earliest stages of the follow-up, much of the planning had been concerned with ways of getting beyond the questionnaire data about further education, salaries, jobs, and so on, into the realm of values. The philosophy of the school gave a primary place to the optimum development of every individual, both intellectually and in his personal-social living. Evidence of the attainment of the intellectual objective was sought chiefly in the kinds of positions, responsibilities, and incomes which were reported by the guinea pigs; these data have been examined in Part II of this study. The final section concerns itself basically with two questions: What values are exemplified in the adult living of these men and women? Are these related to the purposes which the faculty believed gave direction to the school program?

This intellect, whose optimum development concerned us whether the potential was high or low, was assumed to be that of a person who was destined to live in a democratic society, within which the most effective use of his endowments demanded not only that he learn to direct himself and realize his potentialities, but also that he approach the problems of living creatively, with a responsible attitude toward his own development, with consideration for others, and with a sense of social responsibility. The school program, both academic and extra-curricular, had been designed to provide actual experience in living by such values within the school; and the progress reports on every individual student throughout his school years included evaluations

201

and suggestions related to this objective as well as to the student's learning of subject-matter. Had these values continued to function and develop?

Five of the purposes of the school were selected for study: (1) self-direction and self-realization; (2) creativity; (3) democratic living; (4) social sensitivity; and (5) the method of intelligence. As a means of getting at this kind of information, questionnaire responses were not promising. Long analytical essays can presumably be relied on for both direct and indirect evidence, but the possibility of drawing any conclusions would depend upon the representativeness of the sample. (For example, *The Unsilent Generation,* edited by Otto Butz, shows a great deal about the values of the eleven young men whose essays were selected for inclusion, but there is no evidence to indicate whether they speak merely for themselves, for all of Princeton, or for their generation.) In any event since the subjects of our study were all busy people in their mid-thirties scattered over the United States, essays scarcely seemed feasible. The only promising device was the interview, a technique used so successfully by Adorno and his associates in collecting data for *The Authoritarian Personality* and the other volumes in the "Studies in Prejudice" series, and by Riesman and his collaborators for *The Lonely Crowd* and *Faces in the Crowd.* Riesman's work was particularly encouraging because his interviewing methods depended upon verbatim recording by interviewers with relatively little training, who were given a schedule of questions to use and were expected to establish friendly relations with the subjects. The transcripts of these interviews could later be read as often as necessary and studied by different people to work out the analysis. Riesman's interviews were analyzed by experts, and we counted on obtaining some expert assistance to help develop our method of analysis.

The first problem was to hold the interviews. Because of the distances over which the class had scattered—Connecticut, Florida, California, the State of Washington, and points between—various sampling schemes were explored in the hope that some smaller and more accessible group might represent the whole class. All of the samples experimented with, however, had such serious weaknesses that they were abandoned. It was decided to interview at length everyone who had graduated in 1938 after attending the University School for more than two years, a total of forty-eight individuals. (See Chapter II for a description of the interview method, pp. 16–20.)

Interview questions were not aimed directly at the purposes of the school which we proposed to study. Rather, they were in the main fairly conventional and superficial questions about hobbies and recreation, uses of the mass media of communication, home and family life, civic and political participation, and attitudes on a variety of topics. The list began essentially as the one used by Riesman; and, as also happened in Riesman's study, it was modified and expanded in use. Five projective questions, originated by Adorno and also used by Riesman, were retained in a form very close to the original.

Each interview lasted from an hour and a quarter to three hours and a half, with the majority taking a little more than two hours; the protocols ranged from fifteen to forty-one typewritten pages. Three were so brief that the analysis was difficult if sole reliance was placed upon the interview; in each case, a large amount of additional information was available from earlier conversations, from informal exchange at the time of the interview, and from the questionnaire. Such supplementary data was also at hand for most of the others, but the other forty-two subjects used the questions as a starting point for thinking out loud, so that their responses revealed a great deal about their functioning value systems.

The analysis of the protocols presented great problems, not the least of which was the richness of the material. A complete study of the characterological data was not attempted because of limitations of time and skill, and because our objective was more narrowly defined. A statement of the five purposes of the school together with four protocols which represented a range of responses were submitted to Alice Seeman, who worked out some of the technical problems of analysis. Her report established categories under each purpose, noted questions in the protocol which were likely to be richest in meaning, and made practical suggestions about the most efficient ways of managing the data. From a study of her analyses and discussions with her about them, and from a study of the procedures used by Adorno and Riesman, the following method of analysis was developed.

Each protocol was read and reread by the researcher as many times as was necessary to get the feel of the interview, both the surface feeling and the overtones and undertones which sometimes had not been apparent at the time. Though the analysis was being carried out by the same person who had done the interviewing, the researcher found the study of a protocol a new experience because of simultaneous involvement and detachment, rather like watching oneself as a minor actor in an old home movie in which one is able to observe oneself in relation to others, knowing what it felt like then and seeing how it looks now. This kind of binocular view has certain advantages and possibly some dangers.

An analysis sheet was prepared for each individual, allowing space for notes and quotations under each of the five purposes, plus a sixth category "general," under which the answers to the projective questions from Adorno's list were analyzed according to his manual.[1] Statements which had a bearing, positive or negative, on one of the five purposes were noted, as were consistencies and inconsistencies. Words and statements, however, were always considered in context, and the *Gestalt* of the protocol was considered in weighing their meaning. The researcher tried to keep a sharp eye out for verbal clues, but may well have missed some that a more highly trained person might have discovered. Like Riesman, "we seldom actually got, in our interviews, anything as neat as the Freudian slip,"[2] but the quotations will show the type of indirect evidence which was found.

Each individual analysis sheet gave a fairly concrete picture of that person in relation to the school purposes. Since the study was trying to discover how well the group reflected the purposes, it was necessary to find some way of equating forty-five individuals of widely varied

[1] T. W. Adorno *et al.*, *The Authoritarian Personality* (New York: Harper and Brothers, 1950), pp. 545–79.
[2] David Riesman and Nathan Glazer, *Faces in the Crowd* (New Haven: Yale University Press, 1952), p. 15.

abilities and living-patterns. Is there one standard of self-direction and self-realization for a gifted individual and another for a handicapped one? Certainly, there must be different expectations for them as to vocation, but should our expectations differ as widely in the field of values as they do for college success or vocational achievement?

The thesis of this study is that values are exemplified in the quality of an individual's living, his relationships with people and society, his understanding of himself, and his capacity for achieving a good and satisfying life in terms of his own abilities and the welfare of others. Thus, the field which is open to a handicapped individual will be very different in size and complexity from that which is within the scope of another who is gifted, yet for each there is a field within which he directs himself or fails in self-direction, in which he is creative or rigidly conformist. The quality is the same though the field is different. This may be objected to as a rubber yardstick; such problems will be discussed in the analysis of each of the school's purposes.

Using the idea of a quality standard for every individual within his sphere of operation, the researcher rated each one on a six-point scale for each of the five purposes: (1) very high, (2) high, (3) some, (4) little, (5) very little, (6) contradictory. When the evaluations were completed, the writer examined them critically to see whether over-all subjective judgments tended to support the rating scale. There were three individuals who had been rated quite low, but who, in the writer's judgment, were functioning amazingly well in terms of their capacities; otherwise, the rating scheme seemed to work reasonably well. It shares the disadvantage of all grading systems in that a subjective weighing of the evidence and the resultant judgments are tabulated and, from that point on, masquerade as objective data. Perhaps this is not a danger if it is recognized.

While the data on values were being analyzed, another value study of far-reaching importance was published—*Changing Values in College,* by Philip Jacob. This study, sponsored by the Hazen Foundation, began "as an effort to find more reliable evidence concerning the outcomes of teaching general education courses in the social sciences."[3] It developed into a large scale study and analysis of the findings of an amazing number of research projects, and came out with the major conclusion that, although values do change in college, courses, instructors and methods usually have little to do with the change. ". . . College has a socializing rather than a liberalizing impact on values. . . . Most students remain fundamentally the same persons, with the same *basic value-judgments.*"[4]

Most of the research studies analyzed by Jacob used a number of well-established instruments such as the American Council on Education "Inventory of Beliefs" and the Allport-Vernon "Study of Values." Because of the nature of the study, it did not need to, and in fact could not, carry through beyond the experience in college to determine the persistance of values, or to note the appearance of delayed-action effects except in rare instances. These differences, in addition to the fact that our study is concerned with high-school rather than college experience, make close comparisons of findings impossible.

However, in the rare cases in which Jacob finds that college experiences produced significant changes in values, they are attributed by him to (1) normal and frequent association of students and faculty, (2) a climate of values created by certain institutions, and (3) "value laden personal experiences of students imaginatively integrated with their intellectual development." He also found an intimate relationship between a student's personality and his ability to reorient his values. As a partial explanation of the differences between institutions, he notes that students tend to select colleges and colleges to select students in terms of expectations. The possible relevance of these conclusions to our findings will be discussed in the last chapter, "General Comments and Conclusions."

[3] Jacob, *Changing Values in College* (New York: Harper and Brothers, 1957), p. vii.
[4] *Ibid.*, p. 53.

SELF-DIRECTION AND SELF-REALIZATION

The Philosophy and Purposes of the University School contains the following statement about self-direction in the school program:

> . . . All experiences should be such as to aid in the process of "growing up," by which is meant the gradual development of mature relationships with others, that is, the cultivation of a growing sense of responsibility for one's own development in the light of a consistent set of values.[5]

In pursuance of this objective, the school expected from each individual student a rising level of responsible self-direction and independence in his work and in his behavior. In the relations of teachers and students, and of students to each other and to their own education, there was consistent emphasis upon the responsibility of every individual to set his goals and to work toward them. The use of teacher-pupil planning, the progress reports which took the place of report cards,[6] group discussions of problems, and conferences between teachers and individual students all played a part. Among the insights contributed by the interviews was an understanding, more than twenty years later, of the reason why one particular, well-remembered conference had been outstandingly effective.

> Well, here again it's case law rather than code law. In my own experience, I am sure, I can remember very well the first year at University School, my ninth year; I had come out of a formal education system, had been transplanted in the year preceding, had lost a father, and I was very much at sea; and I think that the freedom, relative freedom, at the school was something which I abused considerably. In

[5] P. 10.
[6] See Chapter XI of *Were We Guinea Pigs?* (New York: Henry Holt and Company, 1938), by the Class of 1938.

207

fact, I remember an interview which you and Miss LaBrant had with me, that was very important to me. [I wanted to ask you whether you remember that.] Oh, so well! But there was so much acceptance that I could then, having faced the freedom which had been given me, I could accept the fact that here was a responsibility, too, and it was up to me to do something about the school and my adjustment to it. For me, it was wonderful.

It was great therapy and I feel that progress was probably slow from the standpoint of the teachers, but I feel it was one of the best things that ever happened to me. I could not take—I was too rebellious to take a too strict and too formal education, and I had to learn how to live with freedom; and when I did, I'm sure I made a much better adjustment than I would have made in an orthodox, formal education system.

In evaluating self-direction and self-realization in these people as adults, three main categories were considered: (1) faith in capacity, (2) clarity of purpose, (3) independence. Although all are intimately related, the evidence sought for each may be distinguished.

Faith in capacity refers to the individual's picture of himself. A person of limited ability who recognizes his limitations, but also knows the areas in which he realizes his best results and so directs his life that he has achievements in which he can take pride, may rate very high in this category. So may a gifted individual who knows and enjoys the vastly greater achievements which are open to him, or a handicapped one who has learned to make a satisfying life within the limits of his handicap. Men or women on any level of ability whose picture of themselves is one of failure, inferiority, or lack of skill would rate low. Basic to this category is the belief that every individual has some abilities, some interests, and some limitations, and that his own self-realization requires that he understand them and have faith in his own ability to reach satisfying levels of achievement in fields which are important to him.

Clarity of purpose is closely related to faith in capacity, but is more dynamic. The extent to which an individual makes his decisions and choices in terms of self-understanding and an accurate appraisal of interests and capacities is essential in this category. The man or woman whose conflicting decisions cancel each other would rate low, as would the one who is almost incapable of making decisions. Clarity of purpose does not mean that an individual must have complete singleness of purpose or driving ambition. Those who rate high in this category know what they value, and can recognize its implications for both specific behavior and long-term plans.

Independence shows, or fails to show, itself in a multitude of different ways. The very language of the response in any interview shows

TABLE 55

SELF-DIRECTION AND SELF-REALIZATION

RATING	QUINTILE					TOTAL
	I	II	III	IV	V	
Very high	6	3	6	2	2	19
High	2	1	4	5	3	15
Some	...	1	1	1	1	4
Little	...	...	...	...	2	2
Very little	...	...	...	...	...	....
Contradictory	1	4	...	...	...	5
Total	9	9	11	8	8	45

the spirit in which the individual approached the interview, whether he sought to give acceptable responses, or spontaneous and honest ones. The wide range of rather conventional-sounding questions gave many opportunities for answering in clichés, or for thinking out loud along whatever lines of association occurred to the individual. Independence is also revealed in the freedom with which an individual appraises situations and directs himself toward his own goals. In this sense, it is closely related to creativity and the method of intelligence, which will be discussed later.

The summary of the individual ratings on self-direction and self-realization is given in Table 55. Thirty-four of the men and women were in the high or very high classification; and none showed up so badly as to be rated at the bottom in the "very little" classification.

Five were rated "contradictory," a category reserved for those who, on the basis of responses in different parts of their protocols, could have been given very different ratings.

It is interesting that all five of those who were rated "contradictory" were in the two top quintiles, whereas four of the six who were rated "some" or "little" were in the two lowest quintiles. In the upper quintiles the evidence tended to be positive, so that an inconsistent individual showed clearly both his successes and his failures in self-direction. In the lower quintiles the chief evidence of failure was apt to be the lack of evidence of success; in these protocols the positive indications of self-direction, when they did occur, did not present such obvious inconsistencies. However, the fact that five times as many women as men showed inconsistencies may be significant. An analysis of a few selected protocols will illustrate the kinds of data on which judgments were based.

The first is that of one of the most intellectually capable members of the class. In high school his interests were mainly bookish, and his level of interpersonal social skills was low—he continued a small boy's disregard for cleanliness, grooming, and manners long after the other boys had begun dating, and on one occasion appeared at a dance in tennis shoes and with a chess board. (It is probably significant, however, that he came to the dance at all.) He had a very deep allegiance to large-scale social values, but was indifferent in a benevolently impersonal way to most of the individuals about him. His classmates tolerated his idiosyncrasies and admired his ability; his teachers recognized and fostered his great gifts and tried to help him learn the give-and-take of a social group.

He is now a professor in a field of science at a large state university, is listed in *American Men of Science,* and is called upon to present research papers at international conferences. He is married, and he and his wife and three children have a charming home and garden, and a pleasant social life with friends and neighbors as well as a very warm and satisfying home life. The change raises some very interesting questions about conformity, which are illuminated by many of the same answers which show self-direction.

When asked whether he felt the school had slighted traditional American values, he gave the following reply:

> I would like to comment—perhaps on school, perhaps more on my family background—on not feeling a part of the main currents of the American scene, on feeling a part of the intellectual group which was rather isolated from the main tendencies in American life. Perhaps this opinion was justified. I am not sure it was justified intellectually, but it was not good emotionally.

He commented on changes in attitudes which had occurred in growing up:

> One major change is a greater interest in people as individuals. This change probably started roughly at the time of my marriage twelve years ago. Another change has been the de-emphasis on the importance of being an "intellectual." I substitute for this (1) a professional competence through some superiority in a narrowly limited field, and (2) various non-intellectual pleasures. This has resulted partly from eye difficulties which limit reading, partly from interest in wife and family, while being an adequate and competent worker in a field removes most of the drive for showing off. Along with this, I have taken a less dogmatic attitude on political problems. I believe U. High did work on me in this regard, though the change took place much later.

On the basis of his answers to questions on how he is bringing up his children, it is reasonable to assume that he is distilling the essence of his own experiences as they now appear to him. When asked, "What things do you try to instill in your children?", he replied as follows:

> Good manners! But also being able to have a good time, both with others and in some activity by themselves. We try to stand firm against southern racial prejudices, though not to the point of bringing up the issue or making the children feel particularly different or righteous.

"What plans and ambitions do you have for your sons and daughter?"

That they find something interesting and worthwhile to do—
"worthwhile" is so ambiguous—something interesting they think is
worthwhile—no, I'll go back to the first.

Questions about ambition and about happiness elicited comments
which showed clarity of purpose.

Ambition, tempered with realism about one's abilities, can lead to a
very happy life.

Happiness is very important, and my happiness is closely connected
with other important things such as having happy times with family
and friends, doing a good job at work, and doing what one can on
social problems.

His attitudes toward his job, his place in the academic and the
broader community, and his social life gave a consistent picture of a
man who is directing himself with confidence and with a high level
of self-realization.

I like both the opportunity to learn and to do research myself and
the opportunities to help others learn. I don't like having to deal with
poor and uninterested students. I also don't like the rather great com-
petitiveness in research in my field . . . .

Most important in my future are: (1) A moderate amount of fame
and associated respect, though I do not expect to be really great or
famous in my work. (2) Self-respect and respect of friends for doing
a good job, even if not a great one. (3) Some money for luxuries.
(4) Having a good time with wife and family and friends.

Throughout the protocol, it is obvious that his wife has been a
major element in bringing warmth and happy human relationships to
him to round out his intellectual self-realization. The choice of marriage partner appears in many cases in this study to have been of
critical importance in the later development of the individual, a statement which is doubtless a truism. One can only note in passing that
marriage is not a grab bag, and that a successful marriage depends
far more on the qualities in the individual that led him to make a
particular choice than it does on chance.

There are many more quotable answers in this particular protocol, and the whole tone of the interview was consistent. This man ranked very high in all categories of self-direction and self-realization. The evidence is strong that as a high-school boy he was conforming to his stereotype of the "intellectual" and the "liberal," and that as an adult the change toward an appreciation of the amenities of life represents freedom and autonomy, not conformity.

Another man who has achieved distinction in his profession, and who has developed some unusual hobbies into almost a second profession, was ranked as contradictory. His protocol gave a picture of self-direction and self-realization which was consistently very high except for one area—he felt very unsure of himself in any business dealings; adult experiences in making major financial decisions seem to have added to his distrust of himself in this area.

A man who was near the middle of the class on the various indicators of academic promise is now a successful industrial executive. His protocol showed a very high degree of self-understanding, self-confidence, and self-realization. When asked whether he had found any deficiencies in the teaching of subject-matter in high school, he remarked easily that his wife kids him about not knowing history, but that he hasn't felt it a serious lack.

> My interest really has been in other fields, so perhaps had I been exposed to a more conventional forced-study technique, with examinations out of history books as such, why I probably still wouldn't have retained very much of it, because I wasn't as interested in that as I have been all along in mechanical things.

He evaluated the school program in the following way:

> The first thing that comes to my mind is this business of teaching or helping the students to root for themselves a little bit—that is, to seek out the facts and draw their own conclusions from those facts. . . . Funny thing I've often recalled since, Mr. Moore, in Industrial Arts, was a stickler for drawing a plan before we started a project. And I have quoted him a number of times since in talking to other people; and I have been reminded a number of times since that I have been off base where I had not sufficiently planned what was

about to take place. I think it's very desirable to instill in students, whether they go toward the profession that I have or whatever field, that they know how to seek out facts, draw their own conclusions, and plan what they're going to do, and to think logically.

He answered the question as to whether men or women have an easier time as follows:

Some people can make a very easy life seem very difficult, and some can make a very difficult life seem very easy. My work in industry has involved so much personnel or human relations, conversations, counseling, and trying to determine what the deuce to do about this fellow who can't work with that fellow, but I am just more convinced every day that if people can get the right viewpoint on life, why problems are not so great.

When asked if he wished he had more ambition, he answered in an easy, good-humored manner:

I wish I had more ability. [Laughs.] Ambition—to me that means a drive to do something, and I think I have the ambition, but I don't have the ability. [Laughs.] So the decision is to keep on tryin'.

He made the following comment on getting ahead in life:

I would take hard work first, and brains next, and good personality third, education fourth. Patience has got to be there, too, and good connections might help get a foot in the door, but no further than that. And luck, I think there is a lot of luck in getting ahead. I mean some people just happen to be placed in a situation that they fortunately are able to handle, and can progress ahead much faster than the next fellow. That doesn't mean the ability is greater; it is just chance, that the opening occurred, the individual was there, he saw the opportunity, and stepped in and really worked on it.

From such quotations and an abundance of other evidence, all of it consistent, it is evident that this man has an accurate appraisal of and a great deal of faith in his own capacity, and that he has clear purposes and independence in working toward them.

The kind of statement which caused individuals to be rated "little" may be illustrated by the following. It comes from a man of limited academic ability, who has not married. He is doing quite well in a routine white-collar job, is active in his church, and makes an excellent appearance. But he says,

> I myself think I don't have too much of a chance of getting ahead you might say. . . . I always like to go forward, I hate to go back. I hate to think I'm going backwards, I'm slipping. I think I try to do the best I can.

Another man given the rating "little," who seemed emotionally blocked during all his high-school years and who still seems so, has nevertheless established a home and, through his affection and concern for his wife and family, has a measure of purpose. However, he wonders what the purpose of life is; he always has difficulty deciding what is right and what is wrong, and is always in doubt. He reported that nothing yet has given him a sense of personal worth and achievement; he believed his worst characteristic was that he does not have much strength of character, and his best that he can love and be kind to and understand people. The small amount of self-direction and self-realization which he has attained seems totally dependent upon his marriage, though there is a kind of independence in his discouraged search for answers.

Of the twenty-two women who were interviewed, twenty-one are married and seventeen have children. Hence, their patterns of self-direction and self-realization have been worked out in most cases within the role of the mother and homemaker, though illustrations will also be given of those who have no children. Mothers of families often gave their most revealing answers in reponse to questions about their children. The statements of a woman who had been a leader in high school, and who was rated "very high" in self-direction and self-realization, both academically and socially, serve as a good illustration. When asked, "What things do you try to instill in your children?", she made the following reply:

Well, independence from each other and their parents as well as dependence upon the family—loyalty to the family as a group and individuals. The idea that one can be unique and independent—the idea of individual worth, that all people, black, red, or yellow, are equal and fine to be friends with. Appreciation of money, so they learn to spend wisely but not overvalue it—that some have lots and others little, but that doesn't alter the value of the individuals. Appreciation of the ideas of others, face to face as well as in books. I try to teach them that breakfast is the most important meal of the day. [Laughs.]

On plans and ambitions for her children:

I hope my daughters will be happily married and my sons the same. I hope they will find satisfactions in work.

On differences in parental ideas about bringing up children:

My husband is more strict; it is a matter primarily of his tension and fatigue. He thinks I have had more experience, so he will do what I think is best. He would be much more cautious about freedom and independence than I am. [She then told how she taught the children safety rules, and then let them ride bicycles to school, though many people were afraid of the traffic.]

"What do you like most, and what do you like least, about being a homemaker?"

My time is my own—[laughs]; but at least I don't have to do something at 9:00, 10:00, and 11:00. It is a very creative life; one can see evidence of one's handiwork in material ways and in the development of the family.

I wouldn't say [what she liked least]. One thing is that I don't have freedom to say "yes" to Girl Scouts, Sunday school, etc. What I like least is that I'm too tired to do well the things I do.

Asked how and why she got into outside activities and whether she ever refused to do things she was asked to do, she gave the following responses:

I like to do things outside. I get a real lift out of getting out of my own family and seeing how the rest of the world lives. Also I feel I have a responsibility outside the family to the community.

I enjoy participating in any size groups, where my husband doesn't have any feeling for people or thinking with them. I'm not a group leader any more, but in feeling with a group, getting their ideas, and being able to understand them—that ability was cultivated at University School.

I definitely do refuse to do the things I am asked most of the time. My first responsibility is my family and I don't have enough energy to devote much of it to other things.

"What do you think is most important in your future—money, fame, the respect of your community, something else, or don't you know?"

The love and respect of one's family are the most important; the respect of the community is fine. Money and fame are immaterial. Inner satisfactions are very important; one can live a wonderful life without anyone else knowing about it.

"Is ambition something you admire in other people?"

Yes, to a certain extent. I do not admire it for itself; it depends on how the person uses it. In the test, it needs to be qualified in the person with other qualities such as humility. I guess I admire it where people use it to better the world or help others rather than for their own gain. Ambition to be a creative artist—yes; to make a lot of money—no.

"Do you wish you had more ambition yourself?"

I'm kind of happy the way I am, but there are times when being more ambitious would be helpful. I want my children to be ambitious—I don't want them to be lazy, but I don't want them to be President or the *best* tennis player.

"Do you think that, on the whole, ambitious people have happier lives than unambitious ones?"

Yes, definitely. You have to have something to point to, a goal, and that is what ambition is. The happiness seems to me to depend on the kind of goal.

These quotations give the tone of the whole protocol. This woman gets very tired, finds herself cut off from much of the community participation that she enjoys, and has had to give up her art, her music, and many other personal interests. But she is finding tremendous satisfaction in her job of homemaking and child rearing; her purposes are clear, and she is meeting daily experiences with confidence and independence. She is able to meet the challenges without self-doubt or confusion.

Another woman, who is married but childless, was also rated very high in self-direction and self-realization. She had had a very unhappy childhood, dominated by a mother who tried to realize her own frustrated ambitions through her daughter. Only a job away from home some years after college enabled her to achieve independence, and she worked for several years before she married. She was very explicit about the role of the school in helping her formulate her goals and objectives, though she wished the teachers had helped her specifically toward an understanding of her home situation.

When asked, "Do you consider that you and your husband have a pretty democratic relationship?", she made the following reply:

There is only one thing I want in our home, and that's all the things that my other home didn't have, and I'll work the rest of my life to make it that way. Above board, with privacy, respect, all the warmth, and giving, not taking. I like to have our home be a comfortable, warm, friendly place, and a place that both of us are awfully, awfully happy to come home to, whether it's from work, or from vacation, or what. That's all I want to furnish in our house, and I think we have it.

In response to a question about her jobs, she gave extensive information about the various positions she has held since graduating from college, ending as follows:

I went into it when I came down here, and then headed up the research department for the Air Force Museum program, and I liked this too. Then for the first fiscal year of Air Force recruiting, I was special advisor to the commanding general for publicity and advertising, wrote all his speeches, monitored the whole program. Now—then I retired [laughs] last October, but they've called, I think, about four times now from the field and have offered me a job back in the Air Force Historical Properties program, and I don't see how I can possibly turn it down. I think I'm going back to work after the shortest retirement in history. [Laughs.] [Is it the interest of the work chiefly? How important has it become to you to have your own paycheck?] You know, that's one reason I quit last fall, because I didn't know how important it was; and I quit work completely with the thought in mind that I would never go back, just to see how important it was. The first couple of weeks it was terribly important, and then it became completely unimportant, and my husband showed me that it was terribly unimportant. See, what we do, any money that I make is either—I mean I spend it for lollipops or groceries or savings account or anything, but I'm not allowed to contribute anything to our living. If I want to save it, all right, if I want to spend it, all right, but it has to be spent on something that doesn't contribute to our home. That's his job, and he has encouraged my going back [to work] because a golf professional's hours, particularly during the summer months, and that's about eight months of the year, are just desperate. He may leave at seven in the morning, and we may not have dinner until eleven at night; and if you sit and look at four walls for three-quarters of your waking hours, you can get pretty dull and pretty sloppy in your way of thinking; and I think it's nice to keep sharp, and have contact with other people, and golly, I can't stand it over a back fence. It's got to be something a little bit more challenging than that. [Laughs.]

Her answers to questions about ambition and about happiness were very revealing. "Do you wish you had more ambition yourself?"

I wish I had a little less, because it drives me sometimes. Not an aggressive sort of thing, but it's an ambition to—I don't know what it is that I'm ambitious to do, but I'm just ambitious. Whatever I'm doing, I like to do it as well as I can.

"Do you think that, on the whole, ambitious people have happier lives than unambitious ones?"

Well, it depends. If you're ambitious and you don't do anything about it—for years I was, and I didn't. I was completely and totally frustrated because, as I told you at luncheon, I didn't know where the edge of the earth was, whether it was the outskirts of Columbus or whether it stopped at the state boundary in Ohio, or just how far it went. It was terribly necessary to me to get out and find out, just to see how big it was and how many people there were and how many situations and how many opportunities, and in so doing I was satisfied somehow. If you're ambitious and don't have that opportunity, it could be destructive; but if you're ambitious and have it, it's a wonderful thing, it's exhilarating—like standing in the wind—you know, a fresh feeling.

In the protocols of three of the women, there was evidence of a fairly high degree of self-direction which operated in a relatively narrow area. These were the individuals who placidly accepted their roles as wives, mothers, and community members, managed their affairs competently, and seemed to have no thought of any other possible roles for themselves.

Three of the women showed contradictory tendencies in this category, in each case because of a self-image which could not be completely reconciled with the domestic role which she found herself playing. The evidence indicates that each has been handling her life with a fair degree of success, but probably with a heavy cost in nervous fatigue. A fourth woman showed some inconsistencies, but since she is thoughtfully working them out, and is demonstrating considerable self-direction and understanding in the process, she cannot be rated "contradictory."

The frequent voluntary references in the interviews to the encouragement of individual initiative and responsibility at University School are indications that such aspects of the program contributed to the surprisingly consistent result in this part of the analysis—thirty-four out of forty-five individuals were ranked "high" or "very high" in self-direction and self-realization.

CREATIVITY

Creativity, as used in this section, is a broad term which denotes a spontaneous, expressive, inquiring reaction toward living. A creative individual maintains a fresh and clear-eyed view of his relationship with others and with events and objects in his world. He is interested in exploring ideas and in reaching out into new fields. He works within routines and institutions, but understands that they are created by human beings to serve human ends, and therefore must be subject to change. The new, untried, and deviant proposal is, by its nature, interesting and challenging and worthy of examination, though not necessarily of acceptance. To him, the new is not threatening and subversive because of its newness, though he knows that examination will frequently prove it unsound.

It will be immediately apparent that creativity in this sense is not sharply divided from self-direction and self-realization, which has been examined in the previous section, nor from the method of intelligence, which will be discussed later. It is the spontaneous nature of creativity which in the main distinguishes it, the explorativeness, the avoidance of clichés, the playing with ideas, the pleasure in discovering novel but satisfactory solutions to problems.

Most experts agree that young children are spontaneous, curious, and creative. However, somewhere along the way something tends to stifle the explorativeness of youth. In a recent review of a children's art show which he considered highly creative, Meyer Levin wrote, "One could sense the creeping conservatism of the older age groups up to 14, the very end of childhood. The forms and concepts became more and more commonplace." [7]

[7] "Children's Imaginations Run Riot," *Columbus Citizen,* July 6, 1958, Sec. B, p. 3.

Colleges are frequently disturbed about a lack of curiosity and imagination among their students. A small minority of the most extreme cases are described by Jacob as follows:

> Some students have a set of mind so rigid, an outlook on human relations so stereotyped and a reliance on authority so compulsive that they are intellectually and emotionally incapable of understanding new ideas, and seeing, much less accepting, educational implications which run counter to their pre-conceptions. This particularly limits their responsiveness in the social sciences and the humanities whenever controversial issues arise. Such students quail in the presence of conflict and uncertainty. They crave "right answers." They distrust speculative thought, their own or their fellow students'. They recoil from "creative discussion." [8]

Massachusetts Institute of Technology has received a great deal of attention because of a course which has been introduced for engineers to stimulate them to think in more creative ways about engineering problems.

There is no agreement among educators as to whether the loss of creativity is a natural result of the acculturation of a growing individual, whether it results from something in the education of children, or whether it arises from a combination of factors. Eric Fromm believes that society, not the school alone, is the agent which enforces conformity through the suppression of spontaneous feelings.

> It is important to consider how our culture fosters this tendency to conform, even though there is space for only a few outstanding examples. The suppression of spontaneous feelings, and thereby of the development of genuine individuality, starts very early, as a matter of fact with the earliest training of a child. This is not to say that training must inevitably lead to suppression of spontaneity if the real aim of education is to further the inner independence and individuality of the child, its growth and integrity. The restrictions which such a kind of education may have to impose upon the growing child are only transitory measures that really support the process of growth and expansion. In our culture, however, education too often results in the

8 Jacob, op. cit., p. 10.

elimination of spontaneity and in the substitution of original psychic acts by superimposed feelings, thoughts, and wishes. . . .[9]

The University School believes that one important cause of the loss of spontaneity may be an emphasis in the educational process on "right" answers and "right" ways of doing everything. Absorbing authoritative information about a great many things can be and sometimes is the whole curriculum of a school and, for many people, the meaning of "education." In *The Philosophy and Purposes of the University School,* the following belief is stated:

> . . . So far as possible, the school should provide experiences which demand novel adjustments to situations rather than those which emphasize routine and repetition. Good citizenship calls for individuals who have the ability to synthesize elements of experience that are seemingly unrelated into unified wholes. Such experiments are not confined solely to the arts but should characterize every area of school life.[10]

Teachers in all areas tried to take this responsibility seriously, by handling the children's ideas with respect while encouraging careful examination of them, by fostering individual initiative and responsibility, and by using the children's interests and curiosities as a starting point for many phases of the work. The students themselves noted one aspect of the emphasis on creativity in the book which they wrote in their senior year.

> . . . Student-teacher planning has been a valuable experience, and has proved very successful. It has stimulated us to think about a problem more carefully, and has made us more interested in our work. We have never had the feeling of having education handed to us all ready to be absorbed, but have been stimulated to the desire to learn, discover things in our own way, and think for ourselves.[11]

[9] *Escape from Freedom* (New York: Holt, Rinehart and Winston, Inc., 1941), pp. 241–42.
[10] P. 10.
[11] *Were We Guinea Pigs?* (New York: Henry Holt and Company, Inc., 1938), p. 296.

During the six years that many of the members of the Class of 1938 were in University School, the teachers found enormous differences in responses within the group. A few students were fairly consistently and persistently unimaginative and pedestrian year by year, whereas a larger number were highly creative. In general, the class respected creativity, and, as seniors, had a high level of confidence in themselves and in each other, as demonstrated by their undertaking and completing the writing of *Were We Guinea Pigs?*

TABLE 56

CREATIVITY

| RATING | QUINTILE | | | | | | | | | | TOTAL | |
| | I | | II | | III | | IV | | V | | | |
	Men	Women	Men	Women	Men	Women	Men	Women	Men	Women	Men	Women
Very high...	2	2	..	3	1	2	1	..	1	1	5	8
High....	2	2	1	1	2	2	1	..	1	..	7	5
Some....	..	1	2	2	2	1	3	1	..	1	7	6
Little....	..	..	..	..	..	1	1	1	2	1	3	3
Very little...	..	..	..	..	..	..	..	..	1	..	1	..
Total..	4	5	3	6	5	6	6	2	5	3	23	22

Table 56 shows the distribution of the forty-five class members on the basis of responses during the extensive interviews. Thirteen, or nearly one-third, ranked "very high," twelve "high," thirteen "some," and only seven "little" or "very little." Although no comparisons with other groups are available, it is probable that this is unusually high for any group.

In order to assign individuals to the various levels, only those whose protocols showed clear and fairly consistent evidence of creativity in total outlook were rated "very high." Similar evidence, with a lapse in one important area or perhaps two less important ones, constituted high creativity. Those rated "some" were (1) individuals who showed high creativity in a few areas, but uncritical conformism in others, and (2) individuals who gave lukewarm evidence of cautious creativity.

Those rated "little" showed some creativity but put a high value on conformity, whereas the one person who was rated "very little" showed rather consistent conformity and almost no positive evidence of creativity.

As will be clear from the above discussion, contradictions and inconsistencies in this category were averaged out. This had the odd effect of assigning two of the most highly creative people in the group to the average ("some") rating because of the relatively narrow range within which the quality operated in their lives.

The evidences of creativity upon which the tabulations in Table 56 were based were scattered through each protocol, not always in the expected places. One type of evidence which was used was the extent to which the responses contained clichés or were rich with imaginative twists. Examples of this type of evidence are given in the following three quotations, the first two from women, the third from a man:

Question: If you knew you had only six months to live, but could do just as you pleased during that period, how would you spend the time?

Answer: Well, I think I would just do what I'm doing, unless I would take my children traveling. They might travel after I was gone; but I want them to see the country and the world, and it would be fun to do it with them.

Question: On the whole do you think that you had a pretty good break in your own upbringing?

Answer: Oh, I suppose I do now. I sure fought it when I was being upbrought. [Laughing.]

Question: If you had your choice as to when you would be born, would you have preferred to live in some other age than this?

Answer: No, I think the only regret I have is I would like to—well, I would like to live longer than I know I'm going to live. Because so many things are going on. I know what has happened. I don't know what's going to happen. There is a security problem, that if I lived before I'd know I wasn't going to be blown up by an atom bomb someday. There is this uncertainty; but I guess from all I've read that there have been uncertainties of all sorts all the way through the ages, and there probably isn't any difference. I'm happy the way I am. I've got lots of interesting things to do now.

Among the questions which frequently revealed the extent to which individuals valued creativity were those which concerned their children. The three following illustrations are from different protocols, the first two from women, one with two children and the other with three between six and ten years of age, the last from a man with three children, the oldest aged three and a half.

Question: What plans and ambitions do you have for your sons?

Answer: To be happy, and to be happy in what they are doing, to do something within their own ability, to be fortunate in choosing a nice wife if they care to be married, and I think be able to do creative things.

Question: What aspects of bringing up your children do you enjoy or find challenging?

Answer: Oh, explaining things that are very difficult for them to understand. It's very hard; you find the questions they ask are so far reaching and you think you have it all figured out and then you get— it's so difficult to explain it at their level, but it's fascinating. And encouraging them in this creative work—I thoroughly enjoy the interpretations of their art work. I have just gotten hysterical over this middle girl's drawings. I'll have to show them to you.

It's hard to make them believe in things and people and then have to also develop cautiousness about strangers and the realities, the things that occur. It's very difficult to hit a happy medium there. I enjoy the naïveté in them so much, and I just dread tearing down these illusions. [Laughs.]

Answer: Oh, I think just being with them, and—oh, the whole thing is so tremendous that—Gosh sakes alive! I like to take these guys [aged one and a half and three and a half] with me pretty near every Saturday. We'll take off for a half day anyway, sometimes more, and we go to the tractor shop, and we get things that are needed for the house, and just get out and get away. I love to hear them talk, and I love to hear them express ideas.—It's just fascinating, I think, to see those little guys come up with perfectly startling ideas, and that's the most fascinating angle of it to me, of having children around.

Another important aspect of creativity is the reaction of the individual to the new, the untried, the deviate. A member of the class who has risen rapidly to a highly responsible position in the engineering-development side of the communications industry put a finger on the problem very accurately from the industrial viewpoint:

Well, the type of work that I do, a great part of it is sort of a creative type of thinking—that's when we get our best engineering. If you get people that have the inability to "free think," in a sense, in our type of work, you don't have new ideas, you don't get new concepts; and you find that from those individuals who can run free, you do get new ideas.

Another member of the group, a businessman, who holds a responsible position in a large retail organization, saw the same problem in his field:

In our social-science class, for instance, we were given quite a range of freedom there with definite responsibilities for accomplishing something, the same thing that we do right now, or I do on my job. I'm given a lot of room, but I have to make up my mind and form my outline and arrive at decisions and accomplish certain things.

The minister in the group, who has had training in social work and psychiatry, and who works with a council of churches, made the following comment which exhibited this aspect of creativity:

Then after finishing seminary, I had experience in a couple of churches and received, we call it a "call," to the Council of Churches up in northeastern Michigan, Bay City, a city of about 55,000. There they were looking for a man who would be an executive of their Council of Churches and also give half time to what was known as co-ordination, liaison, or referral work between the social agencies in the community. Now this seemed a natural to me, and I couldn't pass it up because it did combine some of the factors that had been present in the high-school training itself, the social-work training, the ministry, and then the psychiatric side; and I've had a *wonderful* time ever since that. I enjoy this work more than the parish. I miss some of the personal contacts of the parish and I miss the youth work which I did in local churches; but I feel like I'm on a frontier, and this is exciting to me because my interest in this *rapprochement* between psychiatry and religion continues strong and keen and occupies some of my reading. I've incorporated into the Council of Churches in Michigan and then again here in Albany courses for clergy on coming to grips with this, learning something, becoming more effective pastors in their counseling work; and I find it very exciting. Also from the standpoint of the Protestant churches, Protestant and orthodox churches, it's exciting because they are experiencing a coming-to-gether, and, therefore, it has a lot of dynamic quality which appeals.

Among the women with families, many indicated a willingness to consider novel solutions to problems and a good deal of satisfaction from working them out in individually creative ways. Most of these answers are scattered, and extensive quotation would be required to develop them. Perhaps one may be representative. The woman in this quotation, who is analyzing her own operations as a parent, had been left an orphan and brought up by older sisters; she now has three children of her own.

I grew up in a girl's family, [in] a typical, I would say almost Victorian, way, because you see those sisters were almost a generation apart. And then my mother was fairly old when they were born, so they had that kind of an upbringing and probably passed some of that on to me. It was a very girlish kind of a family, whereas now with the boys I am not sure that I'm too good. There are a lot of things—soldering irons and radios, wires all over the bedroom, little clips and pins and needles, boats and glue. Not that that sort of thing bothers me; we don't keep a museum here at home, and the house is just sort of a working laboratory; but still I'm not sure I'm too good at it. I need more experience, more of a rough and ready kind of living.

And I think I keep them a little too close. I tend to keep our oldest boy a little too close to me. He wanted to go downtown alone when he was ten and we thought that was too young, and I bet I was downtown when I was ten. The towns are bigger, and living in a suburb as we do, you think of it as complete within itself; but the child does want to go out and look things over while they're away from home.

I'm questioning a lot of things right now, in the last four to five years, that I just didn't question before. I think it's maybe the thirties and maybe—I don't know what it is. I mean when you have a teen-ager I think you stop and look around a little bit.

The question which most consistently produced evidence of creativity, as well as social sensitivity, was the following: "What kinds of activities and experiences give you the greatest sense of personal worth and achievement?"

From a research scientist:

1. Satisfactory, close personal relationships with another person or persons.
2. Having the abilities and judgments of your own, and in which you have confidence, be[ing] effective in affecting the actions of groups of people. This is the "good" aspect of the power drive.

From an artist and teacher of art:

Well, in my own work when you get a student who comes to you with a problem and not interested in anything—if you can get him interested in school and start him out there, it gives you a great sense of satisfaction. You really feel like you have accomplished something. I expect I get more accomplishment in relationship to society as a whole from that. Now personal achievement—I think if I do a piece of painting or sculpture, and it turns out well and a few people recognize it, particularly people you admire their opinion, they recognize it, then it gives me a very personal satisfaction which is terrific.

From a homemaker who had held an important administrative-supervisory job before marriage:

Well, I think bringing up children is one of the most satisfying, or educating them. Now at this late point, I almost wish I had been a teacher. I think it would be such a source of satisfaction working with young people. Or any kind of job, especially a difficult job, one where it is difficult to work with people—if I am successful in working it through, it makes me feel good even though there is no credit involved; I don't really care about credit, but I like to see a job well done and done without hurting people's feelings; and if it can be done smoothly like that, that gives me a source of satisfaction.

From a homemaker who had been an art teacher before her marriage:

Having children. [Laughing.] In the future, I plan to go back to painting and writing and teaching.

From another homemaker:

I felt that I was contributing something to society when I helped out at this nursery for these underprivileged children. I felt that seeing a different, interested face—someone different than the regular teachers—meant a lot to them, and they were all from underprivileged and broken homes. I get a great deal of personal satisfaction in working in my garden, and creating works of art, and seeing things grow and raising good sweet corn; and I get satisfaction from having a nice home and keeping it up. Not the day to day keeping it up, but the over-all picture. And naturally, a great deal of satisfaction from seeing our family growing from day to day.

The typical answer resembles those quoted—a combination of creative satisfactions, interest in helping other people, and enjoyment of warm family relations. A few mentioned only one of these, but in terms which show creative satisfactions. Two answers from men, however, mentioned only job success in highly conventional terms—more orders, from a salesman; "a good day at the office," from a clerical worker. Another man answered only, "I haven't found any yet."

In conclusion it may be noted that a high proportion of these men and women appear to approach life with freshness, zest, and confidence in the possibility of solutions. There are no data from other groups with which the Class of 1938 can be compared; however, the proportion who are creative seems to be high, though not so consistent as in the category "self-direction and self-realization," which was analyzed in the previous section. It is perhaps of some interest and importance that a great many of the significant protocol responses referred back specifically to the influence of the school. Some of the over-all limitations of the fields in which the class members' creativity operates will be discussed in the section on "democratic living."

It may be of some significance that, although there are creative individuals in all the quintiles, the minority which showed little creativity is concentrated in the two lowest quintiles, and the highest concentration of creativity is in the top group.

SOCIAL SENSITIVITY

Social sensitivity is used here to describe an individual's feelings about himself in his relationships with others and with social institutions. If he respects other personalities in his family, among his friends and associates, and in ever widening circles in the world community, and gives understanding and consideration to the rights and desires of others, even when they limit his own, he is a socially sensitive person. A truly sensitive person values and respects himself, and recognizes the importance of institutions to people; but he also believes one should be able to evaluate, and willing to modify, social institutions in order that they may better serve human ends.

Social sensitivity was a positive value for many but not all groups on the American scene when the University School opened its doors in the autumn of 1932 at the bottom of the depression and on the eve of the Roosevelt landslide and the beginning of the New Deal. The members of the Class of 1938 were in high school during the great period of American soul-searching which resulted from our experiences of the depression at home and our observation of totalitarian regimes abroad. The school was conceived from the first as an expression of democracy and an experience in it. An essential part of its task was felt to be the development of social sensitivity in its students.

> . . . Experiences which develop an awareness of, and responsiveness to, human values should be the constant concern of the school. Democracy is based upon the mutual respect for personality. This implies that each person will respect differences in social or racial groups and strive to elicit the unique contributions of others to the common good.[12]

[12] The Faculty of the University School, *The Philosophy and Purposes of the University School* (Columbus, Ohio: Ohio State University, 1948), p. 9.

232

In one sense the composition of the student body itself did not help in this, for it was not a cross-section of Columbus (see Chapter II). There was an occasional child from the family of a laborer. Negroes, hard hit by the depression, did not begin to enrol till the late 1930's. There were a few refugees from the Nazis in Columbus at that time, and occasionally one of their children entered the school. Most of the students, however, came from well-established white Columbus families, families which were affected by the depression in various fundamental ways, of course, but which belonged very nearly to the same general social stratum.

The weakness of this situation from the standpoint of experience was expressed as follows in two interviews, the first a statement from a woman, the second from a man:

Our class had quite a variety of different types of people. Of course, I don't believe there were any in our class that were very poor, but that's someone you meet out in the world and maybe don't know how to react to. I'll give an example. There is a couple that lives in a trailer across from the barn. They are from Kentucky, and illiterate, and very poor, and I had never really met anyone quite like them until they moved here, and it was a sort of shocking experience to me. I realized that I didn't know how so many of the people in this country really are or how they live until I met that couple. Of course, we didn't experience any type of person that way in school.—But I think that our democratic attitude in school has helped. I mean I didn't look down on those people because they're illiterate, uneducated, poor.

I think it [human relations in the class group] was good. As long as you're in the same category, I think I missed knowing the—sounds snobbish—so-called other side of the tracks. I know during the war I went to work in an aircraft factory, and I was a little bit at a loss how to get along. I was amazed at the different attitudes. I know I spoke about, "Why don't we go down to the Deshler [hotel] and have a good time tonight?" And they said, "We never go to the Deshler. That's a snobbish place to go." And that just illustrates the attitudes, the type of people I met which had a completely different set—I mean so many things I just took for granted, but I found here was a whole set of people [who didn't]. Then when I went into the service, I found that they had a completely different attitude toward life, people, and what they said, and the way they said it, and that their whole set of morals was so completely different that I wondered whether I had missed something in the protective society we lived in in University School.

There was, however, an awareness of social problems on the part of the students and a readiness to try to understand them. One woman expressed it in the following way:

> From my mother and father I would have learned to be nice to the person next door, or to people who are poor, or to stupid or boring or misinformed individuals. You know one has this pattern of behavior in the Middle West anyway; this is a regional thing of being nice to everybody no matter how you feel.

Participation by the pupils in planning capitalized on this social awareness, and trips into the community were a regular feature of the work. There were many kinds of joint endeavors within each class and the school in which the children learned to accept each other's differences and respect each other's problems and achievements. Units of study in the core course, in social studies, and in other areas were planned to contribute to broader human and world understanding. In conferences with the students and in written reports on their progress, the teachers tried to help the boys and girls understand themselves, the people whom they met, and human beings in general.[13]

Social sensitivity in the protocols was analyzed under two categories. Under the first, evidence of the importance to each individual of human-relations values was included, and under the second evidence of how broadly the individual defined the social world to which he was going to be sensitive. The ratings in the two categories have been tabulated separately in Tables 57 and 58.

Table 57 shows the primacy of human-relations values in the forty-five protocols. Thirty-seven of the forty-five, or 82 per cent, indicated high or very high sensitivity to these values, and only eight were below the top ranks, with none in the "very little" group. No significant

[13] For a description of this process in operation, see *Were We Guinea Pigs?* (New York: Henry Holt and Company, Inc., 1938), pp. 274–94.

differences appeared between the ratings of men and women. There seemed to be no real differences, either, among the quintiles, with the possible exception of that between the top quintile, which was consistently high, and the lowest, in which half of the subjects were rated "some" or "little." The lowest quintile contributed half (four) of the total number of individuals (eight) in the "some" and "little" categories. Since the numbers are so small, it would be unwise to give more than passing notice to this fact.

TABLE 57

SOCIAL SENSITIVITY: PRIMACY OF HUMAN-RELATIONS VALUES

RATING	QUINTILE										TOTAL	
	I		II		III		IV		V			
	Men	Women	Men	Women	Men	Women	Men	Women	Men	Women	Men	Women
Very high...	2	4	..	5	4	3	3	..	1	1	10	13
High....	2	1	2	..	1	2	2	2	1	1	8	6
Some....	..	..	1	1	..	1	1	..	2	1	4	3
Little....	..	..	..	..	..	..	..	..	1	..	1	..
Very little...	..	..	..	..	..	..	..	..	..	..	..	..
Total..	4	5	3	6	5	6	6	2	5	3	23	22

In most cases, there was abundant evidence of social sensitivity in interpersonal relations. It appeared in replies to questions about the school program, about bringing up children and other family relations, about community participation, about ambition, about what kinds of people were admired most, and in various other often unexpected places (see Appendix C, Questions 2, 3, 6, 21, 22, 27, 34, 35, 36, 37, 49, 63, 79, 89, 90, 91, 92, and 94). The twenty-three individuals who were rated "very high" showed consistent and abundant evidence in their protocols of the primacy of human-relations values; the evidence was not quite as pervasive for the fourteen in the "high" group, but it was still very consistent. The seven individuals who were rated "some" showed either inconsistencies or blank spots in the area of social sensitivity, even in face-to-face contacts. The protocol of the one classified as "little" gave only a very small amount of evidence, but it was all positive. Nobody showed himself to be egocentric, exploitative, or domineering, attitudes which would have caused the individual to be rated at the bottom. If we were rating a group which included a number of individuals showing such traits, it is probable that by comparison certain of the individuals in our study in the "little" and "some" groups might be pushed up into a higher classification.

A few illustrations will indicate the kinds of responses on which evaluations were based. One of the productive questions was, "Is ambition something you admire in other people?" One response from a woman and two from men are typical of a large majority.

> Well, it depends on what kind of ambition it is. If it's to improve—if it's the same type of ambition I have—to improve our living standards and give opportunities to everyone, why that kind, yes. I don't believe in ambition for ambition's sake.

> Depends on how that ambition goes. Ambition to do a good job, get it done quickly, I admire. Ambition to get ahead as long as it is not at the expense of someone else, I admire. A person who is convinced of his own ideas, who will go ahead with his own ideas, I admire.

> I admire ambition if it is an incentive. I believe that an ambition is something that everybody should have, but it's the way it's applied; in other words whether you walk over people because of [your] ambition or whether it is an incentive that is coupled with getting along with people. I think there are two types of it.

The questions which were concerned with bringing up children were also productive. One quotation from a man can represent this group.

Question: What things do you try to instill in your children?

Answer: I think honesty and sense of fair play; to have respect for others and themselves and to think of others rather than just themselves all the time; belief in God. You could write a whole book on that. An interest in books and reading—we have enough twenty-five-cent Golden Books around here to start a lending library. Randy is more interested; until lately Nancy wouldn't sit still to hear one story through. He is more calm than she ever thought of being.

We have made a concerted effort to see that they were not dependent on us, so they will accept sitters and we can get away.

Sometimes social sensitivity was evident as individuals explored their own feelings, described their activities, or discussed issues. In the next quotation, the fact that the man suspects himself of a selfish point of view and examines his own reactions in that light indicates a fairly high level of sensitivity.

Question: Do you think that labor is getting too much power and too high pay lately, or are you glad to see such things as guaranteed annual wage, $1.00 minimum wage, and the merging of AFL-CIO?

Answer: Well, I have certain negative feelings about labor—I hate to say that—but I don't know why I should deny them the chance to make a living. I do feel it a little bit personally in that some of the guys that work machines and don't have any training can make more money than I do with my professional training, but what I think we should do is raise the professional's training and salary rather than cut down the guy who runs a lathe. He does a dull job, and he has to get paid to make him do it. I am fortunate in some respects, doing a job I like, so I don't have to be paid so much. But I don't—it bothers me a little bit, but I think I'm being selfish there again about it. If I was getting increases as well, I know I would think, "Well, they've got to live too."

In the next quotation, the sensitivity is implicit in the relationships which emerge as the person talks about political discussions.

Question: Do your friends talk much about politics?

Answer: Oh, we discuss them I would say an average amount. [Can you remember the last time there was a discussion and what it was about?] Oh, let's see, the last one I think was about a week ago, and it concerned, if I recall correctly, a local education problem before the board of education. [Do you mostly talk or listen to those?] Oh, it's a give-and-take proposition. Sometimes I'll listen entirely, sometimes I'll just bait them to try and draw them out, and then see if I can learn a little more about it. By the same token, if I think they're wrong, sometimes I can bait them and bring it out and prove to them they're wrong.

I think the last heated discussion that I was in happened to be a bait-ing like that. A friend of my wife's lives in the north end, and they've been quite up in arms over the annexation that's going on; and in-stead of talking she just gets livid about it. Well, that's no good. You can't discuss any problem when you get that way. So I baited her on purpose, trying to calm her down, and it did; and after about a half hour of that, why she started laughing and then we actually discussed it. And they've got reason to be up in arms. By the same token, they're better off discussing it rather than getting mad. [Well, I'm surprised that your baiting got her calmed down. Usually that gets people more livid, doesn't it?] Well, there again, we're such good friends. We know each other so well that—I don't know how to put it —you can bait her so far and then she'll start laughing, and as soon as she starts laughing, why then she's, as we used to say, "over her mad"; and then you all laugh, and you go back to talking about what she was mad about a minute ago, but you're talking about it in a nor-mal tone of voice. It's been rather a hot issue in the north end.

The final quotation is from a woman, who is describing a phase of her community participation.

We have started a crippled Girl Scout group, plus we have helped get the Cub Scouts going out there; and for the last five years we have been working towards getting two weeks of camping for crippled children in this area, and I think this year for the first time we are succeeding. We had a hard time getting the Girl Scouts here to ac-cept unusual children into the large group, and as I said before, I'm a little bit of a rebel and so I have been fighting that. Last year we went to the Camp Fire Girls and asked them if they would take our children for a week, and they were delighted because it gave them community recognition and they could use it for their publicity. It was a little bit of a backhanded way to go about it, but this year the Girl Scouts have come to us with open arms and our girls are going to get ten days of camping. I have gone outside of Junior League to get volunteers to work out there and really had a lot of success; I mean I co-ordinated between Kiwanis who gives us some money, P.T.A. at boarding school to give us some money, and we have to be in agree-ment with and we work with the principal of the school and Junior League. I have to report back because I'm doing the work for them, so it has been a lot of fun and a lot of groups getting together, and I've learned lot about red tape and some of the community groups.

It seemed important to examine separately the scope of the social world to which each individual felt himself committed, since it is possible (perhaps even common) for people to have value systems which function effectively in their relationships with people whom they regard as members of their in-group, but which break down completely for out-groups. The size of the in-group ranges from the family outward through the whole complex range of human relationships to include at its maximum the human race.

A factor which may complicate an analysis of this kind must be taken into consideration. One type of individual, whose social world extends only a little beyond his face-to-face relationships, will probably see the wider world in stereotypes, but regard it in a benevolently accepting way. Hundreds of thousands of Americans can travel and even live abroad without any significant change in this point of view or enlargement of the area of social sensitivity. Of course, many similar millions remain contentedly at home. Another type also sees the world in stereotypes, but feels threatened by it and reacts with intolerance and aggression toward a variety of groups.[14]

In the whole group of forty-five protocols, there was none which showed an authoritarian personality. The limits on the scope of the social world were very real in many cases, but they were limits of imagination, information, understanding, and experienced relationships. Table 58 shows the distribution of the class on a scale which ranges from a "very wide" to a "very narrow" social world.

Whereas 82 per cent of the group scored in the two top classes on the scale of "Primacy of Human-Relations Values," only 55 per cent are in the two top groups on the scale of "Scope of the Social World." At the other end of the scale—whereas only one individual (2.1 per cent) was below the midpoint on the first tabulation (Table 57), ten, or 22 per cent, are below on this one. The lowest group, which tended

[14] The work of Adorno and others in *The Authoritarian Personality* indicate that this is a real personality type.

TABLE 58

SOCIAL SENSITIVITY: SCOPE OF THE SOCIAL WORLD

RATING	QUINTILE										TOTAL	
	I		II		III		IV		V			
	Men	Women	Men	Women	Men	Women	Men	Women	Men	Women	Men	Women
Very wide...	2	3	..	3	3	2	2	..	1	1	8	9
Wide....	2	1	1	..	1	1	2	..	..	..	6	2
Some....	..	..	2	3	1	..	2	2	..	..	5	5
Narrow..	..	1	..	..	..	3	..	..	2	2	2	6
Very narrow	..	..	..	..	..	..	..	..	2	..	2	..
Total..	4	5	3	6	5	6	6	2	5	3	23	22

to limit its responsibility to face-to-face relationships, may be represented by a comment from one man:

> I don't understand about "making other people happy" unless we're talking about my wife. If we're talking about some third party I don't even know—well, I'm not a philanthropist, and I don't feel that I'm too responsible for this nebulous "other" people. I don't even know who they are.

Evidence of a broader and deeper concern came out in such responses as the following from a woman.

> *Question:* When you are in a group of people where the discussion is being dominated by individuals expressing very prejudiced views on questions on which you have strong opposing convictions, what do you do?

> *Answer:* Sometimes I leave and burst into tears somewhere else, as I did when my brother was discussing Negroes once. Sometimes I put in a kind of mild disagreement. It depends on who the speakers are. If it is a question of national politics and people who are very Republican, then you can understand why they feel as they do. It is more or less a question of what their jobs are (perhaps they have always been in high positions), and if they have always been high up and always in Republican circles, then I don't argue with them. Just as I do not

argue with political *émigrés* who believe things would be much better the way they were before the revolution or war which cast them out. There is no sense in arguing with them. They have often stopped being able to think rationally on this subject since their expulsion. But when the speaker's life is not involved and his social relationships are not involved, then I think I might argue. If it were a violent point on the Negro, then I think I would almost undoubtedly speak my piece, even if it broke up some kind of relationship.

The question, "What do you think is most important in life: (a) trying to make the world a better place; (b) happiness; (c) making other people happy; (d) living according to your religion?", was a very revealing one in most protocols. The following quotation is from a man.

Well, I don't think any of those really defines it. I think it's a combination. I think if you define happiness in a broad sense and bring in lots of other things, it's one of the most important things; but I don't think you could go out and try to be happy and get anyplace. I think it's a result of doing something which you think is worth while. I think you have to think that you're contributing something to the world or civilization or to other people or something. You have to feel that your existence is somewhat important. I think that's the reason why that at least I can justify teaching without too far reaching; you can justify your existence as part of the community. That's why some other jobs I've thought about you really couldn't.

In Table 58 a significant difference between the fifth quintile and all the others appears: the lowest group is the only one in which a large majority of the respondents are living in a world of narrow or very narrow social relationships.

In regard to the value, social sensitivity, it appears that this group stands very high in face-to-face relationships and probably fairly high in scope of the social world, though comparisons are not available. To what extent this is due to the climate of the times and of the place, and to what extent to the influence of the school, cannot be conclusively determined. It is of some significance that a great many of the protocols credit some phase of it—"getting along with other people"—to the influence of University School. The differences between Table 57 and Table 58 may mean that successful experiences in sensitive and understanding interpersonal relationships are more potent than well-thought-out efforts to enlarge the areas of social concern through the curriculum of a school.

DEMOCRATIC LIVING

In a basic sense, the American public school has always been a creation of the democratic spirit; but the University School had a special philosophical commitment from the beginning to think out its total program in democratic terms. The following quotation is from the school's report to the Eight Year Study in 1940:

> The democratic way of life is based upon the assumption of respect for human personality. The optimal development of the individual is the basic criterion of value. . . .
>
> . . . .
>
> A distinctive personality cannot be developed in isolation. It develops only where there is free interplay with other personalities. Full and free participation within a given group, and among groups, is the best way of promoting desirable individual development in a complex, interdependent society. . . .
>
> . . . .
>
> Evolving conceptions of the meaning of democracy are reflected in the various interpretations of the democratic methods which are found in America today. . . . The school attempts to provide a program which will help boys and girls to understand and to meet their needs, to extend and enrich their interests, to solve their problems in such a way as to contribute to the development of consistent and unified outlooks on life, and to grow in sensitivity to the values and ideals of our democratic way of life. . . .[15]

In a later section of the same report, a specific aspect is carried further:

[15] Progressive Education Association, Commission on the Relation of School and College, *Thirty Schools Tell Their Story* ("Adventure in American Education," Vol. V [New York: Harper and Brothers, 1943]), pp. 720–21. (Material used with the permission of McGraw-Hill Book Company, Inc.)

The school has been concerned with developing democratic discipline. As stated before, to the faculty this has meant as much freedom as individuals and groups were able to handle with profit to themselves and without detriment to others. Instead of many fixed rules governing every situation, it is expected that children will consider each situation and adjust themselves to it. For example, conversation which is socially acceptable about the sewing tables in home economics is unacceptable about library tables. Order is a function of the total situation.

The acceptance of this definition has many implications which were not immediately obvious, but have gradually been recognized. One is that violations become the point at which one guides the learner, not the point for punishment. It has taken courage to permit a student to make mistakes which might have been prevented by the teacher. We believe, however, that if the penalty of the mistake is inherent in the situation, is not too serious, and will fall on the child himself rather than on someone else, he should be allowed to make mistakes when he cannot see the value of the advice which would have helped him to avoid them. It is the responsibility of the teacher afterward to help him think through the whole situation, and to make sure that he capitalizes on the experience.[16]

In *The Philosophy and Purposes of the University School,* printed in 1948, these ideas are restated in somewhat different words.

Developing co-operativeness. The school program should provide continuous opportunities for young people to work together toward common ends. This includes co-operative planning of programs in every area of school life, and carrying out and evaluating such programs.

.   .   .   .

Developing skills in democratic living. Students should learn to choose leaders in terms of the qualities needed for the particular job at hand. All students should have opportunities for leadership at their level and all should be able to co-operate with leaders. All should have a growing understanding of how to enlist effective participation for common ends by enabling all to take part in defining goals and in selecting their own part in working toward goals. Leaders should become increasingly skillful at distributing responsibilities in terms of

[16] *Ibid.,* pp. 736–37.

the abilities, interests, and preferences of individuals so that all may participate effectively. Before the end of the high-school years these experiences in democratic participation should have reached out beyond the school into the community at many points.

Interpreting democracy. It is not enough that young people should live democratically. They should know what they are about, in the sense that they should become increasingly aware of the value of such living, not only within the school but in life outside of the school. This does not imply dreary "talks" by the teacher on the meaning of democracy, but rather that the democratic life of the school shall be so dynamically related to life outside that the students will be led to understand its meaning, and seek to extend it to all situations in which they are involved.[17]

The faculty tried to make their operations democratic in all aspects of the school program and in their relations with each other as well as with the students. As the school prepared to undertake an experimental program, it was necessary to hold many long meetings in order to develop common agreements and basic understandings. Critical issues were threshed out in protracted evening sessions which lasted until eleven o'clock or later. The enthusiasm and interest of discovering and working on common curricular concerns helped faculty members through a long and inefficient period of direct democracy, during which they were themselves discovering in their own experience the inadequacies of their democratic concepts and practices, and were working toward refinement and clarification.

The same problems provided excellent teaching situations for the faculty to use with the students who were even less accustomed to participating in decisions which affected them, and who had to learn the processes of discussion and decision. Besides participating in the planning and evaluation of their work, the students also organized their student government, planned much of their social program (setting aside time for the planning of social events within school hours gave the teachers an opportunity to retain a role in regard to them, while allowing the students a high degree of independence), put out

[17] Pp. 9–10.

various publications, and acted as responsible citizens in numerous other situations.

The extension of active citizenship into the community was attempted in various ways. Some study of community agencies and community needs always accompanied organized giving at Thanksgiving and Christmas. Many units, especially in social studies, Nature of Proof, and science, used social data and were enriched by trips into the community. English classes attended plays, art classes went to art shows. Studies of such areas as propaganda, conflicting ideologies, and housing brought in world-wide data. It is obvious that many of these studies revealed situations in which action was needed, but in which the student had little or no possibility of acting; this is the continuing problem of the social-science teacher.

Evidence of "democratic living" in the protocols, as in the school, was a complex of behaving and believing. The three aspects of this quality which were analyzed are the following:

(1) *Interpersonal democracy.* Many of the questions on bringing up children and on family relationships gave direct and indirect evidence of respect for personality and for the rights of other people. (See Appendix C, Questions 3, 11, 21, 22, 23, 24, 25, 27, 28, 34, 35, 36, 37, 52, 53.) Important side lights appeared frequently in discussions of jobs and satisfying experiences, and in a variety of other places.

(2) *Democratic ideology.* The interpretations which an individual gives to human-relations values as he deals with them indicate his concepts. This aspect of democratic living is closely related to interpersonal democracy and to social action, but is more a matter of the thought and feeling which accompany behavior.

(3) *Social action.* This aspect is concerned with an individual's participation both in voluntary organizations and in the activities which are usually termed "political"—in other words, with the whole range of activities in which an individual joins with others to further common ends. At a time when the organized garden clubs have just helped win a major victory over the advertising fraternity in getting Congress and many state legislatures to act against billboards on

through highways, it surely is not necessary to labor the point that voluntary organizations have potential political importance. The tremendous significance of the welter of voluntary groups on the American scene has not been sufficiently recognized; too often "social action" has been treated as though it were a synonym for politics. As it is used here, it comprises a continuum of associations for common purposes, beginning with those on quite a small scale and including at the other end all levels of politics.

In evaluating the protocols, the most difficult problem was to establish a standard of social action for both voluntary association and political action. Among the experts consulted by the writer, some insisted that in a democracy *everyone* ought to be politically active, that activity in voluntary organizations and in the local community could not be a satisfactory substitute. Others believe that an individual might work out a pattern of democratic citizenship which was adequate for him and for society, but which included very little interest in politics. Riesman, for example, discusses "politics as a human need" in the following way:

> But it does not follow, from the fact that people can, that they *should* deploy in politics the abilities they can muster in other fields of culture. There are many people who, choosing among their various needs and potentialities on the basis of their temperament, their situation, and their gifts, can build a very satisfying life without the slightest attention to politics. Their gardens are enough, and their osmotic pressure against the news of the day, coupled with their intense activity in other fields, saves them from anxiety. Until conditions become far more desperate, and in some circumstances even if they do, it would seem ascetic, a kind of secularized Puritanism, to suggest to such people that they concern themselves with politics when it is evident that their lives are full and rich and adequately oriented without it. Since we do not live forever, no one can satisfy all his human needs on all levels of living, all the more so as these needs develop with the growth of civilization and the greater ease and length of the average life. And in these people there is choice to avoid politics, not flight from it.
>
> Yet such people seem to me exceptional. . . .[18]

[18] David Riesman and Nathan Glazer, *op. cit.*, p. 48.

Because of these differences among the experts, two separate tabulations have been made in the social-action area for purposes of comparison—the first is a rating of work in voluntary organizations (Table 60) and the second, a rating of political activity (Table 61). Although there is an assumption in Table 59 that a high level of interpersonal democracy and democratic ideology is "good," the same standards may or may not be applicable to Tables 60 and 61.

Table 59 shows the distribution of the group on the scale of interpersonal democracy and democratic ideology. The descriptions which were used for each rating are as follows:

Very high. Consistent respect for other personalities, including those who differ, except when they are trampling on the rights and individuality of people. Evidence that the individual has generalized his specific attitudes into concepts.

High. Evidence similar to that in the highest category, except not quite so extensive, or perhaps showing minor inconsistencies.

Some. Wide respect for others, but with little evidence of a conscious theory of democracy. Or a certain narrowing of the field of respect; no evidence of prejudice against others, just obliviousness.

Little. Very narrow field of interpersonal democracy and evidences of prejudice, which the individual recognizes as such but finds himself unable to reject.

Very little. Belief that everybody is out for himself, and that the law of the jungle operates outside the immediate group, usually the family.

Contradictory. Reserved for individuals who, on the basis of different parts of the same protocol, would have to be placed at very different points on the scale.

It is striking that thirty-five of the forty-five subjects are in the two highest groups and that seven of the remaining ten were rated in the middle of the scale. Quotations from three of the subjects will illustrate the kind of information about interpersonal democracy which was looked for in the protocols and the ways in which democratic ideology appeared.

TABLE 59
DEMOCRATIC LIVING: INTERPERSONAL DEMOCRACY
AND DEMOCRATIC IDEOLOGY

RATING	QUINTILE										TOTAL	
	I		II		III		IV		V			
	Men	Women	Men	Women	Men	Women	Men	Women	Men	Women	Men	Women
Very high...	3	3	..	3	3	3	3	..	1	1	10	10
High....	1	2	2	3	1	2	3	..	1	..	8	7
Some....	..	..	..	..	1	1	..	2	1	2	2	5
Little....	..	..	..	..	..	..	..	..	1	..	1	..
Very little...	..	..	..	..	..	..	..	..	..	..	..	..
Contradictory	..	..	1	..	..	..	..	..	1	..	2	..
Total..	4	5	3	6	5	6	6	2	5	3	23	22

A woman replied to the following question, "What things do you try to instill in your children?"

Respect for property and respect for other children's wishes and other children's differences, not to tease or to make fun or overly criticize other children in their abilities. I suppose honesty, to believe in God. I don't think you sit down—I haven't been conscious of sitting down and thinking out what I'm trying to instill in the children—it just seems that, I suppose, the things that are important to me I unconsciously try to instill in them.

In answer to the same question, a man made the following comment:

Well, I think—I think one of the hardest things to get across to a youngster is to gradually endow him with an increasing sense of responsibility, and I use the term responsibility in an over-all sense. When they first start off in life, it becomes very readily apparent to a young parent that his child is completely selfish, completely self-centered, completely grasping, completely interested only in his own material welfare and his own creature comforts, and as he—only gradually does he arrive at a sense of—of being a member of a larger society. First he is a member of his family unit; later on he acquires

playmates from generally nearby homes. Then, of course, at five or
thereabouts he starts to school, and he—immediately new concepts
are thrust upon him. But as he grows up, as he advances in age and in
experience and in education, there is a constant conflict, I think,
which is part and parcel of everyone's life, learning how to mature,
which is a struggle, learning how to deal competently and fairly with
other people, learning how to satisfy his own wants and needs which
we all have, but also in learning that—that in doing so he can't—
other people have rights and privileges and responsibilities towards
him and he has in turn responsibilities towards other people. To me
that—that is the most difficult thing to do. To try to impart to your
youngsters an awareness that as they grow older, necessarily, they
must learn to accept more responsibility in every sense of the word.

The following analysis of family relationships clearly shows concepts of democracy.

Question: Do you think of your family—the one in which you grew
up—as a democratic situation?

Answer: Yes, if you mean participation of all the family somewhat
in family decisions—yes, I would say so. Father was boss in the
final decision, but there was no totalitarian rule there. The rest of the
family all had their say and could participate. [And were considered?]
Yes, very much so.

Question: From what you know about your wife's family, how would
you answer the same question about it?

Answer: I would say not quite the same, on the surface. Down
underneath, I would say that her father was more inclined to make
his own decisions; but I think he weighed the feelings of the family,
but never let them know it—and still doesn't let them know it—because anything that happens is always a surprise to the family, like a
new automobile or a vacation or something like that always comes
abruptly at the moment. But I really think he plays dumb and listens
to what goes on and pretends to be hard of hearing, and then makes
his decisions and surprises them all. I think he gets kind of a kick out
of it. But that's quite contrary to the way our family is—it's upsetting
to them I know, this being an in-law—still we have our vacation
with them enough that I can see a little change there, so not quite the

same. But I think essentially it is a democratic operation, but it doesn't appear to be so on the surface.

Question: Do you consider your own family—you, your wife, and children—as a democratic institution?

Answer: Yes, I think so. I think that perhaps maybe we go a little more overboard on that than our parents have—to a point. Certain things—certain people are supposed to make certain decisions you might say. Certain ones I think that I should make the final decision on, but really between my wife and me, we hold a directors' meeting about almost everything we do and consider the thing pretty carefully.

Finally, here are two brief quotations which show how casual comments revealed insights:

Democracy requires not only faith in the individual but ability to communicate.

As you grow older and have your own family, you learn to look at parents as adults and human beings, and to understand their problems. When father was in a good mood, he was wonderful to us; I always understood mother. I now understand their relationship with each other better.

Table 60 shows the ratings of the class members in the phase of social action which concerns work in voluntary organizations. The following descriptive phrases explain each classification in the table.

Very high. Active and creative participation in significant community groups.

High. Active (self-propelled) participation, but not necessarily as creative as in the highest classification.

Some. Broad but routine participation, or fairly active participation in a narrow range of organizations or in groups of slight importance.

Little. Minimum (duty) participation, or temporary withdrawal from all participation.

Very little. Withdrawal or habitual lack of participation.

A prodemocratic orientation of diminishing strength and/or consistency was assumed throughout the five levels of participation. One possible situation, which the writer fortunately did not have to face, would have raised problems. If one of the guinea pigs had been an active member of the Ku Klux Klan or the Communist party, how should his responses as a member of a voluntary, actively antidemocratic organization have been handled in such a tabulation? A sixth

TABLE 60

DEMOCRATIC LIVING: SOCIAL ACTION—WORK IN
VOLUNTARY ORGANIZATIONS

Rating	Quintile										Total	
	I		II		III		IV		V			
	Men	Women	Men	Women	Men	Women	Men	Women	Men	Women	Men	Women
Very high...	2	1	..	1	2	1	..	..	1	1	5	4
High....	..	2	1	3	2	2	2	1	1	..	6	8
Some....	1	2	1	..	1	2	2	1	..	..	5	5
Little....	..	..	1	2	..	1	1	..	2	2	4	5
Very little...	1	..	..	..	..	..	1	..	1	..	3	..
Total..	4	5	3	6	5	6	6	2	5	3	23	22

classification might be the answer. The nature of the voluntary organizations with which these people allied themselves is discussed in Chapter VI.

Twenty-three of the forty-five individuals participated actively and creatively, or at least actively, in voluntary organizations, and took leadership responsibilities. Another ten appeared to assume a rather routine but regular part, nine kept their participation at a minimum, and three (all men) abstained from group associations entirely. It will be noted that these figures show a sharp drop from those in Table 59.

A group of excerpts from different protocols gives an impression of certain common elements in the participation of the group. The responses come from men and women, one or more from each of the five quintiles. No single question solicited these comments. Rather, they came spontaneously as each individual explained some other response that he had given.

Well, I think we live in a committee society, which we were very basically taught here. Everything is run by a committee, I don't care what it is, you got to have a committee to do it. I don't necessarily agree that in all cases the committee is the way to do it, but it is something that we live with, and it is something that I certainly wouldn't want to see given up [in the school program] as long as we still are more or less by committee rule. [Even boards of directors are sorts of committees aren't they?] Same thing, the church has umpteen committees, this group has a whole bunch of committees. I think very definitely that we did learn how to express ourselves, especially in a committee, how to give and take in ideas before a final decision was reached. And after seeing how some committees operate, those people who have apparently never had that training or chance to be in a committee before, it certainly indicates that what we had was good training.

There was competition, but the emphasis wasn't on it. [Perhaps the faculty felt you didn't have to learn so much about that, that it was more innate.] Well, that's true. And on the other hand, I think the factor of competition in the outside world is somewhat overemphasized, too—at least apparently in this day and age. [You think the outside world is more co-operative than people sometimes say?] Oh, I think so. I mean you go to almost any neighborhood, and you will discover that the neighbors are co-operative, they're co-operative in the church, they're co-operative in the factory. You'll always have persons with driving ambitions that are the epitome of competition, in fact, who will only co-operate to their own ends; but I don't—the average person goes along and co-operates to the best of his ability. It makes good writing, it makes fine stories about competition, but I don't think it's as big a factor as it's put down to be.

I think there were only a few that have been graduates of the University School—of our class, that is—not willing to get up on his feet if he thinks he should, and get up and talk before any size group about a problem; and after all, that is the key of democracy in action, and I think the school was very successful in that. Now, how much it has been practiced since then, I don't know, but I bet you in P.T.A. meetings, or church meetings, or wherever you are asked to find a group, I don't think you will find a shy violet of our class about getting up and speaking. In that respect, I think the school program was excellent.

As I recall it was a course in design and no one else would talk, and I suddenly found myself being the leader of the class.

Well, it seems like any organization I get into I've a bad habit of talking, and if you're talking, before you know it you're an elected officer. I have been officers in all the organizations I've been into, either on the board or president or vice-president, practically all of them I've been associated with.

I enjoy participating in any size groups. . . . I'm not a group leader any more, but in feeling with a group, getting their ideas, and being able to understand them—that ability was cultivated at University School.

You know what it [integrated courses in high school] seems to have done more than anything else—I have found with myself that I am able, in groups and faculty meetings, when it comes time to summarize—I'm the one that summarizes, because everyone else is off, while I seem to want to pull threads together, and summarize for a very individualistic bunch too.

I find it very deeply satisfying when I can bring people together, and they can begin to see the things which they have in common, which are more important than the things which divide them. Now, whenever that seems to be symbolizing itself, whether it's in a service of worship or more importantly in a committee session or a decision which they've undertaken in which you can see this play of their different backgrounds, and then when they rise to a situation and recognize, "This is bigger than I am or even my denomination or my church's point of view—this is big enough so that I can thread myself to this unreservedly in company with people who come from different backgrounds," and this to me is great. I love it. *It happens.*

Table 61 shows the level of social action of this group as expressed in political activity and attitudes. The definitions for each level of the scale are the following:

Very high. Active in politics at some level well beyond voting and being familiar with issues, with a conviction of real accomplishment.

High. Active but not quite so intensely as in the highest classification—far more than voting, however—with faith in politics as an effective instrument.

Some. Feels obligation to vote at elections and to understand issues (frequently worries over not being adequately informed); tends to look down on those less active.

Little. Seldom votes or takes any part; certain issues might enlist interest.

Very little. Cynical about politics (antipolitical orientation), or complete withdrawal.

TABLE 61

DEMOCRATIC LIVING: SOCIAL ACTION—POLITICAL ACTIVITY

RATING	QUINTILE										TOTAL	
	I		II		III		IV		V			
	Men	Women	Men	Women	Men	Women	Men	Women	Men	Women	Men	Women
Very high...	..	..	..	..	1	..	1	..	..	1	2	1
High....	1	1	..	2	4	..	..	..	1	..	6	3
Some....	2	4	1	3	..	5	4	2	2	1	9	15
Little....	..	..	1	1	..	1	1	..	..	..	2	2
Very little...	1	..	1	..	..	..	..	..	2	1	4	1
Total..	4	5	3	6	5	6	6	2	5	3	23	22

There is a striking drop in the numbers of men and women in the high ratings of Table 61 from those in Tables 59 and 60; only twelve class members, or slightly more than one-fourth, took a more active part in politics than merely acquiring political information and voting. Nine of the group, or one-fifth, fell in the "little" or "very little" class, abstaining almost entirely from politics. The following quotations show attitudes which are probably fairly general among the abstainers and perhaps even among the half of the class which votes dutifully.

Question: After all, does what happens in politics make any difference to the way you work and live?

Answer: I think everything influences your living. I get very depressed when I listen to news; I have stopped listening because I either had to do that or get into it actively.

Answer: I like the C.B.S. "World News Roundups." Both the newspapers and radio are so limited [lives in Far West]. I think we'll have to take *Time* magazine. I don't like magazines like *The Nation* anymore—they just get you all excited about what is happening to poor people, and you can't do anything about it.

Answer: I could either become terribly interested or so terribly disillusioned that I wouldn't be interested at all. I like anything where there is a situation where you can contribute or do something to help correct it; but I don't ever want to get into a situation where you beat your head against a stone wall, and there isn't anything you can do. I think politics is something sort of like that.

On the opposite side of the ledger are a number of people who have played important parts in local good-government campaigns, or who take a regular part in political party organizations or the League of Women Voters, or who have a habit of writing to their representatives in Washington. Two quotations will serve to illustrate the attitudes of these people.

It's amazing what can be done in the art of governing oneself with just even a little effort. I mean I could cite personal example after example of that. What has been accomplished here locally just because of the interest of a relatively few people. . . . I think many things that I have seen happen in my own environment here within the city are traceable to some of the things which we envisioned four years ago. I can name lots of specific things: storm sewers, sanitary sewers, street paving, the extension of our park system, the establishing of a municipal court here in the beginning of this new year. Those are just a few specific things right off the bat.

Question: Is there anything you can personally do about it [large-scale political questions such as war and depression], or is it all up to the experts in Washington?

Answer: Oh, my gracious no! There certainly is something we can do about it. I've found that, surprisingly enough, these so-called experts in

Washington are very receptive to feeble voices that they might hear from their constituents, and I think that a letter now and then to your congressman or your senator I've found to be very effective. In fact one of my favorite senators in Washington is Wayne Morse, who, I think, is probably the most independent thinker, the most honest and realistic man I can think of in Washington. I have corresponded with him two or three different times, and I think that maybe an idea or two that I have expressed to him may definitely help his actions on the floor in Washington.

I know the State Department is very receptive to ideas. I wrote a letter to Secretary of State Dulles one day here a year or so ago when the French were piddling around down in—where was it?—yes, down in Indo-China, and there were great trial balloons being sent up by our honorable Vice-President Nixon about whether we were going to send troops and planes and ships over there. And you'd be surprised, but John Foster Dulles said some two or three months after they decided not to do it that he had received such an avalanche of mail from people opposing—that it had quite a bit to do with it, and happily my letter was one of them.

TABLE 62

A SUMMARY OF THE RATINGS OF THE CLASS OF 1938 ON
THREE ASPECTS OF DEMOCRATIC LIVING

| | DEMOCRATIC LIVING | | |
RATING	Interpersonal Democracy and Democratic Ideology	Work in Voluntary Organizations	Political Activity
Very high	20	9	3
High	15	14	9
Some	7	10	24
Little	1	9	4
Very little	..	3	5
Contradictory	2	..	..

Since none of the three tables that are concerned with democratic living showed any clear differences between the sexes or between the very rough ability groups represented by the quintiles, these divisions have been discarded in making the summary in Table 62.

When examining the striking differences among the three aspects of democratic living in Table 62, it is well to keep in mind that no generally accepted standards of what is "good" or "right" exist for the last two categories—work in voluntary organizations and political activity. The researcher, however, is somewhat disturbed to find that more than one-fourth of the group have rather slight ties with community organizations, and one-fifth take little part in political activities.[19] A cross-check of the original data revealed that seven individuals were rated low on both work in voluntary organizations and political activity: two were rated "little" on both; four were rated "little" on one and "very little" on the other; and one was rated "very little" on both. Yet, almost all of these people have established and satisfactorily maintained democratic interpersonal relationships.

Jacob suggests that one element which many value-oriented programs have in common is the attempt "to involve the students in an experience which will make some social problem vivid to them and require a substantial investment of effort on their part to do something about it." He also says, "Scattered bits of evidence from other programs tend to support the hope that incorporating carefully designed student experience in their college education can have considerable influence on values." [20]

Perhaps the experience in democratic living at University School is one of the factors which helps to account for what appears to be a reasonable degree of success, especially in interpersonal democracy. But if that is true, why did it fail in some cases? Does the number of failures indicate that the program actually had little to do with the results one way or the other? Another quotation from Jacob suggests an alternate explanation:

> This evidence suggests that the response of students to education, especially general education, is vitally conditioned by their own personalities. A course or curriculum, a teacher, or even a college as a whole, will affect students differently, depending on what type of persons they are. The educational impact is twisted and re-directed by

[19] The rates of participation are higher, however, than those found in the only comparable study, by Wright and Hyman, which has been discussed in Chapter VI.
[20] Jacob, *op. cit.,* pp. 96, 97.

its collision with a particular student's personality. The personality acts as a filter, allowing only certain elements from the educational process to get through to the student and influence him.[21]

Although this comment refers basically to college students and programs, there is abundant evidence in the protocols which bears it out. Almost 87 per cent of the men and women reported that they felt the school had helped them develop tolerance for minorities. One who was in the remaining 13 per cent made the following comment:

Well, I'm still intolerant of minority groups and I try to fight it and overcome it, but I don't think that that was developed in high school. I think that was farther back. [You mean you think your intolerance was developed farther back?] Yes, much farther back, and I think perhaps in my outside environment, because a high school had so little to do with forming ideas and philosophies, inhibitions, that it didn't mean anything. [Now do you think you brought most of those things with you when you came?] Yes, they may have been leveled off to some degree, but they still appear, crop up.

Opposed to this is the judgment of another student who was in the school for only two years, but whose personality filtered out different values.

Before I went to University School, I really think I was somewhat of a snob; but I learned to accept all sorts of people there, and enjoyed them, and still do. I'm very tolerant of all religions and races and creeds now, and before I went to the school, I was not. My family beforehand were very prejudiced about people in different religions and faiths.

[21] *Ibid.,* p. 118.

THE METHOD OF INTELLIGENCE

In *The Philosophy and Purposes of the University School,* the following paragraph deals specifically with the method of intelligence:

Developing the ability and zeal to utilize the method of intelligence in solving all problems of human concern. The method of intelligence in a narrow sense includes the following factors: (a) recognizing problems, (b) formulating hypotheses, (c) discovering and organizing data, (d) arriving at tentative conclusions and acting on them. In a wider sense it also means striving to employ reflective thinking in as many areas of living as possible, to develop a consistent pattern of behavior, and to regard truth as tentative and experimental rather than absolute.[22]

In other sections of the same document, the faculty stresses the central importance for a democracy of intelligent judgment and responsible action in terms of a highly developed social consciousness. One of the basic beliefs at University School is that all the values which have been studied in this report—self-direction and self-realization, creativity, social sensitivity, democratic living, and the method of intelligence—are so intimately related that any separation is essentially artificial and temporary. The reader may already have noticed quotations from the protocols included in other chapters that might just as well have been given as illustrations in this section.

The curricular materials and teaching techniques which were used in the attempt to develop in the students ability and zeal in the method of intelligence have been described in earlier chapters. Everything which tended to move individuals forward into more responsible self-direction and group participation served this purpose. Critical evalua-

[22] P. 9.

tion of both individual and class results made an important contribution. *Were We Guinea Pigs?* shows the processes of critical thinking on almost every page. As noted in Chapter IX, the subjects of this study were in unanimous agreement that the school tried to teach them to think for themselves, and almost all, 96 per cent, believed it had succeeded, at least to some degree.

In analyzing evidence of the method of intelligence in statements made seventeen years after graduation, certain problems appear. One concerns the relation of feeling to intelligence. The quotation from the faculty's statement of purposes with which this chapter began seems to present a very cool, collected, unemotional kind of intelligence. Was the method of intelligence assumed to be divorced from feeling except for the zeal the individual might feel for the method itself?

A rereading of the literature about the school that was produced in that period tends to bear this out. The students in their book began the chapter "Putting Our Minds in Order" in the following manner:

> We have made the following definition of critical thinking for the purpose of writing this chapter: Critical thinking is considering a problem unemotionally and searching out all the factors of which it is composed and all the terms on which an understanding of it depends.[23]

The faculty gave major attention in the report which was included in *Thirty Schools Tell Their Story* to "The Development of Critical Thinking." One paragraph near the beginning of the chapter of this title may be quoted:

> Critical or reflective thinking originates with the sensing of a problem. It is a quality of thought operating in an effort to solve the problem and to reach a tentative conclusion which is supported by all available data. It is really a process of problem solving requiring the use of creative insight, intellectual honesty, and sound judgment. It is the basis of the method of scientific inquiry. The success of

[23] *Were We Guinea Pigs?* (New York: Henry Holt and Company, Inc., 1938), p. 201.

democracy depends to a large extent on the disposition and ability of citizens to think critically and reflectively about the problems which must of necessity confront them, and to improve the quality of their thinking is one of the major goals of education.[24]

This statement omits any reference to emotional elements and hence by inference may be considered to deny them.

However, after multiplying illustrations of learning situations in all areas, the teachers remark later in the report, "If the problems mentioned in these numerous illustrations have one characteristic in common, it is that they are of genuine significance to the students who study them." [25] Implicit in the words "genuine significance" is a recognition that some emotional involvement on the part of the student is almost a necessity for his doing real thinking. However, if the writer's memory serves correctly, faculty members differed widely in their understanding of the relation of emotion to clear thinking. Some, with psychological training, stood for the acceptance of emotional biases and attitudes as normal, and attempted to integrate them with thinking by promoting understanding of their causes. Some believed that critical thinking could best be taught by providing experience in the logical analysis of emotion-free situations. Still others held the faith that any undesirable emotional reactions or prejudices could be changed by thoughtful and non-emotional examination of the data.

Mental-health studies of emotion were not yet widely disseminated, though men like Bruno Bettelheim and George V. Sheviakov were consulting with the Thirty Schools. The work of Gordon W. Allport, T. W. Adorno, and the others who have promoted an understanding of the personality factors in prejudice still lay in the future. Perhaps under those circumstances, the variations in the approaches of different teachers provided learning situations of desirable variety.

Data on the method of intelligence were analyzed in three categories: (1) intellectual control versus freedom-excitement, (2) level of logical analysis, and (3) level of tolerance for ambiguity.

[24] Progressive Education Association, Commission on the Relation of School and College, *op. cit.*, pp. 745–46.
[25] *Ibid.*, p. 750.

"Intellectual control versus freedom-excitement" was a category which was difficult to identify in the protocols because of the number of variables, including the variations in the personalities of the subjects and in their expressiveness in the interviews. The following descriptive classes were developed and the individuals were grouped under them; but in the absence of generally accepted standards of what is a desirable relation between thinking and feeling, the writer would not presume to make judgments as to whether the first class is the "best," and those later on are less "good"; or whether the middle is more desirable than the extremes. In general, they present a progression in the relation between thinking and feeling, although even the progression is not clear in the last classes.

1. *Generally uses method of intelligence, but accepts the validity of his own feelings, and enjoys the emotional lift of his activities.* Eight of the forty-five individuals fell in this group, four men and four women. Many sections and questions shed light on this trait, especially 49, 75, 79, 80, and the "Paths of Life." (See Appendix C for the interview schedule.) The single most revealing question was often number 79: "When you are in a group of people where the discussion is being dominated by individuals expressing very prejudiced views on questions on which you have strong opposing convictions, what do you do?" Typical answers from the eight in this group were the following:

> Well, I think that's a real problem. I know that has been a real problem with me, and that's something my husband and I have a difference of opinion on. He thinks sometimes I'm much too outspoken —well, I don't think he thinks that I'm outspoken so much, but he thinks that I could put my arguments in a slightly more tactful way that would be more apt to win people I completely oppose. I guess I tend to say what I think, maybe too much so.

> I get red in the face no doubt, and I see red definitely. I'm afraid I speak up and probably not very pleasantly.

> Oh, I just talk. [Laughs.] That is where I think lies part of my difficulty. I try to listen to what they say, but I do get very indignant on

prejudices. And maybe then I try to dominate a little bit by expressing my views, too.

I usually go berserk, I'm afraid. I have one that maybe is becoming a phobia with me—that's the race question. Because we live in a zoned town you see, and it comes up all the time, and everything is always blamed on—you know—another race. I really get rabid, and I have made enemies at the bridge table, I know, on this score.

Well, I'm afraid that from time to time I am likely to be such a person, stridently expressing my views, and I've never had trouble verbalizing. My feeling is this, though, that where I can, I try to first insinuate a few questions to more or less slow them down; and secondly I'm not averse to expressing my views, although I don't think I get angry over issues—I used to more, but I now realize it only raises the blood pressure—but I wouldn't hesitate to say what I thought.

An answer from a different individual is slightly at variance with part of the last quotation, but both attitudes were included in this group.

Question: When you get excited, how do you feel about it afterwards?

Answer: You mean on a political issue? I usually feel mad, but it's sort of exhilarating too. I rather like to get excited in arguments, I guess.

2. *Generally uses the method of intelligence and accepts the validity of his own feelings, but is a little cautious about his feelings.* Perhaps those in this classification were more concerned about the impression they were making in the interview, or were aware of other values in the situation. Again data were found in many places, but Question 79, which was quoted under the first classification, again produced many clear pictures. Ten of the forty-five were in this group.

This has happened a good many times to me, especially in the family. I soon learned not to say anything if we wanted to keep the love and affection of our family.

I take great delight in needling them if I can possibly get in the position of the needler instead of the person who is expounding the so-called fact. I think that's a lot of fun. I get a lot of enjoyment out of that. It sometimes develops into something that may become a little bit unfriendly; but I think as long as it stops at that point, or before that point, it's a very healthy thing.

Well, a lot of that will depend on the individual. I'll generally express my opinions, but if it's an individual that makes known his opinion only by volume rather than by logic or sense, I'll probably be talking to somebody else before very long.

Well, I generally go at it maybe a little bit indirectly; rather than strictly saying they are wrong with a counterstatement, I try to pick out a particular fallacy in it to see if they really know what they are talking about—rather than because they have the floor, let's say, or the louder voice—to see if they really know what they are talking about—in other words it's indirectly tearing the argument apart.

Usually when it's at home, I keep still; but if it's at somebody else's house I might voice my opinion.

Well, I wait as long as I can, and usually shoot off my mouth.

3. *Intellectual control is dominant and emotions are recognized but kept subordinate.* Many individuals seemed to consider emotions, their own or others, as a possible danger to order, logic, and moderation, which appeared to be important values to them. The distinction between this classification and the previous one is often difficult to make from the information in the protocols; and others analyzing the same material might well reach different conclusions. Ten of the forty-five individuals were in this classification.

Sometimes I speak up and sometimes I keep quiet depending on who the person is and how old they are. I see no point in causing hardship or misunderstanding or ill feeling because of politics and religion.

That depends on the group. Sometimes I'll argue with them. I think most of the time I'll either leave or help change the subject. [Under what circumstances do you argue?] As long as I don't get mad and as long as the group itself is not mad, I'll argue.

Well, that's a problem. I often wonder what to do. Usually I keep my mouth shut, and I'm not sure that's the right thing to do at all. I absolutely never get into it and get heated up or argue. That I never do. I either keep quiet or I try mildly to express my opinion or at least get the person to think of another side. It doesn't really come up too often. I've thought about it, though, and wondered what to do if somebody did do something like that; and I think if it were an important question, I think I probably would speak up a little bit. At least I'm trying to work myself up to have the courage to do that if I thought it were important. Right now I wouldn't though; I'm afraid I'm a little backward that way.

4. *Assigns a dominant position to intellectual control and distrusts strong emotions, his own or others, as a definite threat to order and logic.* This group also lies so close to the previous one that differences are not striking. Seven individuals were assigned to this group.

Well, it—like they taught us in the army—it depends on the technical situation in the terrain. [Laughs.] You can't always answer that, I don't think. In the first place, I'm not one to—just by nature—to force my views on anyone else; I will discuss them, I think, without getting mad. I'm happy that I can discuss them without getting mad, but everyone is entitled to their own opinion on such things; and I can state my opinion and argue mildly towards it, and beyond that point I'd just rather drop the matter than get all up in a huff.

I don't know that the situation arises very frequently. I would probably express my decided opinions briefly, not make much of an argument, and get out.

6. *Has achieved a very orderly pattern with a subdued intensity level of both emotions and intellect.* Six persons seemed to have achieved this pattern in the relation between emotion and thinking, although either one might break through at times.

Finally, one individual appeared to be stalemated by a conflict between thinking and emotion. Four very interesting individuals escaped any classifications that the writer was able to devise, perhaps because they had some conflicts of values which helped account for inconsistencies in their protocols.

"Level of logical analysis" is the next category of the method of intelligence to be considered. Here we encounter the same problem discussed at the beginning of Part III—the wide differences to be expected from individuals because of their native endowments. A person who is using the method of intelligence should be bringing his best thinking to bear upon the problems which concern him and upon the events in his world; but his "best thinking" is all that can be expected of him, whether his I.Q. is 70 or 170. Similarly, "the problems which concern him" and "the events in his world" will vary enormously in range and complexity. However, as citizens of a democracy, everyone's world includes community and political questions. Thus, the analysis of each protocol was carried out with the particular individual very much in mind; each was assigned an informal handicap as in a golf match, but each was assumed to be playing at least an important part of the same course.

For the analysis of this category, the text of the protocol was given great weight. That is, an individual who talked freely and intelligently before the interview began, but gave unrevealing answers to the questions in the course of the interview, was judged entirely by his protocol. Although this undoubtedly resulted in a false picture of at least three individuals who had talked volubly before the tape recorder was turned on but "clammed up" in front of the microphone, the measurable injustice seemed vastly preferable to the confusion of allowing memories and impressions from other sources to intrude into the ratings.

Evidence was sought in the way the respondent went about the analysis of events in his world: the depth of focus, assignment of causes, understanding of motivation, and perception of relationships. Also relevant was his degree of sophistication in the handling of concepts by which specific events or problems might be interpreted.

Evidence of the last aspect of the method of intelligence, "tolerance for ambiguity" was chiefly sought in the sections of the protocol which asked for specific answers to unanswerable questions: "Who do you think have an easier time in present-day America, men or women?", "What people or groups in this country do you think of as having interests similar to yours—that is, they are more or less on your side?", or "Do you think an individual is really responsible for what becomes of him?" In this category, the respondent who was rated high recognized the ambiguity of the question, but as he explored it further, found that life itself was ambiguous, that the question asked had at least two sides, or that it was a legitimately unclosed question. The person who can comfortably recognize, live with, and work on the

TABLE 63

METHOD OF INTELLIGENCE: LOGICAL ANALYSIS
AND TOLERANCE FOR AMBIGUITY

Rating	Quintile										Total	
	I		II		III		IV		V			
	Men	Women	Men	Women	Men	Women	Men	Women	Men	Women	Men	Women
Very high...	4	3	1	2	3	1	1	..	1	1	10	7
High....	..	..	2	4	1	2	3	..	..	..	6	6
Some....	..	..	..	..	..	3	..	1	1	1	1	5
Little....	..	1	..	..	..	..	2	1	2	1	4	3
Very little...	..	..	..	..	..	..	..	..	..	..	..	..
Contradictory.	..	1	..	..	1	..	..	..	1	..	2	1
Total..	4	5	3	6	5	6	6	2	5	3	23	22

myriad unanswered questions of our age has a high tolerance for ambiguity. The alternatives are discomfort, despair, or some form of flight —a closing of the mind or withdrawal of attention. Since this aspect seemed closely related to the level of logical analysis in the protocols, the two phases were tabulated together. In the few cases in which there were serious differences between the answers in different parts of the same protocol, the individual was rated "contradictory."

Table 63 summarizes the results of the ratings on two aspects of the method of intelligence. Twenty-nine of the forty-five men and women were rated "high" or "very high," thirteen were rated "some" or "little," and three were rated "contradictory." For these ratings, there was a strong tendency to use an intra-class standard in the absence of any standard that had been developed for and applied to the general population. Since the group tended to be high, it is possible that the judgment of the lower members may have been unduly severe.

There is a regular drop from quintile to quintile in this table, a circumstance which has not been evident in any of the other tables in this section except Table 58, "Social Sensitivity: Scope of the Social World." The method of intelligence appears to be more dependent on I.Q. than the other qualities which were promoted by the University School program, but it is noteworthy that none of the class members in any of the quintiles was rated "very little." The individuals who were rated "very high" in the lowest quintile were the same ones who were considered by the writer as probably misplaced by the arbitrary scheme on which the quintiles were originally set up. (See Chapter III, pp. 39–40.) With such small numbers involved, it is probable that the slight differences between the ratings of men and women are of no significance, though the men appear to have a slight edge at first glance.

The quotations which are offered as examples of several aspects of the method of intelligence will be largely positive, showing the kinds of responses which contributed to a high rating, though there will be an occasional illustration of a contrasting one. In general, the responses which were given low ratings were brief, superficial, or evasive.

Some examples which reveal an analysis of motivation will lead off. Each is from a different respondent, and both men and women are included.

Question: Do you think of your family—the one in which you grew up—as a democratic institution? If not, who was boss?

Answer: No, father was boss; but mother made a lot of decisions behind his back. As an adult I can see that the decisions behind his back made him more dictatorial.

Question: Are you bringing up your children more strictly than you were raised, less strictly, or about the same?

Answer: I don't know. The reason I don't know is that I don't remember what my parents did. I think I am more readily willing to be strict than my parents were because I have more faith in myself. But I would not say in absolute terms that we are strict with our children, but I believe firmly in the axiom that "parents are at least as important as children."

Question: If you had your choice as to family, would you now choose to have had another set of parents?

Answer: No, not now. Oh, pshaw. That's a hard question to answer. Of course, I had a lot of antagonism at home, with my father particularly; and yet now—you know, when you said, "Does school build individuals?" it wasn't just the school. It was my parents and their friends—they were individual types too; and now that I like people like that, I look back and think it was great. But I was an adolescent, I was unhappy that we didn't have a radio, and that we took trips in the summer instead of going to a cottage at the beach, and so on— we saw the world. I wouldn't change it though, I don't think.

Question: Do you think of yourself as a realistic person on the whole or more on the idealistic side?

Answer: I would say more trending to be a realist. I am accused of being an idealistic person at the plant sometimes because of the things that I think we can do, but sometimes that's just the natural resistance to change. Something can be done, someone else says it can't be done—then they feel they're being realistic and I'm being idealistic; but I think no one likes things to change, though no one admits it to himself. [When it works out, then they admit you're realistic on that?] Yeah.

Question: Do your own parents or your in-laws or other relatives ever try to interfere in decisions which you regard as purely matters for your own family?

Answer: Oh yes, we have to contend with that. [How do you and your wife handle—] Well, we try to be understanding and we try to be diplomatic, although at times I suppose we don't succeed in being either. Yet it's awfully difficult for older people, our seniors in terms of years and in terms—certainly in many respects in terms of wisdom and in terms of understanding some of the basic problems of life—

it is difficult for them not to advise or to insist that we do certain
things, or that we see that our children are raised in a certain manner,
or that certain things are done for them, or that they are required to
do certain things. It's difficult for older people not to advise or demand in those respects. We try not to offend, we try to be thankful
where possible. Where we just have to put our foot down, well, we
do so.

The common factor in all of these responses is the attempt to find
the reasonable cause for the behavior of others who, in most cases,
are opposing or have opposed the respondent. In none of the protocols
are other people pictured as threatening, vindictive, or completely un-
reasonable.

Most closely related to the understanding of motivation (in the
logical analysis of events) is the assignment of causes.

Question: Do you think that there will always be wars?

Answer: Well, I don't think necessarily—I think eventually we'll
probably do away with them, but that won't be in my lifetime. [What
do you think can be done to make war less likely?] Well, I wish I
knew. I really don't know. I used to think that the United Nations
would be the solution. I had great hopes. I think something like the
United Nations would be the only thing I'd know to make it work;
but when people believe so strongly different, as we do with the
Russians, of basic concepts of human rights and functions, it's a little
hard to see how you can co-operate. But I think it's the only thing we
can do, and I think there is a chance of us eventually getting together
someway. I think there's also a chance of the thing blowing up in
our face.

Answer: I don't think there always has to be war. I think that—I
hope in time that the—oh, I don't know what it is—that psychology,
philosophy, social studies can somehow get it across to the people—
and also the view in bringing up your children—that war accom-
plishes nothing. I see no reason why there should be war. [What
do you think could be done to make war less likely?] I think
the United Nations is a step; I think having foreign students come
over here and sending students over to other countries; trying to
accept their way of life and not trying particularly to have everything
democratic, because I'm not positive that democratic—I don't think

it should be *forced* upon people. I think they should have a chance to see it and apply it in their own ways in their own countries.

Question: A number of people felt that one outcome of the program should be "the ability to think for yourself." Do you think that was one of the things the school stressed?

Answer: I think definitely that was one of the strengths. [Can you explain what makes you think you do or do not have this ability to think for yourself?] Well, I think I do have the ability to think for myself in that I want—I definitely don't agree with everyone nor do I feel that I must follow what is the popular way of thinking. I believe that is my only excuse for saying I have learned to think for myself. [Do you think that thinking for yourself is related to self-confidence?] Not necessarily, because I have never felt, or at least I don't feel that when I was younger anyway, that I had much self-confidence. I have gained self-confidence, but I'm not sure that I have ever tried to relate the two.

Question: Do you ever get as worked up about something that happens in politics as about something that happens in your personal life?

Answer: I think more so, because I actually know less about what happens in politics than I do in my own personal life. [That is, you feel the amount of working up depends on not knowing so much?] In a way. I mean you can fly off the handle a lot faster about something if you don't know all there is to know about it.

Two responses to the same question will illustrate the difference between the individual who explores causes and the one who avoids the issue.

Question: Do you think it is easier to avoid war or to avoid depression?

Answer: I believe it would be possibly easier to avoid depression. In fact, I am sure it would be easier to avoid depression rather than war. [Why?] Well, I believe that the government can subsidize a lot of things—projects, anything connected with putting more money on the market, even though it's inflationary and everything else—I believe they could do that. Whereas when a belligerent country wants

to fight, there is nothing you can do except fight—I mean argue, but
if they are dead set they are going to fight, there is nothing you can do.

Answer: Avoid war or avoid depression? I think it's easier to avoid
war. [Can you explain why a little bit.] I don't know. [Laughs.] [You
don't have any opinion between those two?] Well, if you don't have a
war once in awhile, they say you are bound to have a depression.

The kinds of concepts which lay behind responses offered another
kind of evidence that could be evaluated. Shallow and stereotyped
responses like the following were rated low:

Question: Who do you think runs the country now?

Answer: I'd say big money.

Answer: Well, I think the country runs itself. The officials interfere
with it a great deal and fool around and tinker with the mechanism a
great deal, but actually I think it runs itself.

In contrast, consider the depth of focus and understanding of concepts in the following answer to the same question:

Well, that would be hard to say. The country is run on a series of
compromises, compromises of force—forces of one single congressman here, another one there, a bill here wants to be passed so he votes
for this, and the administration wants this done, somebody else on the
outside says, "We want this done," the public feeling over here is
definitely against it; and it's all a series of compromises. That's been
the history of our whole government. It's, if anything, run by Mr.
Compromise. I mean it's power against power, it's the old checks and
balances, but not as simple as the framers of the constitution envisioned it to be.

Answers to a particular question may be very different and yet both
show mastery of the handling of concepts. Consider the following
examples.

Question: A number of people felt that one outcome of the program
should be "the ability to think for yourself." Do you agree? Can you

explain what makes you think that you do or do not have this ability? Is it related to self-confidence?

Answer: Yes, one should get the ability to think for one's self in a fairly large area of human thought. However, along with this thinking for one's self, there must be associated a knowledge of the approximate limitations of success in thinking for one's self. I think I do have this ability to a reasonable degree in certain limited fields, and it is related to self-confidence. I gained this ability many years after leaving University School, so the causal relation is not clear.

Answer: Yes, indeed. Without any question whatsoever, I felt that I was always encouraged and I never forgot it. I found in college that there seemed to be more professors who felt that this was a heretical viewpoint that any student was supposed to do it; but I am very grateful to the school. I certainly feel that this is true. [You think it's related to self-confidence?] Well, yes; of course, it breeds its tensions, too, because it will push you often toward nonconformity in so far as conforming means accepting rather pat and glib answers. You take the risk of setting yourself emotionally apart from a group every time you think for yourself. On the other hand, I suppose it contributes somewhat to self-confidence, assurance.

Question: How do you feel about the government's present loyalty-security measures?

Answer: Our country is awfully large and we try to have a great amount of freedom—understanding those two things, the security program would be a most difficult one to administer. It seems that at times while they were picayune about small things, outsiders got into the inside of the big things like the atomic programs and uh— know-how. But it would be difficult to all ends to police the country in that respect.

Answer: I think they need to improve them a great deal. The McCarthy business brought to a head the horrible business of what can happen when people can malign others with great publicity and those maligned cannot defend themselves with equal publicity.

Question: What do you think is most important in life: (a) trying to make the world a better place; (b) happiness; (c) making other people happy; (d) living according to your religion?

Answer: You'd better live according to your religion—you won't get very far with the others. [Laughs] If you try to make yourself happy, you won't get far. If you try to make others happy, you won't do what they want. Better live according to your religion, and let the chips fall where they may. Making the world a better place to live in is an awfully big assignment.

Answer: Well, of course, my religion would encompass several of those others; but happiness, I feel, is a by-product of reaching your goals and accomplishment and living with other people in a manner which you enjoy. In other words, I feel, in my instance at least, it's a mistake to seek happiness as such. I think happiness is a result of other things.

Other responses illustrate the wide range of questions which shed light on the level at which an individual handled concepts and theories.

Question: Do you think an individual is really responsible for what becomes of him?

Answer: In a purely academic sense, no. In a practical sense, he is responsible for not getting in his own way. He cannot control what he will be; but it is up to him to accept what he is, whatever that is.

Question: Do you think that labor is getting too much power and too high pay lately, are you disturbed about things like this merger, or do you think it's a good thing?

Answer: I'm not so sure that anything that's too big—maybe even General Motors—if it's too big it has its drawbacks as far as the welfare of the country is concerned. That might apply to the combined sixteen-million-member labor organization. I don't think labor is getting too much. I think some of labor's bosses are without a great amount of reason, and I blow a fuse every time one of them says that certain technological advances should not be put into effect because it will put certain numbers of labor's force out of work. That to me is a dastardly thing to say, and if put into effect, would reduce the standard of living. The only way we can increase the standard of living is to produce more for every hour that a man puts in working.

Evidence of the third category of the method of intelligence, tolerance for ambiguity, appeared in a great many places, including a number of responses already quoted, in which the respondent analyzed events with some care but indicated that there were still uncertainties. Responses will be quoted from both men and women in all quintiles; each quotation is from a different protocol.

Question: On the whole, and considering people in all walks of life, who do you think have an easier time in present-day America, men or women?

Answer: I don't know. I can see advantages both ways; in certain respects I can say men, in other respects women. A lot will depend on the particular individual. Of course, I think they have done a lot of things to make homemaking easier for the women, but sometimes I wonder about that. Women have emancipated themselves, but they try to run a house and do three or four activities on the side when one would keep you busy.

Answer: Well, it depends on what they're doing. I don't know whether you could put it into two separate categories. Some men, I think, have it easy and some women; but I don't think I can say.

Answer: Well, I think it is very difficult for both of them. I think that the educated woman is an enigma to the men. I don't think that we are quite as equipped to make them comfortable as they think maybe we should. I think it's hard on both of us. We are emancipated and we have our outside interests, and they are a combination of trying to understand us and co-operate and still expecting a little more of life than the past generation, and I think it's a difficult time for both. I think the pressures are great in business; and maybe women don't stop and consider their comfort because of the pressures and all. There are many deaths among the men from your heart attacks and all, and I think it's very difficult for both of us.

Question: If you had your choice as to when you would be born, would you have preferred to live in some other age than this?

Answer: No. I think so far—why, the age that we are living in right now is fine to me. It's mixed up and confused, but every other one has been, too, so I see no point of wishing that we were born any other time.

Question: Do you think an individual is really responsible for what becomes of him?

Answer: Within limits, yes. [What are the limits?] Well—you would ask that! A coal miner in the hills of Kentucky, for instance, is not responsible for what happens to him. He's poorly educated, if educated at all. He's had very little choice of job; and even if he has a job, he has someone that tells him how long, when he can work, and how much he can get for it, and somebody else to take the money away from him for this purpose, [inaudible list, spoken very rapidly], and so forth, especially investments, and all that. He can't do much with himself, or for himself. A person who has a fairly decent education can usually make of himself what he wants, but then again there are limitations. Everybody can't be President of the United States. I don't have to do what I am doing now, if I want to do something else.

Answer: I think the degree of responsibility which an individual person has for what becomes of him varies extensively from individual to individual and from time to time. [What makes the difference?] (a) The more intransigent characteristics of the individual, such as race, intelligence, personality type, etc.; (b) the various situations in which he is—certain situations are conducive to development of a type of personality.

Question: Do you have any feeling now about how well the balance of co-operation and competition in the school prepared or failed to prepare you for competition and co-operation as you met them outside?"

Answer: Well, certainly the school stressed co-operation. I mean this was impressed upon me in my experience in the school. But I cannot evaluate that in terms of really knowing how much impression was made upon me. I know that the school stressed co-operation, and it seemed to me that a great deal of it existed; and as I have talked to people who came from a different educational process, I'm quite sure it existed to a high degree. In so far as how it prepared me, I don't know.

Question: Which of the following are the most important in getting ahead in life: (a) education, (b) brains, (c) a good personality, (d) hard work, (e) good connections, (f) patience, or (g) luck?

Answer: What do you mean by "getting ahead"? You mean financially successful, or what are you thinking of that way? [Well, that's an undefined term that you'll have to define for yourself.] That makes it difficult. Assuming that it means basically that, I think they are all important. I think education, as far as formal education goes, isn't overly important. I think you can gain a lot of that yourself, if you want to. A good personality would be—. It's hard. There again, a personality in some phases of getting ahead doesn't even enter into it. There are some strictly technical fields where personality is of no importance. I would say hard work is important. There's a little luck in it always, too.

Answer: I think it's hard to say, because it depends so much on what "getting ahead" means. If it's a career—in some phases brains are especially important, in others a personality. If you think of your education as your formal schooling, I don't think it is too important. If you think of it as your general background of knowledge or anything, I would say it is probably the most important. Does that answer your question?

To summarize, it appears from the data that the method of intelligence is used at a higher level by the academically gifted individuals. It is present as a method, however, among all groups, and at every level some individuals are significantly more adept at using it than others.

XI

GENERAL COMMENTS AND CONCLUSIONS

The previous chapters have examined from many points of view the patterns of adult living of fifty-four men and women who graduated from the University School in 1938. The study was undertaken as an attempt to evaluate the long-term results of the specific educational program to which they had been exposed; the findings of the study may be of general significance as evidence of the degree of effectiveness that is achievable in secondary education, and of the promises and limitations of experimental programs.

Part II, which was based largely upon responses to the questionnaires, is primarily concerned with the objective data of further education, income, health, reading habits, marriage, families, and so on. Throughout that section, except in Chapters VIII and IX, there is comparatively little attempt to relate the separate findings to the school program. In contrast, Part III was concerned specifically with certain values which the school consciously tried to foster. Using data from the interviews, supplemented by any other information which was available and pertinent, the writer studied the ways in which these values functioned or failed to function for the members of the class, who were now in their middle thirties. An examination of the consistencies and inconsistencies of the data and of their cumulative significance is an important function of this final chapter.

Whether the material gathered in this report really shows the influence of the school program, or whether it has been so contaminated by other intervening influences that it cannot show anything, is a question which was raised in the beginning and must be re-examined.

That these individuals in high school and in their adult living were and are influenced by their times cannot be disputed. In matters which the school program was not designed to influence—religious participation, age at marriage, size of families—this group quite closely follows national trends. In areas with which the school was actively concerned, most of the data indicate that the times were a contributing rather than a dominating influence. Whenever comparative studies were available, they emphasized the marked resemblances among the members of the Class of 1938 and the significant differences between them and the comparative groups. The widely disparate educational, vocational, and military experiences and the geographical scattering of the class members since their graduation in 1938 suggest that there are only two probable sources for the high degree of similarity: (1) the school program, and (2) the selective factor which caused them to come to and remain in the University School.

These two factors probably cannot be separated. However, the boys and girls and their parents were not all equally sympathetic to what the school was trying to do. Some few dropped out for that reason, although other marginal individuals remained to graduate. There were other members of the class whose analyses, as adults, of their high-school family situations showed clearly that the reasons their families had chosen University School were certainly not based on an understanding of the values and purposes that the faculty held. In the majority of cases, however, it appears that the homes and school were working toward essentially the same ends.

Taking all these points into consideration, it seems reasonably safe to give major emphasis to the role of the school program in producing general likenesses, provided such similarities are true for a very large proportion of the class and are not more readily accounted for by some other influence. This conclusion is even more likely when data from different parts of the study support each other, and when other studies of similar groups yield quite different results.

The data on social sensitivity and democratic values were obtained from an analysis of the protocols, the data for community participation from both the questionnaire responses and the protocols. It is assumed that the data in these two areas should be closely related, and such is, indeed, the case. For assigning primacy to human-relations values, 82 per cent were ranked "very high" or "high," 15.5 per cent "some," and only 2.3 per cent "little." Similarly, 77.7 per cent were placed in the two top groups on "interpersonal democracy and democratic ideology," the same 2.3 per cent in "little," and the rest in either "contradictory" or "some." In the analysis of scope of the social world and work in voluntary organizations, only a few more than half were ranked in the two top classifications; however, 18 per cent of this number volunteered unsolicited comments which revealed that they played leadership roles. Only three of the total number interviewed had joined no voluntary organizations; the questionnaires indicated slight or no participation for 18.5 per cent of the men and 12 per cent of the women, and extensive involvement for 81.5 per cent of the men and 88 per cent of the women. This contrasts sharply with the results of the studies by Wright and Hyman. They found that college-educated people joined the most organizations; but that 30 per cent of this group were members of none, another 25 per cent belonged to one, and only 36 per cent belonged to two or more. In a similar study in Denver, only 56 per cent of the women reported belonging to one or more organizations; in the same study, 82 per cent of the married men with children under eighteen years of age were members of at least one, the only figure which approaches the record of the guinea pigs (100 per cent of the married men of the Class of 1938 belonged to voluntary associations). It appears that the guinea pigs are far more actively involved in their communities than their counterparts.

Leadership qualities were revealed in some other connections. In the Second World War, 73 per cent of the men who entered the army were privates; when the war ended, only one remained a private. All of the men who joined the navy became commissioned officers. Their records of peacetime jobs, and of earned incomes, show that the same leadership qualities are reflected in their day-to-day living.

There is abundant evidence that few of these people are conformists, though none is self-consciously and assertively nonconformist. Most of them are quite aware of being individualists and of liking other people who are. Magazine subscriptions are highly individualized, as are their uses of the other mass media. Recreational patterns are varied and personal. For a significant proportion of the group (15.5 per cent), community participation, highly organized as it is, takes on an individual style.

One aspect of the extent and degree of individuation may be represented by the analysis of creativity, which has been treated in this study as an expressive, spontaneous, inquiring reaction toward living. Twenty-eight and nine tenths per cent were very highly creative, 26.7 per cent were rated "high," 28.9 per cent were creative to some extent, and only 15.5 per cent showed little or no creativity. The last group includes those individuals with relatively strong tendencies toward conformity. Riesman speaks of the autonomous person as one who recognizes conventional behavior, but has the inner freedom to make his choice in any situation about whether or not to conform. It would appear that the guinea-pig group includes an unusually high proportion of relatively autonomous people.

This quality is also shown in their attitudes toward money (82 per cent felt that a certain amount was necessary; but beyond that, it was less important than satisfaction with work, happiness of the family, and self-respect and self-realization), and toward living in the present age (82.2 per cent were either satisfied or enthusiastic, whereas only 15.5 per cent would prefer the future and 2.3 per cent the past). Princeton Class of 1944 reported in 1954 that only 34 per cent of their number "accepted the chills and vapors of the cold war cheerfully." A large proportion of the guinea pigs (79 per cent) liked their jobs very much or fairly well. They felt they were getting, or will get, what they want out of life; they admired ambitious people unless they tread on the rights of others; they believed that each individual has a major part in determining his own fate, though circumstances often take a hand.

Data which contradict each other would be important evidence that chance was playing a large part in the results for this small group. No such contradictions were found for the group as a whole. However, there were individuals who revealed contradictions within themselves—the uncompromising intellectual who revealed in the relaxed atmosphere of the interview a warm, spontaneous, creative personality which the interviewer was forbidden to report; and the dogged introvert who was still searching the world around him for the explanations which lie in his own personality.

The latter person appears in every tabulation at the bottom of the scale; he and a very few other individuals account for a disproportionate number of the low scores in each category except "Scope of the Social World" and "The Method of Intelligence." In these two, and especially in the latter, there is a tendency for high and low scores to be distributed according to intelligence level. The individuals in the two lowest quintiles who rated very high in these categories were those who were, in the writer's opinion, misplaced by the device used in establishing the quintiles, with the exception of one who was and apparently remains a consistent over-achiever.

It seems reasonable to expect that the more intelligent a person is, the more able he will be to see the breadth and depth of his social world and the more adept at using the method of intelligence. There is, therefore, an interesting problem raised by widely differing results in closely related categories. Interpersonal democracy is high, but democratic action in volunteer groups is relatively low and in politics lower still. Social sensitivity is high, but many interpret the scope of their social world narrowly. Is it inevitable that problems less closely related to the individual shall be perceived with less clarity by many? Or is this a failure of the method of teaching? Might more use of the kinds of experiences advocated by the Citizenship Education Project, or of those described in the quotation from Jacob (pages 106–7), make a difference? Or are these results—high in comparison with other groups—the most that one could hope to get?

The groups which offered the most interesting comparisons with the guinea pigs were Terman's gifted children, Barbe's major work-program graduates from Cleveland, and Princeton Class of 1944, with some interesting side lights from McIntosh's low I.Q. trade-school group.

Terman's group was homogeneous only in having I.Q.'s of 140 and

over. Their school and college experiences were completely heterogeneous. In most respects, the guinea-pig class as a whole, with its complete range of abilities but with its exposure to a carefully planned
school program, has made a record equal to Terman's group of
"geniuses." What this actually means is not that students of low ability
can be made into geniuses, but that when a large majority of the members of a class perform somewhere near their best potential the group
can reach surprising levels of achievement.

In 1953 Barbe studied the graduates of a major work program in
Cleveland, in which classes for gifted children were set up in the
elementary grades and continued through the high-school years. All
of the students in these classes had I.Q.'s of 120 or over, came mainly
from upper–middle class homes, and were given a special school
program in elementary and high school. The proportion of this group
which graduated from college was much smaller than that of the
Class of 1938; the proportion who belong to professional groups
was the same. The guinea pigs expressed satisfaction with their school
experience in about the same numbers as the students in Cleveland
(85.5 and 88.5 per cent respectively), but with rather more enthusiasm. Not nearly so many of the Cleveland group were satisfied
with their jobs.

The chief comparisons with Princeton Class of 1944, which was assumed to be a highly selected group of men of similar age, concerned
income (similar), reading (Princeton graduates read a few more
books), and attitude toward living (the guinea pigs seem to have
learned to tolerate ambiguity and insecurity better than the Princeton
graduates though the data for this comparison are tenuous).

The study by W. J. McIntosh of one thousand graduates of a trade
school is interesting for several conclusions that may help to explain
some of the results obtained from our group. He remarks, "Other
factors, such as emotional stability and personal drive, were as important [to later vocational success] as even 20 points in the I.Q.
scale within the range of 65 to 95." "The experience of success at
school, in some form, helps to build up a sense of personal worth
within the boy, and does more to stabilize his emotions and give him

the drive necessary to succeed in life than years of drill on phonics or arithmetic facts." [1]

The data show clearly that, twenty years after their graduation from high school, this group of young adults is an outstanding one; the data do not, however, offer a clear basis on which the influence of home and school may be separated. In the cases of three individuals whose home situations were deeply disturbing to them as high-school students, the influence still persists strongly today; four or five others who lived through situations which seemed equally disturbing appear to have surmounted the difficulties and to have integrated them successfully into adult living. Pondering these and other individuals, the writer concludes that education is most effective when home and school share common concerns and methods, but that the school can help enormously to make up for the deficiencies of certain homes, and can, to an extent, substitute for some missing elements of great importance. The limiting factors in this process appear to be the personalities of pupils, teachers, and parents.

The evidence indicates that a dynamic education can have a marked influence on the later lives of students. The essential elements seem to be faith, on the part of the teachers and the students, in growth and in the ability of the pupil to go on from where he is; in the necessity of respecting every individual; and in the ability and responsibility of each person to use the method of intelligence to solve academic, personal, and social problems. Although these fifty-four men and women are now leading very different lives, there are striking resemblances in their vital, forward-looking atttitudes toward living and their basic consideration for other human beings. Only one member of the group seems to be trapped in a blind alley, and even that is not certain.

The fact that this was a heterogeneous group does not seem to have penalized any ability level—high, average, or low. The students who criticized their high-school science courses (which were also criticized

[1] "Follow-up Study of One Thousand Non-academic Boys," *Journal of Exceptional Children,* XV (March, 1949), pp. 191, 170.

by the faculty in the same period) nevertheless went on to specialized work in science in college. A look at the achievements of all of the fifty-four since their graduation from high school—jobs, income, personal adjustment, patterns of living—gives an impression of possibilities quite richly fulfilled for most and completely missed by none. This means that almost everyone, in terms of his own level of ability, has become reasonably successful. The curricular organizations and devices which made this kind of development possible in high school have been noted at many places in our study; nobody was trained to expect constant failure or easy success.

There is convincing evidence that the values to which the school is committed can be made operational in the lives of most students through appropriate experiences and techniques in the curriculum. Students seem to learn these values through the process of valuing in experiences that are significant to them, rather than by indoctrination. The success of this type of education appears to be closely related to healthy personalities—people who know themselves, accept themselves, find learning significant, and can work with others.

A student who, for some reason, does not feel himself a valued part of the group and who puts small value on himself receives little education; in extreme cases, such students may experience negative learning from situations which are positive for others. Hence, a basic necessity for effective learning for any student is a sense of status and involvement in the educational process. Three elements seem to be of basic importance for effective learning: (a) acceptance by the teacher of every individual *as he is,* but with faith in his ability to learn and skill in stimulating him to attack meaningful problems; (b) participation by the pupil in planning so that each student may have a share in establishing his individual goals; (c) a class atmosphere of co-operation and mutual aid, supplemented by competition whenever it is appropriate (i.e., in situations in which all those competing have a chance of success if they work hard).

Philip Jacob, in *Changing Values in College,* makes a number of surmises as to the reasons certain college programs are more effective than others in changing the values of students: close faculty-student relationships, active involvement of the student in learning, use of situations real to student, and so on. Our experience tends to support his hypotheses.

This kind of education is very challenging to teachers and very demanding. It requires creative teaching, and offers rich opportunities for successes and failures. Excerpts from recent letters from two guinea pigs may appropriately close this report.

One of them, who was concerned about the problems of his very bright child in a laboratory school in which much of the instruction is done by student teachers, made the following comment on "progressive education":

> We think there's a great deal to be said for emphasis on "old fashioned subjects," combined with ability grouping so the bright kids can go through the material at a reasonable rate and not be bored. Long division can be *more* exciting than a six weeks unit on cactuses. The "progressive system" with units and democratic planning of what to study next can work well with extremely good teachers, but can be a dreadful mess with the ordinary teacher.

The other ended his letter in the following way:

> I want you to know that I will never cease being truly grateful for my four years in University School. Those years began for me in a state of disturbance, confusion, and rebellion. They ended as golden years, exciting, absorbing, and rich beyond expression. Of course, I emerged a pretty callow kid, but insights and stimulus and perspective gained in my high school helped give me pointers and directives and opened up areas of intellectual and social interests that I should feel poverty-stricken without today.

APPENDIXES

BIOGRAPHICAL QUESTIONNAIRE

The University School
The Ohio State University
Follow-up of Class of 1938

Date of filling out form _____

Full name _____ Birth date _____
     Married women include maiden name

Address _____
1. Education since leaving University School.
    a) Circle highest grade completed. College: 1 2 3 4; Postgraduate
    work in college: 1 2 3 4 [Special courses—technical, business,
    professional, artistic—to be entered under (c)]

b) Name of college	Dates of at-tendance	Degree received Date	Scholastic honors

291

c) Name of technical or other school	Dates of attendance	Diplomas or other recognition

2. Military service, if any: Date entered _____ Date of leaving service _____ Reason for leaving _____

_____

Branch of service _____ Grade or rank on entry _____

Highest grade or rank reached _____

Unusual experiences, assignments, associations, or responsibilities

_____

_____

_____

_____

_____

Special citations, decorations, etc. _____

_____

_____

3. Volunteer war work and postwar civilian defense. List all kinds you have done since 1941, including work with Ration Boards,

Blood Bank, USO, Air Raid Filter Centers, relief agencies, etc. Give approximate dates.

_____

_____

_____

_____

_____

To be detached   (see letter)

· · · · · · · · · · · · · · · · · ·

4. Occupation and earned income. (Under income, report annual salary before income tax deductions are made.) If self-employed (doctor, lawyer, business owner, etc.), give equivalent of salary, i.e., earned income less operating expenses. Women who are devoting the full time to homemaking, enter that in first column and earned income of spouse in last column.

Year	Profession, job, or position	Nature of the work	Earned income per year	Earned income of spouse
1950				
1951				
1952				
1953				

Do you own your own home or apartment? _____

5. List your publications, if any, giving full bibliographical references. Make a separate classification for any work published by your husband or wife on which you gave major assistance, though

you are not listed as joint author. Use a separate sheet if space below is insufficient.

_____

_____

_____

_____

_____

6. Your health since 1938.

 a) Physical condition has been (underline) very good, good, fair, poor, very poor.

  Illnesses, accidents, or surgical operations since 1938: _____

  _____

  _____

  After effects _____

  _____

 b) Has there been any tendency toward emotional disturbances, nervousness, worry, special anxiety, or nervous breakdown in recent years? _____

  Nature of such difficulties _____

  How handled _____

  Present condition _____

7. Marriage.

 Are you married now? _____ If so, give date _____ Age at marriage _____ Living with husband or wife? _____

Name of spouse (maiden name of wife) _____

Spouse's age at marriage _____ Highest grade or college year of

spouse's schooling _____ Degree received _____

What school or college _____ Scholastic honors_____

Present occupation of spouse (if in military service, give branch

and grade or rank) _____

Have you been married before? _____ Date _____ Was the marriage terminated by (underline) death of spouse, separation, divorce?

Date and cause of separation or divorce _____ Any chil-

dren by first marriage? _____ Had spouse been married previ-

ously? _____ Any children by previous marriage? _____

8. Offspring:

Name	Sex	Birth date	Adopted or stepchild?	If not living, age at death

9. *a*) Avocational interest. Mark a cross on each of the 12 lines below
to indicate the amount of your interest in each subject or activ-

ity. Place it at any point that most nearly indicates your interest.

(1) Travel

_____

Very More Average Slight None
much than
     average

(2) Outdoor Sports

_____

Very More Average Slight None
much than
     average

(3) Religion

_____

Very More Average Slight None
much than
     average

(4) Mechanics

_____

Very More Average Slight None
much than
     average

(5) Social Life

_____

Very More Average Slight None
much than
     average

(6) Literature

_____

Very More Average Slight None
much than
     average

(7) Music

_____

Very More Average Slight None
much than
     average

(8) Art

_____

Very More Average Slight None
much than
     average

(9) Science

_____

Very More Average Slight None
much than
     average

(10) Politics

_____

Very More Average Slight None
much than
     average

(11) Domestic Arts

_____

Very More Average Slight None
much than
     average

(12) Pets

_____

Very More Average Slight None
much than
     average

b) Be as specific as you can in a few sentences about what sorts of things you do in your principal avocational interest. (Collecting particular kinds of records, participating in chorus or orchestra, climbing mountains, or whatever.)

10. (For those gainfully employed. Housewives and others who do not receive paychecks for their work should omit this.)

Did you definitely choose your present work or get into it more or less accidentally or casually? _____

_____

_____

Would you prefer some other kind of work? _____ If so, please specify _____

_____

_____

11. Politics.

   a) When you were in high school, did you consider that your parents were (underline) radical, liberal, liberal on some things and conservative on others, fairly consistently conservative, reactionary. (If father was in one classification and mother in another, indicate by putting F or M above the phrase you have underlined.)

   b) Were their political affiliations or votes fairly consistently (underline) Democratic, Republican, Socialist, Independent, Don't know. (If father and mother usually differed, put F or M above the party name.)

   c) How regularly do you vote? (Check)
   All elections _____   Only state elections _____
   Only national elections _____ Only local elections _____
                   Only school elections _____

   d) What political work have you done within the last four years? (List such things as working in campaign offices, running for office, acting as judge of elections, passing out literature, addressing meetings, etc.)

   e) Have you contributed money to any political cause or organization in the past year?

    f) Have you done any fund-raising work for any political cause or organization?

    g) Do you count yourself as (underline) Democrat, Republican, Independent, Other.

12. Religion.

    a) When you were in high school, were your parents church members?_____ Did they attend church regularly?_____ Did you go regularly?_____

    b) Were you and your spouse of the same religion before you married?_____ If different religions, how did you work it out? (Underline) Both kept our own faith; I changed my church; my spouse changed churches; we both pretty much gave up church; other (specify).

    c) Do you send your children to Sunday school regularly?_____

13. Careers for women. [Feminine members of the class please answer (a); all males will please skip to (b).]

    a) 1. How many years have you worked for a paycheck since you graduated from high school?

        2. Do you feel that your work was or is interesting enough to you and valuable enough to be considered a career?

        3. Are you keeping on with it after marriage?_____ Would you hope to continue if you have children?_____ If not, would you want to take it up again when they are old enough so you are relatively free?

        4. If you have not worked since your marriage, what plans, if any, are you making for the time when your home responsibilities will be lightened enough to leave you with time on your hands?

        5. If you have never worked for a paycheck, do you feel that you have missed anything?

6. How does your husband feel about
   (*a*) other men's wives working to earn money or have a career?

   (*b*) your working now or in the future either for a career or to supplement the family income?

b) All male members of the class who are married answer this. Unmarried men may answer 2.

1. Had your wife worked before your marriage?_____
   Has she held any paid jobs since you were married?_____

2. How do you feel about
   (*a*) other men's wives working to earn money or have a career?

   (*b*) your wife working now or in the future either for a career or to supplement the family income?

---

14. Community participation. In what community activities are you interested and active? List such things as Children's Hospital, Community Houses, P.T.A.'s, etc., and indicate part which you take.

Community activity	Role I have played in it

15. Write at as great length as you wish on any or all of the questions below. (Use separate sheets for different questions, and please write on one side of paper.)

   a) Do you feel *now* that the things we emphasized at University School actually were the important things, the things which *should* have been stressed?

b) Do you feel that your University School experience has had any significant bearing, positive or negative, on your over-all capacity to *enjoy* life (as contrasted with your ability to do particular things)?

c) Are there particular experiences since you left high school which have been so challenging to you or so rewarding that you want to tell about them?

d) Are there particular values in living that you have come to prize very highly or particular causes that you watch for opportunities to further? If so, do you want to tell about them?

e) A future inquiry will deal in some detail with your reading. There are, however, sure to be questions concerning other types of information which you would like answered by the class. If you will send these in, they can also be circulated (with or without use of your name, as you prefer).

USES OF COMMUNICATION MEDIA
QUESTIONNAIRE

Please use other side of questionnaire or add extra pages if space is inadequate for your answers.

A. What is (are) your major source(s) of *news?*

    1. Newspapers (please name)_____

    2. Magazines (please name)_____

    3. Radio and television (please name programs, favorite news-

       broadcasters and commentators, and so forth)_____

       _____

       _____

       _____

       _____

B. What are your chief sources of *information and opinion* on political and social issues, national and international?

    1. Books (please name any recently read)_____

_____

_____

2. Magazines (please name)_____

_____

_____

3. Radio and TV_____

_____

_____

4. Other_____

_____

_____

C. For what magazines (including trade and professional) do you subscribe?_____

_____

_____

_____

_____

Name others you read occasionally or frequently?

_____

_____

_____

_____

_____

D. 1. Do you use either of the following as guides to reading?

   Book reviews (if so, give source)_____

   Advice of friends_____

   2. Where do the books you read come from? Public library_____

   Rental library_____ Borrowing from friends_____

   Purchases_____

E. What is the approximate size of your *Private Library?* _____volumes

   Does it emphasize professional books?_____ Literary material?____

F. Name, if any, a book or books you are reading or have been reading within the past month. Please do not limit your reply to books of importance or high literary quality.

   _____

   _____

   _____

   _____

   _____

G. Approximately how many books do you read per year? (Guess)____

   What types are included? Professional_____ Fiction_____

   Poetry_____ Travel_____ Political discussion_____

   Biography_____ Mystery_____

H. Can you name one or more books you would like to read if you could find time? If so, please list.

_____

_____

_____

_____

_____

I. Can you name a half-dozen books read during the past ten years which you have found unusually stimulating? If so, please name.

_____

_____

_____

_____

_____

Same for outstanding movies, legitimate plays, lectures, concerts,

etc._____

_____

_____

_____

_____

_____

K. If you attended college, please state effect of college on your reading and other related habits.

L. What do you consider your greatest reading problem?

M. If you have children, indicate what you are attempting to do with their reading attitudes and habits, and the methods, if any, you are using. If you will, comment similarly on radio, television, and movies.

N. Add other information about your own reading and listening (or viewing) that may be interesting and significant. This might concern family habits, reading aloud, use of television, rereading, subscriptions to book clubs, attendance at study clubs, leadership in reading groups, demands of professional business reading, and so forth. You may work on securing better movies or similar matters. I think this may, for many of you, be the most significant part of the questionnaire.

INTERVIEW SCHEDULE

GROUP I

Questions raised by responses on Biographical Questionnaire

1. Various people mentioned inadequacy of factual knowledge. Can you recall situations when you were handicapped by not knowing something which others seemed to know and you felt the school should have taught you in grammar, spelling, geography, history, science, famous quotations—all of which were mentioned—or any other?

2. One mentioned the understressing of traditional American values and an overemphasis on change, as though change were good in itself, another the development of a world picture with no room for God or faith. Were you, or have you become, aware of such tendencies?

3. Tolerance for minorities was mentioned by one student as something learned at school; others mentioned respect for individuals, that you were not forced to conform, that you learned to accept yourselves. One thought this might have been overdone in the direction of too much individualism. What is your opinion?

4. Many people mentioned values derived from Nature of Proof. Can you recall a specific instance when you used methods learned in this course, or can you trace any habits of thinking to it?

5. Some mentioned "learning without drudgery," "enjoying learning," acquiring the attitudes and skills which have fostered later learning. Others felt they should have been compelled to learn more things, that some things should have been "rammed down our throats." What is your attitude?

6. One said that for him the school overstressed the intellectual; another said that it understressed the intellectual. Many commented that they learned to get along with others, but a few felt that human relations was a neglected area. What is your opinion?

7. A number of people felt that one outcome of the program should be "the ability to think for yourself." Do you agree that this is something for which the school was working? Can you explain what makes you think you do or do not have this ability? Is it related to self-confidence?

8. A number of people felt that there was not enough "disciplined learning" in the school. Can you look back and say where you felt you got this, and where you felt that you needed more than you got?

9. Do you have any feeling now that integration of subjects gave you any more habit of seeing relationships than most of the people you go around with?

10. Do you have any feeling now about how well or how badly the balance between co-operation and competition in the school prepared you for competition and co-operation as you met them later?

11. The faculty talked a great deal among themselves about trying to make the school an experience in democratic living and about helping you to verbalize about democracy from your experience. Were you aware of that at the time and has it been of any value to you later?

12. Of course the process of growing up and assuming adult responsibilities brings some changes or at least redefinitions of our standards and our values. Were any of these changes sudden enough or drastic enough so that you were aware of them? Can you be specific about what they were and what brought them about?

13. A number of people felt as they looked back that they wasted a good deal of time in high school. Do you feel that you wasted much time? If so, was that just a part of the process of growing up, or do you feel that the faculty should have done something about it?

14. Of course you know the school as a human institution must have changed, but since you do not know just what the changes are, assume that it is still just as you knew it. Tell the faculty what things about it were particularly valuable and should be conserved, and what parts were weak and should be improved.

Group II

(To be asked of all students in the school three or more years.)

15. Do you watch TV? What are your favorite programs?

16. (For people with children.) Do you regulate the children's TV?

17. Do you regularly listen to radio? What kinds of programs? Do you like any particular news programs or commentators? Any special music programs?

18. *a*) How often do you go to the movies?
    b) What kinds of pictures do you like best?
    c) What ones have you enjoyed recently?

19. What newspapers and magazines do you read regularly?

20. *a*) Are you reading a book now? If so, what is it?
    b) What was the last one you read?
    c) What kinds of books do you like best?

21. (For those with children.) Are you bringing up your children more strictly than you were raised, less strictly, or about the same? Can you be specific about the ways in which you hope to differ from what your parents did?

22. (For those with children.) Do you and your wife (husband) have different ideas about bringing up the children? In what specific ways are they different, and how do you work that out?

23. On the whole, do you think that you had a pretty good break in your own upbringing?

24. Which of your parents do you think was fonder of you?

25. Which of your parents were you fonder of?

26. Was that always true, or did you feel differently at some time in your life?

27. (For those with children.) What things do you try to instill in your children?

28. (For those with children; ask questions in terms of number and sex of children.) What plans and ambitions do you have for your son(s)? For your daughter(s)?

29. On the whole, and considering people in all walks of life, who do you

think have an easier time in present-day America, men or women?

30. If you could be born over again, would you rather be a boy or a girl?

31. If you had your choice as to when you would be born, would you have preferred to live in some other age than this? Which one?

32. If you had your choice as to family, would you now choose to have had another set of parents? Any in particular?

33. If you knew you had only six months to live, but could do just as you pleased during that period, how would you spend the time?

34. Do you think of your family—the one in which you grew up—as a democratic situation? If not, who was boss? If yes, how were decisions made?

35. (Ask only of married people.) From what you know about your wife's or husband's family, how would you answer the same question about it?

36. (Omit this question entirely for unmarried persons who are living alone. For unmarried who are living with parents or other relatives, make variations appropriate to the situation; for married, include or omit children, according to situation.) Do you consider your own family—you, your wife (husband), and children—as democratic? If not, who is boss? If yes, how are decisions made?

37. (Ask only of married.) Do your own parents or your in-laws or other relatives ever try to interfere in decisions which you regard as purely matters for your own family? How do you and your wife (husband) meet that situation? (If degree of independence from family of the unmarried has not been covered in question 36, ask here, "Do your parents or any other relatives ever try to interfere in any decisions which you regard as entirely your own to make? How do you handle the situation?")

38. Do you think of yourself as a realistic person on the whole or more on the idealistic side? Would you say you were more or less realistic (idealistic) than the others in your class?

39. Is there someone you think of as your best friend, or are there a number of people with whom you are equally intimate?

40. Did you have a chum in high school? Do you think it is better to have a lot of friends with whom you are not so intimate, or a few very close friends?

41. With how many of the people you go around with do you share your personal thoughts or problems?

42. What kinds of recreation do you enjoy which you share with other people outside your family? (Omit this for unmarried living alone.)

43. (Omit for unmarried living alone.) What kinds of recreation do you enjoy as a family group?

44. What individual recreation do you enjoy?

45. What kinds of sports do you like best as a participant? As a spectator? Or don't you like any in particular?

46. *a*) What kinds of music do you prefer?
    b) How do you feel about jazz?
    c) Do you have a record collection? How large and what types of records?

47. Do you ever let yourself go and just daydream?

48. Are you ever blue or depressed or worried about things in your life? What do you find helps you then?

49. What do you think are the best and worst aspects of your personality?

50. *a*) (For women who are housewives.) What do you like most about being a homemaker?
    b) (For men who are married.) What do you like to do around the house and yard?
    c) (For women who are working and also keeping house for husband and family.) What difficulties do you find, if any, in combining marriage and a career?

(Omit 50, 51, 52, 53, and 54 for the unmarried.)

51. *a*) (For women who are housewives.) What do you like least about being a homemaker?
    b) (For men who are married.) What do you do as household chores which you do not really enjoy?

52. (Omit for those who do not have children.) What aspects of bringing up your children do you enjoy or find challenging?

53. (Omit for those who do not have children.) What aspects of bringing up your children are just necessary routines which you do not really enjoy?

54. (For housewives.) Are you doing any work now which brings in an income?

55. (For all of both sexes who are employed full time or part time.) Do

you want to tell how you got into your present line of work, what you like about it and what you don't like. (For those women who had careers before marriage, phrase the question to ask about that.)

56. (For men and women who are employed full time.) If you had to choose between very interesting work at low pay and uninteresting work at very high pay, which would you choose?

57. What do you think is most important in life: (a) trying to make the world a better place; (b) happiness; (c) making other people happy; (d) living according to your religion?

58. What do you think is most important in your future—money, fame, the respect of your community, something else, or don't you know?

59. To what clubs, fraternal orders, local and national organizations do you belong?

60. In which ones are you active as an officer, committee member, or worker?

61. Which ones hold regular meetings which you attend more or less regularly?

62. Are you a member of a church? Do you do any work for the church? If so, what?

63. What community work have you done in the last two years? (Civil defense, United Appeals, etc.)

64. Do you consider yourself as a person who is very much interested in politics, moderately interested, or hardly interested at all?

65. Where do you think most of the people you go around with would stand on such a question?

66. What kind of person do you think of when you think of someone very much interested in politics?

67. What kind of person do you think of when you think of someone who is not much interested in politics?

68. Do you often change your opinions on national and international political questions?

69. Do you remember the last time you changed your mind on a political issue? What was it? Do you remember what made you change your mind?

70. Does what happens in politics make any difference to the way you live and work?

71. *a*) Do you think Eisenhower will run again? (This question was varied as the political situation developed.)

    b) If he doesn't run, whom do you hope the Republicans will nominate—Nixon, Knowland, Stassen, Dewey, McCarthy, Warren, or someone else?

    c) If the Republican candidate runs against Stevenson, or Harriman, which one do you expect to vote for?

72. Do you think Soviet policy has really changed since Stalin's death?

73. Do you think that labor is getting too much power and too high pay lately, or are you glad to see such things as guaranteed annual wage, $1.00 minimum wage, and the merging of the AFL-CIO?

74. *a*) How do you feel about the government's present loyalty-security measures?

    b) Were the investigations conducted by McCarthy's committee a good thing?

75. Do you often get indignant or very excited about political happenings? When was the last time? How did you feel about it afterward?

76. Do you ever get as worked up about something that happens in politics as about something that happens in your personal life?

77. Do your friends talk much about politics? Can you remember the last time you had a discussion? What was it about? Is there anyone who more or less takes the lead in these discussions? Are you yourself one of the persons who mostly talks or mostly listens?

78. Is there anyone whose opinions you particularly trust when it comes to politics? What kind of person is he?

79. When you are in a group of people where the discussion is being dominated by individuals expressing very prejudiced views on questions on which you have strong opposing convictions, what do you do?

80. Do you ever get indignant or very excited about things other than politics that you read in the paper, or see in the movies or on TV, or hear on the radio?

81. What people or groups in this country do you think of as having interests similar to yours—that is, they are more or less on your side?

82. What people or groups in this country do you think of as having

interests opposed to yours—that is, they are pretty much on the other side?

83. Do you think it is easier to avoid war or to avoid depression?

84. Is there anything you personally can do about it, or is it all up to the experts in Washington?

85. Do you think there will be another world war in the next twenty years?

86. *a*) Do you think that there will always be wars?
    b) What do you think could be done to make war less likely?
    c) What do you think you'll be doing in case another war comes?

87. Who do you think runs the country now?

88. Can you name any people who have greatly influenced your beliefs, understanding, or thinking?

89. What great people, living or dead, do you admire most?

90. Is ambition something you admire in other people?

91. Do you wish you had more ambition yourself? How often?

92. Do you think that, on the whole, ambitious people have happier lives than unambitious ones?

93. Do you personally care very much about happiness, or do you think other things in life are more important?

94. What kinds of activities and experiences give you the greatest sense of personal worth and achievement?

95. What chance do you think you really have for getting what you want out of life?

96. Do you think an individual is really responsible for what becomes of him?

97. What might cause a person to commit suicide? Do you believe in mercy killing?

98. What is the most embarrassing experience you can remember?

99. What is the most awe-inspiring experience you can remember?

100. Are there any things you have failed to do that make you feel guilty? Do you ever feel guilty about neglecting your obligations to yourself, your family or friends, or to the world?

101. Which of the following are the most important in getting ahead in life: (a) education, (b) brains, (c) a good personality, (d) hard work, (e) good connections, (f) patience, (g) luck?

Seven cards, each with a "Path of Life" (see David Riesman and Nathan Glazer, *Faces in the Crowd,* p. 181) were given to the subject for him to read and comment on, and show his agreement or disagreement.

DESCRIPTIONS USED IN CLASSIFICATION

OF POLITICAL ATTITUDES

1. Conservative

a) Tendency to be an admirer of MacArthur, Knowland, Nixon, and many southern Democrats. There may be some admirers of Stevenson and some of McCarthy in this group.

b) Great concern about the power of labor. Tendency to focus attention on certain vulnerable union leaders or union activities and make them symbols of the whole labor movement.

c) Genuine fear of increasing power of federal government, and of most new power groups unless he himself happens to be a member. Tendency to think of government as referee, but to feel that it should not get in the fight. A feeling that government services are debilitating; usually blind to those established ones from which he benefits, and very much opposed to new ones.

d) Willingness to sacrifice many government services for a balanced budget.

e) Recognition of world Communist danger, but tendency to see it mainly as a conspiracy, not making adequate allowance for the political immaturity and naïveté of underprivileged people who are attracted by Communist promises and propaganda.

f) Tendency to want to give limited help to underdeveloped areas, and to expect an immediate *quid pro quo* in the form of gratitude and military alliance.

g) Tendency to feel that our security depends mainly on our own production and armed forces, and to assign a minor role to international organization or alliances.

b) Some concern over invasions of civil liberties in hunt for Communists, but a tendency to feel that it is an unfortunate necessity; some tolerance and even possible acceptance of McCarthy, believing in his aims though rejecting his methods.

2. Middle-of-the-Road

a) Often are strongly pro-Eisenhower, or may be pro-Stevenson. If Eisenhower and Stevenson are running against each other, they would tend to vote on the basis of party preference.

b) See hope for world in greater co-operation in UN, some surrender of sovereignty, some righting of ancient wrongs, more attempts of individual people to understand each other across international boundaries. There is some recognition that other nations may legitimately differ from us.

c) Belief that budget-balancing is important, but that need for services should be equally important.

d) Greater concern over civil liberties than true, dyed-in-the-wool conservatives.

e) Little tendency to see nation as made up of power groups "on my side" or "on the other side."

f) Some concern over labor's possible political power, or over added strength due to merger; not certain this is bad, but wonders.

3. Liberal

a) Admirers of Adlai Stevenson, Averell Harriman, Earl Warren, Paul Douglas, Eleanor Roosevelt tend to fall in this group.

b) Generally glad to see progress of labor, though often concerned about the leadership or policies of particular unions or the wisdom of particular strikes.

c) Tendency to see spread of world communism as largely a reaction against colonialism and exploitation, with our answer needing to be mainly in technical assistance, education, American support for independence movements, and all activities which serve to demonstrate that freedoms and personal liberties are valued in democratic states, in contrast to their suppression in Communist states. Tendency to support foreign-aid budgets, UN, CARE, Voice of America, World Health Organization, UNESCO, etc.

d) Concern over civil liberties and conviction that control of subversion can be achieved without loss of the Bill of Rights. Absolute rejection of the methods of smear, guilt by association, and trial by headline.

e) Willingness to accept and pay for new functions of government made necessary by changing conditions, without necessarily feeling that bigger and more expensive government is desirable for its own sake. Less concern than other groups about an unbalanced budget when circumstances seem to make it desirable; ideas of "compensatory economy."

4. Radical

Sincere and consistent radicalism is a little hard to find or to define today except as the extreme left of liberalism. Much of what used to be radicalism has been taken over or exploited by the Communist party-liners. Most individuals or groups which are trying to speed up change in one area are considered radical by the groups opposing that change (i.e., the NAACP in the South). Such groups must be constantly alert to avoid infiltration or the exploitation of their cause by the Communist party.

5. Non-rational Fringe (emotional reactions masquerading as political opinions)

a) Sees McCarthy as a knight in shining armor, exposing deadly Communist infiltration; or, sees the U. S. government as a tool of "Wall Street" or "The Interests," with the little man in a hopeless situation unless he embraces "the Party" or some other leader; or, believes government is degenerating because masses of politically illiterate people are willing to follow blindly anyone who promises them anything without cost.

b) Violent hatred toward and fear of various groups in the community.

c) Isolationist attitude, with considerable scorn of other nationalities; agitation for international policies which would tend to lose us our friends; lack of understanding of or concern over how people of other nations see us or of how they feel.

d) Very little concern over civil rights or over treatment of minorities.

MAGAZINES SUBSCRIBED TO OR READ

I. Class members reported subscribing to the magazines listed below. Numbers in parentheses refer to the number of persons reporting each magazine; if no number is given, only one person reported that periodical.

AAUP Bulletin
Accounting Review
Advertising Age
Advertising Agency
American (2)
American Anthropologist
American Aviation
American Canner
American Home (4)
The American Scientist
Arizona Highways
Art News (2)
Atlantic Monthly (2)
Aviation Week
Barron's National Financial Weekly (2)
Bent of Tau Beta Pi
Best's
Better Homes and Gardens (10)
Boys' Life
Business Week (5)
The Candle

Ceramic Age
Ceramic Industry
Ceramics Monthly
Children's Digest
Christian Century
Collier's (2)
Consumer Reports (2)
Control Engineering
Cornell Engineer
Coronet (2)
Country Gentleman
Cue
Drug Trade News
Electrical World
Family Circle
The Farm
The Flower Grower (2)
Food Topics
Forbes (2)
Fortune (3)
Girl Scout Leader
Good Housekeeping (9)
Gourmet (2)
Grade Teacher
Growing
Harper's Bazaar (2)
Harper's Magazine (3)
Holiday (2)
Hollywood Reporter
House and Garden (4)
House Beautiful (2)
Humpty-Dumpty's Magazine
The Instructor
Jack and Jill
Journal of Accountancy

Journal of American Folk-lore
Journal of Applied Physics
Journal of Chemical Education
Journal of Exceptional Children
Journal of Forestry
Journal of the International Folk Music Council
Junior League Magazine
Kappa Alpha Theta Magazine
The Key
Kiplinger reports (4)
Ladies Home Journal (8)
League of Women Voters periodicals
Life (27)
Living
Local Agent
Look
McCall's Magazine (3)
Mademoiselle
Mechanix Illustrated (2)
Medicine
Metal-Working
Methods
Michigan Education Journal
Midwest Folklore
Motor Trend
National Geographic Magazine (6)
NEA Journal (2)
New York Conservationist
New Yorker (12)
Newsweek (5)
Opening Doors
Outdoor Life (2)
Parents Magazine (5)
Petroleum Processing
Petroleum Refining

Physical Review
Physics Today
Popular Electronics
Presbyterian Life
Proceedings of the Institute of Radio Engineers (2)
Progressive Grocer
Radio
Reader's Digest (22)
Record of Sigma Alpha Epsilon
The Reporter
Review of Modern Physics
Road and Track
Saturday Evening Post (9)
Saturday Review
Scientific American
Scientific Management
Scouting
Sovetskaya Etnografiya
Sports Afield (2)
Sports Illustrated (2)
Successful Farming
Sunset (2)
Television
Theatre Arts
Time (22)
Town and Country
UNESCO Courier
U. S. Naval Institute Proceedings
U. S. News and World Report (5)
Variety
Vogue (4)
Western Arts
Woman's Home Companion (3)
Yachting (2)

"Technical journals related to radio"

II. In addition to the subscriptions listed in the first section of this Appendix, members reported reading the following magazines occasionally. Figures in parentheses indicate the number reporting each periodical, if more than one person reported. An asterisk before a title indicates that the magazine is not on the list of magazines subscribed for by any class member.

Atlantic Monthly (2)
Better Homes and Gardens (3)
Business Week
Collier's (3)
Consumers' Digest
Cosmopolitan (2)
Esquire
Factory Management and Maintenance
Flying
Good Housekeeping (5)
Gourmet
Harper's Bazaar
Harper's Magazine
Holiday (4)
House and Garden
House Beautiful (2)
Iron Age
Ladies Home Journal (4)
Life (10)
Journal of Speech
Look (9)
McCall's Magazine (4)
Mademoiselle (2)
Mill and Factory
National Geographic Magazine (3)
New Yorker (7)
Newsweek (6)
Quarterly Review of Pediatrics
Reader's Digest (4)

*Redbook
*Revue des Études Slaves
Saturday Review
*Southern Folklore Quarterly
Sports Illustrated (2)
*Steel
*Steel Processing
Sunset
*Tempo
Time (6)
Town and Country (2)
*Training School Bulletin (Vineland, N.J.)
*TV Guide
*Uncensored
U. S. News and World Report (4)
Vogue (2)
*Western Folklore
*Your Life
*Zeitschrift für Slavische Philologie

"About 20 physics journals"
"Folklore periodicals in 8 languages, especially German and Russian"
"Music periodicals, especially in German and Russian"
"Women's magazines"

BOOKS BEING READ

Fifty class members listed the names of the books which were being read at the time questionnaires were returned. Figures in parentheses after the title indicate the number reporting each book, if more than one person reported.

"Air Force technical publications"
Richard S. Aldrich, *Gertrude Lawrence as Mrs. A.* (2)
Fred Allen, *Treadmill to Oblivion*
Robert Anderson, *Tea and Sympathy* (2)
Daisy Ashford, *The Young Visiters*
Roland H. Bainton, *Here I Stand*
Tallulah Bankhead, *Tallulah, My Autobiography*
Margaret Campbell Barnes, *Brief Gaudy Hour*
Lincoln Barnett, *The Universe and Dr. Einstein*
Hamilton Basso, *The View from Pompey's Head*
The Bible (2)
Jim Bishop, *The Day Lincoln Was Shot* (2)
Claude M. Bristol, *The Magic of Believing*
Pearl Buck, "The China I Knew"
Paddy Chayefsky, *Television Plays*
Sheldon Cheney, *The Story of Modern Art*
G. K. Chesterton, *The Amazing Adventures of Father Brown*
Agatha Christie, *Witness for the Prosecution*
William G. Cole, *Sex in Christianity and Psychoanalysis*
Thomas B. Costain, *The Tontine* (2)
Noel Coward, *Present Indicative*

Max Doerner, *The Materials of the Artist and Their Use in Painting*

Lloyd C. Douglas, *The Big Fisherman*

William O. Douglas, *Almanac of Liberty*

C. S. Forester, Horatio Hornblower series

Christopher Fry, *The Dark is Light Enough*

Arnold Gesell, and Frances L. Ilg, *The Child from Five to Ten* (2)

Arnold Gesell, and Frances L. Ilg, *The First Five Years of Life*

Ellen Glasgow, *The Woman Within*

Charles H. Goren, *Contract Bridge*

Charles Gorham, *The Gold of Their Bodies* (2)

Robert Graves, *King Jesus*

Giovanni Guareschi, *Don Camillo's Dilemma*

Jacques Hadamard, *The Psychology of Invention in the Mathematical Field*

Hermann Hagedorn, *The Roosevelt Family of Sagamore Hill*

Lawrence and E. M. Hanson, *Noble Savage, Life of Paul Gauguin*

William J. Hennessey, *Complete Book of Built-ins*

James Hilton, *Time and Time Again*

Bob Hope, *Have Tux—Will Travel*

Hermann Kesten, *Copernic et son temps*

Frances Parkinson Keyes, *The Royal Box*

Russell Kirk, *A Program for Conservatives*

Harold Lamb, *Tamerlane*

Pierre LaMure, *Moulin Rouge*

John A. Leavitt, and Carol O. Hanson, *Personal Finance*

Isabel Leighton, *The Aspirin Age*

Alan Le May, *The Searchers*

Anne Morrow Lindbergh, *Gift from the Sea*

Philip Lindsay, *A Rake's Progress*

Dee Linford, *Man without a Star*

Betty MacDonald, *Onions in the Stew*

John P. Marquand, *Sincerely, Willis Wayde* (2)

André Maurois, *Lélia*

James A. Michener, *Bridges of Toko-ri*

Herbert Miller, *C.P.A. Review Manual*

Margaret Mitchell, *Gone with the Wind*
Lewis Mumford, *Technics and Civilization*
Nuclear Science, Annual Review of
Zoé Oldenbourg, *Cornerstone*
Aleksandr I. Oparin, *Origin of Life*
Harry A. Overstreet, *Mind Alive*
Cesare Pavese, *The Moon and the Bonfires*
Norman Vincent Peale, *The Power of Positive Thinking* (4)
Joseph Petracca, *Come Back to Sorrento*
Fletcher Pratt, *A Short History of the Civil War*
Ira Progoff, *Jung's Psychology and Its Social Meaning*
Robert Raynolds, *The Sinner of Saint Ambrose*
Lillian Roth, *I'll Cry Tomorrow*
Harold Rubins, *Dream Merchants*
Carl Sandburg, *Abraham Lincoln*
Anya Seton, *Katherine*
Harlow Shapley (ed.), *Climatic Change*
Nevil Shute, *Round the Bend*
Vern Sneider, *Teahouse of the August Moon*
Benjamin Spock, *The Common Sense Book of Baby and Child Care*
John Steinbeck, *East of Eden*
John Steinbeck, *Sweet Thursday*
Rex Stout, *Full House*
Morton Thompson, *Not as a Stranger*
Paul Tillich, *The New Being*
Lael Tucker, *Lament for Four Virgins*
Mark Twain, *Innocents Abroad*
Leon M. Uris, *Battle Cry*
David H. Walker, *Digby*
Jerome Weidman, *Your Daughter Iris*
Percy F. Westerman, *The Missing Diplomat*
William S. White, *The Taft Story*
Leonard Wibberly, *The Mouse That Roared*
Sloan Wilson, *The Man in the Gray Flannel Suit*
Christopher Montague Woodhouse, *The Greek War of Independence*

The following books were mentioned but could not be found in the *Cumulative Book Index:*

Handbook of Color Television

Nee-Sa-Wa-Jon (a publication about the Great Lakes put out by some Lake Erie industry)

"Biography of a Seattle lawyer who was something like Clarence Darrow"

Blood and Sugar: A study of hypoinsulinism

STIMULATING BOOKS RECALLED

Forty-six respondents, in the questionnaires and interviews, reported that the following books had proved stimulating reading during some time in the past ten years. Figures in parentheses after the titles indicate the number reporting each book, if more than one person reported.

Louis Adamic, *The Eagle and the Roots*
Elliott Arnold, *Blood Brother*
Harriette L. Arnow, *Hunter's Horn*
Felix Barker, *The Oliviers*
Dorothy W. Baruch, *One Little Boy*
Hamilton Basso, *View from Pompey's Head*
Ruth Benedict, *Race: Science and Politics*
Stephen Vincent Benét, *Western Star*
The Bible (King James Version)
Ambrose Bierce, *In the Midst of Life*
Karen Blixen (Isak Dinesen, pseud.), *Seven Gothic Tales*
Claude M. Bristol, *The Magic of Believing*
Charlotte Brontë, *Jane Eyre* (reread)
Jean Bruller (Vercors, pseud.), *You Shall Know Them*
Martin Buber, *I and Thou*
Ben L. Burman, *Steamboat Round the Bend*
James M. Cain, *Mildred Pierce*
William E. Campbell (William March, pseud.), *The Bad Seed*
Albert Camus, *The Plague*
Rachel Carson, *The Sea around Us* (3)
Joyce Cary, *The Horse's Mouth* (and other books of his)

Miguel de Cervantes, *Don Quixote*
Whittaker Chambers, *Witness*
Sheldon Cheney, *The Story of Modern Art*
Winston Churchill, "War memoirs" (2)
Thomas B. Costain, *The Black Rose* (2)
Thomas B. Costain, *The Silver Chalice*
Richard H. S. Crossman (ed.), *The God That Failed*
Marcia Davenport, *Valley of Decision*
John Dewey, *Art as Experience*
Charles Dickens, *Oliver Twist*
Max Doerner, *The Materials of the Artist and Their Use in Painting*
Edward W. Dolch, *Manual for Remedial Reading*
Lloyd C. Douglas, *The Big Fisherman*
Lloyd C. Douglas, *The Robe* (2)
William O. Douglas, *Almanac of Liberty*
Dwight D. Eisenhower, *Crusade in Europe*
Edna Ferber, *Giant*
Esther Forbes, *Running of the Tide*
Murray Forbes, *Hollow Triumph*
Hugh Fosburgh, *View from the Air*
Ernest K. Gann, *The High and the Mighty*
Kahlil Gibran, *The Prophet* (2)
Davis Grubb, *The Night of the Hunter*
A. B. Guthrie, Jr., *The Big Sky*
Oscar Hammerstein, II, *The King and I*
H. Gordon Hayes, *Spending, Saving, and Employment*
Ernest Hemingway, *Old Man and the Sea*
O. Henry stories (no specific title given)
Thor Heyerdahl, *Kon-Tiki*
History of the Civil War (pocketbook)
James Hymes, *Understanding Your Child*
James Jones, *From Here to Eternity* (2)
Russell Kirk, *The Conservative Mind*
Ralph Kirkpatrick, *Domenico Scarlatti*
Arthur Koestler, *Darkness at Noon*

Harold Lamb, *Suleiman the Magnificent*

Margaret Landon, *Anna and the King of Siam*

Susanne K. Langer, *Feeling and Form, a Theory of Art Developed from Philosophy in a New Key*

Rosamond Lehmann, *The Ballad and the Source*

Emil Lengyel, *World without End*

Olga Lengyel, *Five Chimneys, the Story of Auschwitz*

Joshua L. Liebman, *Peace of Mind* (3)

Charles A. Lindbergh, *The Spirit of St. Louis*

Jack London stories (no specific title given)

Herbert Luethy, *France against Herself*

Norman Mailer, *The Naked and the Dead*

Thomas Mann, *Magic Mountain*

John P. Marquand, *Point of No Return*

Catherine Marshall, *A Man Called Peter*

F. Van Wyck Mason, *Himalayan Assignment*

H. L. Mencken, *Chrestomathy*

James Michener, *The Bridges of Toko-ri* (2)

John Cecil Moore, *The Blue Field*

Lewis Mumford, *Technics and Civilization*

Audie Murphy, *To Hell and Back*

Kimon Nicolaides, *The Natural Way to Draw*

Reinhold Niebuhr, *The Nature and Destiny of Man*

J. Robert Oppenheimer Hearing, Transcript of Testimony of

George Orwell, *Animal Farm*

George Orwell, *1984*

Vernon Louis Parrington, *Main Currents in American Thought*

Alan Paton, *Cry, the Beloved Country* (4)

Norman Vincent Peale, *Power of Positive Thinking* (3)

Alberto Pincherle (Alberto Moravia, pseud.), *The Woman of Rome*

Plato, *Dialogues* (in part)

William H. Prescott, *Conquest of Mexico*

Ernie Pyle's book (no specific title given)

Ayn Rand, *The Fountainhead* (3)

Herbert Edward Read (ed.), *Surrealism*

David Riesman; Reuel Denney; and Nathan Glazer, *The Lonely Crowd*

Robert B. Robertson, *Of Whales and Men*

Henry Morton Robinson, *The Cardinal*

Antoine de Saint-Exupéry, *Wind, Sand and Stars*

J. D. Salinger, *Catcher in the Rye*

Agnes Sanford, *The Healing Light*

George Santayana, *The Last Puritan*

Henry Schaefer-Simmern, *The Unfolding of Artistic Activity*

Lawrence Schoonover, *Spider King*

Anya Seton, *Katherine*

Hugh Seton-Watson, *The East European Revolution*

Fulton J. Sheen, *Peace of Soul*

Samuel Shellabarger, *Captain from Castile* (2)

Hoyt L. Sherman *et al., Drawing by Seeing*

Frank Smothers *et al., Report on the Greeks*

Benjamin MacLean Spock (no specific title given)

Lincoln Steffens, *The Shame of the Cities*

Marguerite Steen, *The Sun Is My Undoing*

John Steinbeck, *Grapes of Wrath*

Robert Louis Stevenson stories (no specific title given)

Joseph Warren Stilwell, *Papers*

Irving Stone, *Immortal Wife*

Irving Stone, *Lust for Life*

Neil H. Swanson, *Unconquered*

Lowell Thomas, *Out of This World*

Morton Thompson, *Not as a Stranger*

Henry David Thoreau, *Walden*

Leo Tolstoy, *War and Peace* (4)

Mika Waltari, *The Egyptian*

Andrew John West, *Way of the Transgressor*

William S. White, *The Taft Story*

Alfred North Whitehead, *Dialogues* (edited by Lucien Price)

Alfred North Whitehead, *Science and the Modern World*

Ben Ames Williams, *The Strange Woman*

Edmund Wilson, *To the Finland Station*

Herman Wouk, *The Caine Mutiny* (5)
Philip Wylie, *Essay on Morals*
Philip Wylie, *Generation of Vipers*
Frank Yerby, *The Foxes of Harrow*
Emile Zola, *Kill*

BIBLIOGRAPHY

Adorno, T. W., *et al. The Authoritarian Personality.* New York: Harper and Brothers, 1950.

Asheim, Lester. "What Do Adults Read?", in *Adult Reading: Fifty-fifth Yearbook of the National Society for the Study of Education,* edited by Nelson B. Henry (Chicago: University of Chicago Press, 1956), LV, Part II, pp. 5–28. Copyright 1956 by the University of Chicago Press.

Babcock, Franklin L. *The U. S. College Graduate.* New York: Macmillan Company, 1942.

Barbe, Walter B. "A Follow-up Study of Graduates of Special Classes for Gifted Children." Unpublished Ph.D. dissertation, Northwestern University, 1953. (Available on microfilm from University Microfilms, Inc., Ann Arbor, Michigan, Publication 7014, 1954.)

"Booksellers Consider Their Rent and How to Cope with It," *Publishers' Weekly,* CLVII (February 11, 1950), 891–93.

Butz, Otto (ed.). *The Unsilent Generation.* New York: Rinehart and Company, Inc., 1958.

Chamberlin, C. D., *et al. Did They Succeed in College?* ("Adventure in American Education," Vol. IV). New York: Harper and Brothers, 1942.

Class of 1938, University High School, Ohio State University. *Were We Guinea Pigs?* New York: Henry Holt and Company, Inc., 1938.

Covert, Warren O. "High-School Graduates after Six Years," *Bulletin of the National Association of Secondary-School Principals,* XXXIV (January, 1950), 270–79.

"The Eight Year Study: A Report of the Ohio State University School to the Commission on the Relation of School and College of the Progressive Education Association by the Faculty of the School" (Columbus, Ohio, October, 1940). This report was later printed in *Thirty Schools Tell Their Story,* pages 718–57.

The Faculty of University School. *The Philosophy and Purposes of the University School.* Columbus, Ohio: Ohio State University, 1948.

Folsom, J. K. *The Family.* New York: John Wiley and Sons, Inc., 1934. Revised and reprinted in 1943 as *The Family and Democratic Society.*

Fromm, Erich. *Escape from Freedom.* New York: Holt, Rinehart and Winston, Inc., 1941.

Fromm, Erich. *The Sane Society.* New York: Holt, Rinehart and Winston, Inc., 1955.

Gerth, Hans, and Mills, C. Wright. *Character and Social Structure.* New York: Harcourt, Brace and Company, 1953.

Harvard 1926. *The Life and Opinions of a College Class.* Cambridge, Massachusetts: Harvard University Press, 1951.

Havemann, Ernest, and West, Patricia. *They Went to College.* New York: Harcourt, Brace and Company, 1952.

Hersey, John. "Yale '36—Look at Them Now," *Harper's Magazine,* CCV (September, 1952), 21–28.

Jacob, Philip. *Changing Values in College.* New York: Harper and Brothers, 1957.

Krutch, Joseph Wood. "Dialogue on Americans," *Saturday Review,* XL (May 18, 1957), 30–32.

LaBrant, Lou L., and Heller, Frieda M. *An Evaluation of Free Reading in Grades Seven to Twelve Inclusive* ("Contributions in Education," No. 4) Columbus, Ohio: Ohio State University Press, 1939.

Link, Henry C., and Hope, Harry Arthur. *People and Books.* New York: Book Industry Committee, Book Manufacturers Institute, 1946.

McIntosh, W. John. "Follow-up Study of One Thousand Non-academic Boys," *Journal of Exceptional Children,* XV (March, 1949), 166–70, 191.

Mills, C. Wright. *White Collar: The American Middle Classes.* New York: Oxford University Press, 1953.

Norton-Taylor, Duncan. "Why Don't Businessmen Read Books?", *Fortune,* LXIX (May, 1954), 115–17.

Progressive Education Association, Commission on the Relation of School and College. *Thirty Schools Tell Their Story* ("Adventure in American Education," Vol. V). New York: Harper and Brothers, 1943. (Material used with the permission of McGraw-Hill Book Company, Inc.)

Riesman, David, and Glazer, Nathan. *Faces in the Crowd*. New Haven: Yale University Press, 1952.

Riesman, David; Denney, Reuel; and Glazer, Nathan. *The Lonely Crowd*. New York: Doubleday and Company, Inc., 1955.

Terman, Lewis, and Oden, Melita. *The Gifted Child Grows Up: Twenty-five Years Follow-up of a Superior Group*. Stanford, California: Stanford University Press, 1948.

Waples, Douglas, and Tyler, Ralph. *What People Want to Read about*. Chicago: University of Chicago Press, 1931.

Wright, Charles C., and Hyman, Herbert H. "Voluntary Association Membership of American Adults: Evidence from National Sample Surveys," *American Sociological Review*, XXIII (June, 1958), 284–94.

Zinsser, William K. "The Class of '44 Today," *This Week Magazine* (*New York Herald Tribune*, Sec. 7), June 6, 1954. The Princeton reunion book, *The First Decade*, from which the magazine article was taken, was privately printed and is not available.

INDEX